Believing Identity

EXPLORATIONS IN ANTHROPOLOGY
A University College London Series

Series Editors: Barbara Bender, John Gledhill and Bruce Kapferer

Jadran Mimica, *Intimations of Infinity: The Mythopoeia of the Iqwaye Counting System and Number*

Barry Morris, *Domesticating Resistance: The Dhan-Gadi Aborigines and the Australian State*

Thomas C. Patterson, *The Inca Empire: The Formation and Disintegration of a Pre-Capitalist State*

Max and Eleanor Rimoldi, *Hahalis and the Labour of Love: A Social Movement on Buka Island*

Pnina Werbner, *The Migration Process: Capital, Gifts and Offerings among Pakistanis in Britain*

Joel S. Kahn, *Constituting the Minangkabau: Peasants, Culture, and Modernity in Colonial Indonesia*

Gisli Pálsson, *Beyond Boundaries: Understanding, Translation and Anthropological Discourse*

Stephen Nugent, *Amazonian Caboclo Society*

Barbara Bender, *Landscape: Politics and Perspectives*

Christopher Tilley (ed.), *Interpretative Archaeology*

Ernest S. Burch Jr and Linda J. Ellanna (eds), *Key Issues in Hunter-Gatherer Research*

Daniel Miller, *Modernity – An Ethnographic Approach: Dualism and Mass Consumption in Trinidad*

Robert Pool, *Dialogue and the Interpretation of Illness: Conversations in a Cameroon Village*

Cécile Barraud, Daniel de Coppet, André Iteanu and Raymond Jamous (eds), *Of Relations and the Dead: Four Societies Viewed from the Angle of their Exchanges*

Christopher Tilley, *A Phenomenology of Landscape: Places, Paths and Monuments*

Victoria Goddard, Josep Llobera and Cris Shore (eds), *The Anthropology of Europe: Identity and Boundaries in Conflict*

Pat Caplan (ed.), *Understanding Disputes: The Politics of Argument*

Daniel de Coppet and André Iteanu (ed.), *Society and Cosmos: Their Interrelations or Their Coalescence in Melanesia*

Alisdair Rogers and Steven Vertovec (eds), *The Urban Context: Ethnicity, Social Networks and situational Analysis*

Saskia Kersenboom, *Word, Sound, Image: The Life of the Tamil Text*

Daniel de Coppet and André Iteanu (eds), *Cosmos and Society in Oceania*

Roy Ellen and Katsuyoshi Fukui, *Redefining Nature: Ecology, Culture and Domestication*

William Washabaugh, *Flamenco: Passion, Politics and Popular Culture*

Bernard Juillerat, *Children of the Blood: Society, Reproduction and Imaginary Representations in New Guinea*

Karsten Paerregaard, *Linking Separate Worlds: Urban Migrants and Rural Lives in Peru*

Believing Identity

Pentecostalism and the Mediation of Jamaican Ethnicity and Gender in England

Nicole Rodriguez Toulis

BERG

Oxford • New York

First published in 1997 by
Berg
Editorial offices:
150 Cowley Road, Oxford, OX4 1JJ, UK
70 Washington Square South, New York, NY 10012, USA

Berg is an imprint of Oxford International Publishers Ltd.

Library of Congress Cataloging-in-Publication Data

Toulis, Nicole Rodriguez.
  Believing identity: Pentecostalism and the mediation of Jamaican
ethnicity and gender in England / Nicole Rodriguez Toulis.
      p. cm. --(Explorations in anthropology)
  Includes bibliographical references and index.
    ISBN 1-85973-104-X (alk. paper). --ISBN 1-85973-109-0 (pbk. : alk.
paper)
    1. Pentecostalism--Great Britain--Case studies. 2. Jamaicans--
Great Britain--Ethnic identity--Case studies. 3. Jamaicans--Great
Britain--Religion--Case studies. 4. Women, Black-- Great Britain--
Ethnic identity--Case studies. 5. Women, Black--Great Britain--
Religious life--Case studies. 6. Blacks--Great Britain--Ethnic
identity--Case studies. 7. Blacks--Great Britain--Religion--Case
studies. 8. Great Britain--Religious life and customs--Case
studies. I. Title. II. Series.
  BR1644.5.G7T68 1997   96-45031
  305.48´89697292042--dc21   CIP

British Library Cataloguing-in-Publication Data

A catalogue record for this book is available from the British Library.

ISBN 1 85973 104 X (Cloth)
          1 85973 109 0 (Paper)

Typeset by JS Typesetting, Wellingborough, Northants.
Printed in the United Kingdom by WBC Book Manufacturers, Bridgend,
Mid Glamorgan.

For Verna whose spirit was and remains indefatigable and
"Bobbie" one generation out of slavery who told me stories

Contents

Acknowledgements   ix

Editorial Note   xi

List of Plates, Tables and Figures   xiii

List of Abbreviations   xv

Introduction
     'Long time gal me no see you'   1

1   The Brethren of the King Street New Testament
     Church of God   37

2   'Moving up the King's Highway': African-
     Caribbean Pentecostalism in Jamaica and
     England   80

3   'Born of The Water, The Spirit and The Blood':
     The Individual and the Collective   121

4   'I may be Black, but we're from the same hand,
     the hand of God': The Construction and Mediation
     of Identity   165

5   Wives, Mothers and Female Saints: Women in the
     Church   212

Conclusion   265

Appendix I   276

Appendix II   280

Appendix III   281

Bibliography   283

Index   299

Acknowledgements

The study on which this book is based was made possible by the emotional and financial support of numerous people. I would like to thank MA, AA, LJ, OP and the members and Pastor of the King Street New Testament Church of God for welcoming me into their fellowship and homes, enduring hours of questioning and for providing constant spiritual support. To my family, Vasilios, Gladys and Tad, who sacrificed for me and supported and encouraged me, thank you. My appreciation also goes to my friends for their endless solace and forbearance.

The research, thoughts and arguments presented in this study took shape through cumulative interactions with many Fellows and fellows. I am indebted to Sue Benson for her unfailing enthusiasm, support and patience during research. I am especially grateful to Esther Goody and Malcolm Ruel for their advice and for helping me to organize my initial thoughts after the original period of fieldwork. I also thank Keith Hart, Sandra Wallman, Tomoko Hamada, Virginia Kerns, Connie Sutton, Greg Johnson, Daniel Bates, Phil Kilbride, Gerald Creed and my fellows Kristi Norget, Simon Coleman, Andre Czlégdy-Nagy, Louise de la Gorgendière, David Sneath, Vinay Srivastava, and Arlene Davila for taking an interest, teaching me, listening and inspiring me to think that little bit harder. Immeasurable gratitude also goes to Professor Alan Macfarlane for all of the above, for sage counsel and for imparting optimism.

The background study and research presented in this book was made possible by an Overseas Research Student award from the Committee of Vice Chancellors and Principals of the Universities of the United Kingdom, the Amy Mary Preston Read Fund of the University of Cambridge, the Audrey Richards Fund of the Department of Social Anthropology, an External Studentship and a Hardship loan from Emmanuel College, and a dissertation preparation grant from the Radcliffe-Brown Memorial Fund of the Royal Anthropological Association of Great Britain.

NRT

Editorial Note

This book contains many passages of direct quotation and reported speech. The source of each quote is given in parentheses following the quote, e. g. (Sermon) or (Sister). Verbatim quotes are indicated with single quotation marks, paraphrased quotes taken from fieldnotes with double quotation marks. Since much of the recorded speech is a combination of patois and standard British English I have not altered the grammatical construction of sentences, verb tenses or prepositions; [sic] is used sparingly for variant spellings and to retain clarity in ambiguous constructions.

Following current usage I use the terms Black or African-Caribbean for persons of Caribbean origin in Britain. The term migrant is preferred to immigrant out of deference to the feelings of the people. While the original name of the denomination is used with permission, all names of persons and local congregations have been replaced by pseudonyms. The term 'member' is used interchangeably with 'saint' throughout. A list of commonly used abbreviations is provided.

NRT

Editorial Note

List of Plates, Tables and Figures

Plate 1	A Main Road in the Study Area	38
Plate 2	A New Testament Church of God Hall	81
Plate 3	The Baptism of a Female Saint	122
Plate 4	Testimony, National Youth Convention	166
Plate 5	Testimony in Song, National Youth Convention	213

Table 1.1	Economic Activity as Percentage of Ethnic Group's Total Population	44
Table 1.2	Socio-Economic Group by Ethnic Group	45
Table 2.1	Jamaican Religious Affiliation in 1943	100
Table 2.2	Growth of Pentecostalism in Jamaica: Claimed Religious Affiliation as Percentage of Population	107
Table 2.3	Growth of The New Testament Church of God in England	118

Figure 1.1	Nucleus of Non-Fictive Kin in the Congregation	55
Figure 1.2	Secular Fictive Kinship	58
Figure 1.3	Local Sacred Fictive Kinship	60
Figure 1.4	General Sacred Fictive Kinship	61
Figure 3.1	Plan of Church Hall and Seating Arrangements	148
Figure 4.1	Ethnic and Religious Identity as Overlapping Constellations	202
Figure 4.2	Ethnic and Religious Identity as Overlapping Constellations but Distinct from Black British Identity	203
Figure 4.3	Religious Identity Transcends Ethnic Identity	204

List of Abbreviations

COG	–	Church of God, Cleveland Tennessee, USA
LM	–	Ladies' Ministry, an auxiliary of the church's 'Ladies' Ministry' department
MF	–	Men's Fellowship, an auxiliary of the church's 'Men's Fellowship' association
NCWP	–	New Commonwealth and Pakistan
NTCG	–	The New Testament Church of God, an affiliate of the Pentecostal denomination of the Church of God in Cleveland, Tennessee
YALM	–	Young Adult Ladies' Ministry, an auxiliary of the church's 'Ladies' Ministry' department
YLM	–	Young Ladies' Ministry, an auxiliary of the church's 'Ladies' Ministry' department
YMF	–	Young Men's Fellowship, an auxiliary of the church's 'Men's Fellowship' association

Introduction: 'Long time gal me no see you'

Racism is a bitter, ugly, vicious spirit. But it is in the world. A person that is not a Christian will use the same thing to combat it – resentfulness, bitter anger. These attitudes are still part of the world, not of Christ. The Christian who supposed to be having and practicing the spirit of Christ – it's not that he accept it, but he is instructed from the word of God that he should not offer back revenge – should leave this to God. Hence, though he don't accept it, but he don't fight back with the same spirit. . . .In other words that [racism] is the spirit of the devil, this world. As a Christian you would say to yourself I'm living on a higher plane than that. Hence, you are able to treat that person with love, with understanding. Not that you accept it, but you don't retaliate. Now we have this to live with in Britain, because personally we detest racism – know it's wrong, but you can't use another wrong trait or attitude to combat it. So we using our God. . . .. They're in a polite, enlightened Britain – people would come talking with you – they kind of feel well you know, because you're not a White person you're not equal. And they'll try to put over you, hoodwink you, that you kind of feel they are so with you. You know in your heart they are looking out some good thing for themself to see if they can get across, take disadvantage. . . .. It's a wicked, vicious spirit that want to strip some people from their dignity. (An African-Caribbean Pentecostal Pastor in Britain)

In June 1948, 492 West Indians, mostly Jamaicans, disembarked from the *SS Empire Windrush*; among them was one female stowaway (Banton 1959: 157). By 1961 the number of West Indians in the UK had risen to 172,379 (Patterson 1965: 47–8). Most of the migrants were under thirty, and unlike some other migratory movements, the proportion of women to men was roughly equal (Davison 1962; Glass 1960; Peach 1968). Once in England, West Indians entered into low-status, low-paying employment, returning

1

after work to rented rooms in the inner city areas of Britain's urban conurbations. By 1991, the 'Black Caribbean' population of Great Britain had reached approximately half a million, of which just under half had been born in Britain (OPCS 1991a, Part I: Table 6). It has been fifty years since the arrival of West Indian migrants in Britain and ethnicity remains an issue for African-Caribbean people, for whom 'race' and ethnic divisions continue to structure access to employment, residence and the nature of their lives. However, throughout this period, and continuing to the present, the meaning of 'race' and ethnicity for the identity of African-Caribbean people has been debated and undergone several transformations.

This book examines the construction of identity among first-generation Jamaican migrants through their participation in African-Caribbean Pentecostalism in Britain. From South America to the former Eastern Bloc, Pentecostalism is one of the world's most rapidly expanding religious frameworks. Pentecostalism is a millenarian movement which promises that the current world order and its inequities will be eradicated with the second coming of Christ. As a form of fundamental Christianity, Pentecostalism demands strict moral rigor from its followers in return for the rewards of heaven on earth. The widespread appeal of Pentecostalism among women, migrants and minorities has been variously attributed to its compensatory functions in the face of rapid modernization; economic, political and social marginalization; the problem of overcoming the culture shock migrants confront as they assimilate to a new society; and the perpetuation of distinctive cultural patterns. This study breaks with previous interpretations of Pentecostalism. Instead, African-Caribbean Pentecostalism is regarded as a powerful forum for the construction of new identities which are used to negotiate the dominant, and often injurious, representations made about African-Caribbean people by others in British society.

Based on anthropological fieldwork conducted from January 1990 through June 1991 in Birmingham, England, the initial aim of research was to document the experiences of African-Caribbean women and understand how they construct a sense of self in the face of negative stereotypes regarding immigrant women. During the course of fieldwork it became clear that this endeavor required an understanding of the mobilization of religious resources in Britain's African-Caribbean population. Hence much of the material reflects the broader processes of religious conversion, experience, participation and identification within the church. The dual focus on women and religious identification provides rich and exciting material which makes it possible to begin to think about the nature of the linkages between ethnicity, gender and religion in the construction of self-identity. The 1990s have witnessed the fierce resurgence of nationalisms in which cultural resources are mobilized in the construction of particularistic and divisive identities. This study of the process of Pentecostal belief and identification is a salutary reminder that religious and ethnic identities are not always coterminous and that in the current age identities are not always exclusive. Members of the Pentecostal church studied here create an identity which engages difference and seeks to integrate others on the basis of a common experience as Christians. This book documents how a migrant minority group redefines, relocates and crosses the boundaries of group identity and gender.

The remainder of this introduction provides three rough sketches concerning what we know about Black identity, African-Caribbean women and African-Caribbean religious participation. The sketch of Black identity traces the debates and transformations in post-war Black identity in Britain and the implications of dominant representations for structuring social interaction between Blacks and Whites in British society. The sketch regarding African-Caribbean women presents the ways in which they were portrayed in early accounts up until the mid 1970s and how recent developments in thinking about gender have informed our way of approaching African-Caribbean women. The sketch of religious participation presents the different academic interpretations of the significance of African-Caribbean religious participation and how in recent years representatives of the churches and Black feminists have entered into the politics of representation by defining the role of Black churches for themselves.

Identity

Over the past five decades Black identity in Britain has been talked and written about in a variety of ways. The following sketch is based upon the empirical evidence of the way Blacks were received and perceived on the streets of Britain, but it also recognizes that a gap exists between the way Blacks feel about themselves and the ways in which these perceptions are presented by academics. The sociologist Stuart Hall (1992) has identified three broadly overlapping phases which mark the changes and developments in post-war 'Black identity.' Roughly speaking, these phases correspond to an initial identity as 'West Indian migrant,' followed by 'Black' self-ascription and a current identity of what Hall terms the 'New Ethnicity.'

West Indian Migrant

In the first phase (1945–1965) the Black person was addressed as a 'West Indian migrant' (Davison 1962; Peach 1968). Following World War II, a shortage of labor in Britain's rapidly expanding economy was resolved by an 'open-door policy' regarding New Commonwealth immigration. At this time the average White English person had little knowledge of the colonies, their people or their cultures. Publicly immigration was a benign issue, but privately White English attitudes towards Black people were characterized by ignorance, ambivalence, antipathy and the conflation of 'race,' culture and class (Banton 1955, 1959, 1967; Glass 1960; Little 1947; Patterson 1965). The general ideology of imperialism, with its assumptions of racial hierarchy and Black inferiority, structured the way in which the colonial migrant was initially received and perceived by others in British society (Banton 1967: 368; also Glass 1960; Little 1947; Patterson 1965; Rex 1973). Visible differences of 'race' were the most important single symbol of alienness and cultural difference, and all those who appeared to be different were grouped together in the homogeneous category of 'dark stranger.' Whiteness was the symbol of a superior, pure and advanced culture, while blackness was associated with an inferior, backward and impure race and culture. The concept of cultural immaturity sustained the contradictory stereotypes of the affable, respectful, law-abiding but simple, lazy, childlike, manipulative person and the potentially threatening and sexually promiscuous savage (Banton 1955: 183–8; 1959: 122; 1967: 368, 374–8; Deakin 1970: 284–5; Patterson 1965: 209–11).

On the level of official ideology and public opinion, the Black colonial migrant was a person to whom the abstract idea of equality should be extended (Little 1947: 223–5). The extension of equal opportunity, however, was structured along the lines of imperial trusteeship, in which Britain as an advanced culture was responsible for helping backward people to advance (Banton 1955: 183; 1967: 368). West Indians were perceived as possessing no authentic culture of their own, only an inferior version of British culture (e.g., Banton 1955: 214; Glass 1960: 104; Little 1947: 250). As Patterson put it (1965: 200): 'Unlike most other coloured migrants from the commonwealth, [West Indians] come from an English oriented sub-culture, and lack any distinct and separate culture of their own. . ..' Hence, the public norms governing interaction were the themes of benevolence, philanthropy, fair-play and patronage, in which the assumption was that migrants would in time learn, change, and 'assimilate' into British society (Banton 1967: 378; Little 1947: 223–5).

However, Little and Banton, early researchers on race in Britain, both noted that between public ideology and private views was a yawning gap where the individual was reluctant to contend with the logical implications of putting abstract ideals into practice (Banton 1959: 99; 1967; Little 1947: 225, 233). In public, people were willing to express a favorable attitude towards Black people, but in private there was a substratum of antipathy and prejudice (Banton 1955: 182; 1959, 1967; Little 1947: 225–38). In private, Black people were not accepted on equal terms in relationships where there was a possibility of social and physical contact (Banton 1959; 1967; Little 1947: 245). Ironically, this stance was legitimated on the same terms which had legitimated the public ideology of benevolence – on the basis of innate cultural difference, or claims that the Black person would not know the rules governing social interaction and could easily overstep the boundaries of social relations (Banton ibid.).

While early accounts offer a clear statement of White attitudes towards Black people and responding Black attitudes towards White people (e.g., Banton 1955; Glass 1960; Little 1947), what is less clear is how the Black person felt about him- or herself. From the very date of arrival a gap opened up between the identities assigned to Black people by the White British and the identities which held meaning for them. Early accounts stress that 'West Indians' saw themselves as socially and legally British:

The West Indians were, initially at any rate, the most assimilationist of all the coloured immigrant groups because of their cultural identification with Britain, an identification which was the product of slavery and colonialism in the Caribbean. The West Indians took their British citizenship seriously, and many regarded themselves not as strangers, but as kinds of Englishmen. . . .. As one provincial spokesman put it, 'We are not immigrants in the true technical sense: after all, we are members of the realm, we are British.' (Deakin 1970: 283)

Working in the London docklands in the early 1950s, Banton sketched an enduring paradigm for Black identity structured along the axis of youth and deviance. He noted a polarization between the young unemployed, who were members of local café society, and the older more 'respectable migrants' and the 'old timers,' who had been seamen prior to the wave of post-war immigration (1955: 211–14). Within this paradigm, the young migrant who challenged the stereotypes of White representation and championed their social and legal status as a British person was seen as having developed a heightened 'racial consciousness.' In the phraseology of early accounts he was seen as being 'hypersensitive' or as having a 'chip on his shoulder' (Banton 1955: 212; 1959: 123; Glass 1960: 95; Little 1947: 250, 261; Patterson 1965: 200, 204). How this transformation in West Indian identity was perceived by others is clearly illustrated by Nicholas Deakin:

. . .what the black immigrant meets is a series of English disqualification exercises, implemented with all the massive ingenuity of English hypocrisy. He meets them with tolerant, unvindictive good humour, although there is clearly a limit to his patience. . . .. Tracing the policies expressed by leading West Indian organizations from 1958 to 1968, a clear shift is observable away from assimilation and multiracialism, towards self-help and emphasis on a distinct West Indian identity. It is also possible to observe the changing reaction to the English community: from expectation of fair play, to apprehension, to a certainty of foul dealing. (1970: 287–8)

However, migrants who did not actively or publicly challenge the representations were understood to lack racial consciousness. They were perceived as respectable, acquiescent, withdrawing migrants who shunned interaction or strove to achieve a higher status by adopting the values of the dominant society (Banton 1955: 201–2, 212–13; Glass 1960: 108).

While the perception of West Indian identity made by English observers suggests a progression along a single continuum from English identification to heightened racial consciousness, Hall (1992), himself a Jamaican migrant, and other writers note that there was actually great variety in the ways in which 'West Indians' negotiated their identities and contested the representations which others made about them. The identities which held meaning for Black people were their parochial island loyalties and their ties to the Motherland, identities that were not necessarily incompatible. A meaningful identity was simultaneously Jamaican and British, Trinidadian and British, etc.; Black people were already beginning to construct identities out of symbols infused with meaning in the Caribbean diaspora. In this period, the meaning of Black identity in Britain was the result of racial divisions in the contexts of interaction and of the complex interplay of definitions made by the self and definitions made by others.

The many ways in which West Indians felt about themselves and negotiated identity and the terms of their inclusion in British society are vividly recorded in fictional accounts. In his novel *The Lonely Londoners* (1993 [1956]), Samuel Selvon records the diversity of migrant circumstances and identification in the multiple characters of 'the boys,' while in *The Mimic Men* (1967), V. S. Naipaul presents multiple identities within the single persona of Ralph Singh.

Selvon and 'the boys' are well aware that British society perceives all 'Blacks' as West Indians and all West Indians as Jamaicans (1993: 28, 52). 'The boys,' however have different origins: Cap is a Nigerian student; Moses, Henry-Galahad and Big City are from Trinidad; Tolroy and Lewis are from Jamaica. Sometimes origins cannot be neatly demarcated; Harris is from both Jamaica and Trinidad, and Bart's origins are unclear. Inside the category of Black, 'the boys' perceive difference among themselves and create their own stereotypes to mark out diversity; for example, Moses sees Jamaicans as successful migrants who always manage to save money, sending home remittances or sending for their families (ibid.: 26).

Despite differentiation among 'the boys' they are all equally subject to the 'old English diplomacy' – the racial antipathy – that structures their place in British society and governs social interaction. Each character adopts a different strategy to negotiate the terms of their interaction with others in society or to challenge

dominant representations. Moses is the quiet, older migrant who
until recently identified with Trinidad and maintained a myth of
return. At work, Henry-Galahad adopts the character of the new
West Indian migrant doing hard, menial, night-shift work in
industry; on his days off he becomes the antithetical character of
the young dandy who takes in the sights of the city in English
suits. Henry-Galahad's two personae parallel very different
feelings he has about himself: the self-assured young man who is
so full of confidence that he can choose to ignore racial slights,
but who is also given to moments of panic, introspection and racial
consciousness (ibid.: 41–2, 87–8). Bart and Harris instead opt to
play the 'gentleman,' but for different ends. Bart wants to be a
gentleman, and he clings tenaciously to a clerical job which
differentiates him from most other migrants, using his light-
skinned appearance to claim an identity as Latin American, which
he believes will deflect racial categorization and discrimination
(ibid.: 61). Harris plays into the hands of outsiders' perceptions.
He believes his own culture is substandard and tries assimilation.
He is embarrassed by the community of 'the boys' and by
extrapolation his own identity. To compensate, he plays 'the
ladeda,' becoming more English than the English (ibid.: 111).

In Naipaul's novel, a question mark is placed beside the identity
of the persona of Ralph Singh, but for Singh issues of identity are
not drawn along lines of 'race.' He regards 'race' as irrelevant to
him because he is a Caribbean migrant of Hindu origin. Unlike
'the boys,' Singh is not an economic migrant but a student and
later a 'political immigrant.' Singh lacks a community or group
which can serve as a reference point in the construction of identity.
He is not only searching for an appropriate identity to use in
interaction with others, he is seeking an integrated identity.
Lacking a clear point of reference, Singh is forced to seek out his
identity in the eyes of others: 'We become what we see of ourselves
in the eyes of others' (1967: 20). On the surface, different characters
spin like reflections in a revolving door, and more often than not
Singh plays a two-dimensional extravagant colonial cruising the
British council in a red cummerbund. Singhs's identity may be
situational, but it is compartmentalized. At Ralph Singh's center
there is no sense of unity or cohesion. The fluidity necessary
to negotiate identity in his Caribbean home society becomes
a pathological sense of disassociation and disintegration in
Britain.

Despite the various identities and strategies for interaction adopted by Blacks, the dominant attitudes and stereotypes which lumped Black people together into a homogeneous category remained critical in structuring the 'objective' position of Black people in the contexts of social interaction. In the context of work, migrants were segregated into certain sectors of employment, like manufacturing, transport and the health service, where they were engaged in low-paying jobs with poor working and employment conditions and anti-social hours. The nature of their employment was justified on the basis of dominant stereotypes and public ideology, not as outright discrimination but as a reflection of migrants' abilities (Rex 1973; Patterson 1965: 68–71 and chapters 5, 6).

Differential economic resources, public ideology and dominant stereotypes resulted in residential segregation, with migrants being squeezed into specific inner-city areas (Smith 1989; also Peach, Robinson and Smith 1981). Having been grouped together, migrants came to live their social lives in what John Rex called 'the colony,' where the social institutions of churches, clubs, pubs and shops catered to a Black clientele and helped 'the new immigrant to sustain a social life of his own' (1973: 124). For Rex, 'the colony' provided an important resource in shaping interaction and identity in society: either it could serve as a 'springboard' launching the migrant into British society as a citizen and worker, but also a retreat where the migrant detached himself from society and entered 'an insulated world' of his own; or else its institutions could serve as the 'organs and agencies' of racial revolt (ibid.).

By the beginning of the 1960s, the growth and consolidation of West Indian settlements in London and other urban areas, the growing politicization of race in the national arena and the debates surrounding immigration control were contributing to an increasingly powerful sense of collective identity in which migrants came to see themselves as a group of people originating in the West Indies who shared similar experiences in the context of Britain. This period witnessed the emergence of formal and informal West Indian associations, like the Harmony Clubs, the Association for the Advancement of Coloured People and political organizations like the West Indian Standing Conference, which stressed integration and inter-racial friendship and partnership; the increased growth and popularity of West Indian Pentecostal sects; and the launching of the *West Indian Gazette* (Ramdin 1987: 222–6, 370–

94, 410–15).[1] It is difficult to assess how important these new publications, political organizations and associations may have been in the process of creating this new identity. It is unlikely that every West Indian saw them as important resources.[2]

From the perspective of research, there was little insight regarding how the migrant felt about his or her own identity. Changes in West Indian identity and acts of potential West Indian resistance like political participation, or participation in West Indian Pentecostal sects, were devalued and interpreted by academics as safety valves to release accumulated emotional frustration (Banton 1955: 197; Little 1947: 263–5) or as a manifestation of the hypersensitive attitude of the migrant which stood as an obstacle in the path of assimilation (Calley 1965: 141, 144; Patterson 1965: 227). What is clearer is that as migrants settled down and started or raised families and found themselves committed to life in Britain, the experience of life in Britain was increasingly incorporated into individual views of self.

The last half of the 1960s witnessed an increasingly confrontational and militant stance among some sections of Britain's African-Caribbean population, who adopted the models of Black Power and separatism from the experience of African-Americans. Ramdin puts the mid 1960s as the turning point in the underlying philosophy of Black identity and action; prior to this date Black organizations and leadership were tolerant and accommodating, but from the mid 1960s onwards several organizations began incorporating militancy and separatism as part of their agenda in the struggle to confront racism and fascism (1987: 371).

Black Self-Ascription

By the end of the 1960s, the 'firm but fair' immigration policy agreed upon by both Labour and Conservative governments had closed the door on the primary phase of West Indian migration. By allowing only dependents – primarily women and children –

1. This is not to ignore earlier pan-African movements in the UK (Fryer 1984), but there is little research on the connections between these early movements and more recent ones.
2. For some of the difficulties which hindered the popularity of these associations, see Ramdin (1987: 222–6, 370–4).

right of entry, this act had a dramatic effect on the demographic composition of Britain's African-Caribbean population and the ways in which they were addressed in public, political and academic discourse. These discourses focused on what were now seen as communities of settlers within Britain and their integration into British society. West Indians were no longer addressed as 'immigrants' but as an 'ethnic minority' among other 'ethnic minorities.' The ambivalence inherent in public and private White attitudes towards Black people were increasingly underscored. Racial right-wingers like Enoch Powell and the National Front mobilized a model of an imagined White Britain containing within it a population of unwanted cultural and racial aliens. On the other hand, officially acceptable discourse mobilized a model of a 'multiracial society' founded on 'good race relations.' Britain is imagined in this model as a 'mosaic of communities,' each with its own cultural traditions and institutions. Considerable attention focused upon the 'second generation' and its problematic relations with mainstream British society. During this period, the diversity of the West Indian population was forgotten and attention focused on a criminalized Black male youth. Racial identity became associated with crime and the problems of a pathologized Black community.

The 1970s marked a watershed in Black identity. The background of 'the mugging panic,' the debates on the 'sus' law and educational provision, National Front marches and the experience of racism and discrimination in Britain acted as an increasingly powerful common point of reference for young Black people. This experience provided a category for a new politics of resistance among groups and communities with diverse histories, traditions and ethnic identities. It was in this phase that the 'Black experience' – the experience of the African Diaspora – gained prominence as a framework creating a Black identity across ethnic and cultural difference. The cultural politics of the 1970s and early 1980s challenged, resisted and attempted to transform the relations of representation which rendered stereotypical representations of Black identity (Hall 1992: 252). Hall notes that it produced a 'counter narrative' of the oppressed in which diverse resources and cultural forms were called in from the West Indies, Africa and the US to construct an Afrocentric identity which could be used by actors to negotiate their own spaces (Hall 1992; Henry 1982). Rastafarianism in particular offered a potent 'factory' where such ideas were worked out. The politics of representation and resistance were not, however, limited to African-Caribbean youth: older individuals and Asians were also drawn into the struggles which confronted their children.

Much research during this period reproduced the paradigm of youth and deviance outlined by Banton and as such focused on a very narrow range of identity issues, especially Rastafarianism and the criminalization of Black male youth (e.g., Cashmore and Troyna 1982; Hall *et al.* 1978) and an examination of the resources used in the construction of Black identity (e.g., Cashmore 1979; Hall and Jefferson 1976; Henry 1982; Pryce 1979). The cultures of disaffection were seen as a response to actors' marginal placement in society as a consequence of the dominant stereotypes about Black people. By seeking to understand identity as a response to marginalization, research relied on the dominant stereotypes for its explanation.

The fascination of social science research with cultures of disaffection makes it difficult to assess just how widespread the commitment to such cultures was between 1970 and 1985, or indeed, what was happening with other members of the African-Caribbean population. While it is clear that the meaning of Black identity varies at different historical moments, there is also evidence to suggest that it is situational and that its meaning varies from individual to individual (Benson 1981) and from neighborhood to neighborhood (Wallman 1978).

Beresford Henry (1982) identified five 'corporate identities' for the African-Caribbean population in Handsworth, Birmingham: 'West Indian' (including perpetual migrants and returnees), 'Colonial Settler,' 'Civil Rights Black,' 'Black Nationalist' and 'Pan Africanists' (including Rastafarian). 'West Indians' called themselves 'Black' but qualified this in terms of their island of origin, and the dominant point of reference for the construction of their identity was the West Indies. They were not hostile towards society but preferred to avoid confrontation by maintaining limited political and social involvement with White Britons. They did not belong to any organization other than African-Caribbean Pentecostal churches (ibid.: 435–46). 'Colonial Settlers' referred to themselves as 'Coloured,' not 'Black.' The dominant point of reference for their identity were the values and attitudes of the deferential section of the British working class. This group desired assimilation and preferred to interact with Whites; they had little knowledge of or attachment to local Black organizations (ibid.: 446–9). 'Civil Rights Blacks' called themselves 'Black,' the dominant point of reference being the experience of African-Americans. They believed that the conditions of Black people would be ameliorated not by changing the structure of society, but by working within the structure of society and educating others about the conditions faced by Black people. They also sought integration into White society without forfeiting their Black identity. They tended to join inter-racial, integrationist organizations (ibid.: 449–56). 'Black Nationalists' also called themselves 'Black' but were committed to political engagement and probable confrontation. They believed that the time for protest was over and that it was necessary to change the structure of society and erect a separate Black nation within Britain. Like 'West Indians' and 'Civil Rights Blacks,' their dominant point of reference was outside Britain, where they tended to draw upon the long history of the African Diaspora. Although half the people in this group did not attend church, a significant cluster attended African-Caribbean churches. 'Black Nationalists' joined self-help separatist organizations (ibid.: 456–66). 'Pan-Africanists' were persons of African descent or Rastafarians who also called themselves Black. Unlike members of the other groups, they refused to accept concessions from society or take part in the political process. They firmly rejected British society and drew upon Africa as a point of reference for the construction of identity (ibid.: 466–89).

A number of important conclusions may be drawn from Henry's study. Black identity is not the exclusive property of any one section of Britain's African-Caribbean population. The term 'Black' masks multiple meanings and very different points of reference in the construction of identity. It is also significant that although women were predominant among the 'Colonial Settlers' and young men among the 'Pan-Africanists,' the remaining categories demonstrate comparable proportions of men and women and continuity between the generations (ibid.: 446–9, 466–89). Thus, the emergence of 'Black' identity cannot be neatly correlated with commitment to a specific politics. No simple distinction can be drawn between first-generation 'passivity' and second-generation 'racial activism.' Lastly, different 'Black' identities cannot be neatly sorted according to gender.

Henry's findings indirectly challenge some of the more popular and politically powerful ideas of multiculturalism that developed in the 1980s. Throughout the 1970s, 'biological' models of 'race' in Britain were increasingly replaced by cultural models of difference in which institutional variations like family or religion were taken as badges of community identity. As was noted earlier, this new emphasis on culture was linked to two very different imaginings of the nation. On the one hand, culturally differentiated groups were tolerantly pieced together under the law into a single, culturally heterogeneous Britain. However, the new meaning of race as culture also had a negative side: where race was coupled with 'ethnic absolutism,' the nation was imagined as culturally homogeneous. Hence the discourse of the 'new racism' was based on inclusion and exclusion: those who had the same culture belonged to Britain, while those who did not, did not. People with different cultures could never be assimilated. Neither liberal nor right-wing interpretations of multiculturalist discourse entertained the possibility that cultural diversity and different identity positions existed among the members of the same externally defined group as well as between the members of different groups.

The 1980s witnessed the emergence of Black voices in academic discourse which were not content to reproduce stereotypes about Black people. Authors like Amos and Parmar (1984), Bourne with Sivanandan (1980), Carby (1982a, 1982b), Gilroy (1987), James (1989), Lawrence (1982a, 1982b) and Parmar (1982) questioned the hegemonic meanings of race, culture, class and gender, and began to disentangle these concepts and to rewrite the history of Black people in Britain. In doing so, these authors attacked the very basis of both popular multiculturalist discourse and the 'new racism.' Errol Lawrence stripped away the 'common sense' notions which had defined African-Caribbean and Asian people by emphasizing the discontinuities between them, re-evaluating the institution of the family as that epitome of cultural difference, demythologizing African-Caribbean and Asian cultures, and positing continuity between generations of African-Caribbean people (1982a, 1982b). Instead of trying to explain the position of race and ethnicity in relation to an overarching class structure, Paul Gilroy sought to understand the formation of 'class' and 'race' (1987: 19). Since 'race' was not an absolute but a politically and socially constructed category, he argued that its meaning can change, accommodating various meanings both over time and simultaneously in a single historical conjuncture (ibid.: 38). By recounting the variety of resources (music, language, religion, political philosophy) which originate in the Black Diaspora and are used in the construction of Black identity in Britain, Gilroy sought to demonstrate that Black culture is complex, dynamic and syncretic. This makes it impossible to accept ethnic absolutism and the static view of culture posited by multiculturalism.

The 'New Ethnicity'

In the 1990s, we can no longer speak of a single homogeneous Black identity. The coherent Black identity and political movements of the 1970s are no longer powerful. While racial disadvantage remains a salient feature of life in Britain, there is also a self-acknowledged diversification of identity among Britain's African-Caribbean population. Current academic work is attempting to move away from ideas of multiculturalism and to account for the diversity of Black identity which is encountered on the streets.

Claire Alexander (1992) analyses the diverse possibilities of Black identity among young Black men in East London. She does not present us with multiple characters like those who inhabit Selvon's London; instead, the diverse possibilities of Black identity are approached as performative alternatives for the single individual – in a more positive and coherent manner than Naipaul's Ralph Singh. Alexander argues that at street level Black men actively construct a variety of alternative identities which can be manipulated according to context and used in the negotiation of representation and interaction (ibid.: 24). Hence the alternative identities which these men hold is best understood as situational ethnicity and symbolic interaction in which the form and content of identity is derived from the different contexts of 'lived experience' (home, work, leisure) and the manipulation of symbols. Among the variety of identities, one's identity at any given moment becomes the enactment of individual choice based upon one's assessment of the situation and one's desired ends. However, the range and nature of alternative identities for these young men are limited by the ways in which others see them and by the resources they command (ibid.: 79–80). The construction of alternative identities and choice of identity at any given moment within the socio-economic and political constraints of society and relations of power and dominance constitute what Alexander calls the 'art of being Black' (ibid.: 80, 296).

Hall (1992) describes the current phase as one of 'hybridity'; it signals the end of the 'essential Black subject.' The Black person has the potential to claim inclusion in several different worlds which are not based on 'pure' origins but on the 'cut and mix' of experience and difference. Identity encompasses the variation of subjective positions, social experiences and cultural repertoires that constitute the category of 'Black.' Black identity is understood as a politically and culturally constructed category which cannot be grounded in nature (ibid.: 254) or tied to the boundaries of nationhood. The question then becomes: If identity is not about nature or citizenship, where and how is it grounded? The 'New Ethnicity' creates a sense of belonging rather than exclusion; it engages difference and is premised upon the commonalty of experience over the purity of origins (Hall 1992).

The shifts in meaning of Black identity in post-war Britain highlight two important issues which form the background for the research and analysis presented here: age and gender. We need to account for the meaning of Black identity for older African-Caribbean people, especially women, in Britain.

Hall is careful to point out that, with reference to identity, the movement from phase to phase does not render the expressions and strategies of an earlier phase obsolete (ibid.: 253). There seems, however, to be a view that while the process which creates new forms of identity is cumulative, with the arrival of new actors in each phase, the experiences and negotiations of the previous generation recede into a passive and acquiescent past. The division between the first and second generations of Britain's African-Caribbean population is reinforced by concepts like inter-generational conflict (Lawrence 1982a) and the shift in labels from 'immigrant' to 'ethnic minority.' As Sheila Allen suggests (1982: 146-7), when reference is made to the experiences of the first generation, it either renders their experiences invisible or offers a foreshortened account in order to sharpen the comparisons between the attitudes and behavior of the first generation and their children.

The corrective to generational discord can be found in the writings of the second generation of Black British authors like Bryan, Dadzie and Scafe (1985), Dodgson (1984), James (1989) and Lawrence (1982a, 1982b). By asking 'Who fought the Fascists and Teddy Boys in Nottingham and Notting Hill in 1958?' Lawrence reminds us that despite the fact that some 'youths have brought new understandings and different modes of struggle' to the conflict, this does not mean they are not 'following in their parent's footsteps or that they don't stand firmly *side by side* their parents in opposition to racism' (1982b: 132, original emphasis). There is not always a disjuncture in the forms and expressions of the two generations. James has argued that due to shared experiences of racism in Britain, there has been a convergence in the perspectives of parents and youth where each new generation has discovered the extent of racism and the strategies to combat it from the existing one (1989: 240–1).

While youth as the vanguard of Black identity continue to mesmerize observers and researchers, it must be remembered that members of the first generation are not dead and that their continued experiences must inform the way we think about current Black identity in Britain (Allen 1982). Although dismissed in earlier accounts and ignored in later work – with the exception of Malcolm Calley (1962, 1965) and Clifford Hill (1963, 1971a, 1971b, 1971c) – African-Caribbean religious participation in the West Indian Pentecostal sects is an expression and strategy adopted by West Indian migrants in the politics of representation. This work spans the generation gap, not by tracing explicit continuities between generations, but by returning the focus of study to the first generation and examining their continuing history and experiences, as well as examining how religious participation in African-Caribbean Pentecostalism persists as a viable strategy adopted by both old and young in the politics of representation.

> The Black Pentecostal Church has provided for the young, for middle-aged, for old, a sense of identity, equality, participation. Young people don't need to go out and plait their hair in dreadlocks to find identity. (Io Smith, Pastor of the New Testament Assembly, in Smith and Green 1989: 104)

Not only does the subculture perspective ignore the varied ways in which the first generation and the majority of Britain's African-Caribbean population structure their experiences, it can also be accused of gender blindness (Allen 1982: 155). Initially, attention focused primarily on the history and experiences of Pakistani, Bangladeshi and Indian migrant women, where the presence of authentic culture was not at issue (e.g., Westwood 1984; Westwood and Bhachu 1988; Wilson 1978). Less work was focused on African-

Caribbean women, though the Black feminist critique has begun to change this. Findings suggest that young women structure their experiences differently from men (e.g., Dex 1983; Edwards 1988; Fuller 1982). Understanding how African-Caribbean women are active participants in the construction of identity and the negotiation of interaction with others requires a specific understanding of their histories and experiences.

Women

Although approaches to identity have become increasingly sophisticated, the experiences of women and of the older generation are relegated to a background position. Research on migrants, whether focusing on the determinants and patterns of migration or attempting to understand the social position of migrants, has for the most part ignored women. However, quite early on a very high proportion of women were migrating from the West Indies: in 1956, over forty percent of Jamaican migrants were women (Jamaican Ministry of Labour, in Davison 1962: Table 4). As of 1992, over fifty percent of the British population who were born in the Caribbean were female, and women who had been born in Jamaica were the only group of female migrants outnumbering their male counterparts (OPCS 1991a, Part 1: Table 7).

Although the arrival of West Indian female migrants was recorded (Banton 1959: 157, Glass 1960: 15), the history and experiences of women in the first decade of post-war immigration is poorly documented. We lack an understanding of the different factors which prompted women to migrate, their circumstances in Britain, the nature of their domestic relationships, how they encountered racism, and how they felt about these issues, made sense of them and incorporated them into views about themselves. When West Indian women and their circumstances were acknowledged, they were interpreted with reference to contemporary stereotypes of Black people and the dominant conception of gender for White women.

Joyce Eggington (1957) and Sheila Patterson (1965) provide early accounts in which economically 'dependent' housewives are contrasted with single women. It was assumed that the 'dependent' West Indian woman had never worked outside the home before. They were depicted as 'home-birds' who had shared domestic responsibilities with other women within the extended family and household (Eggington 1957: 131; Patterson 1965: 75). Brief mention is made of domestic difficulties, of the increased domestic responsibilities shouldered by women in the absence of female kin and of how racism and discrimination penetrated relationships between husband and wife and mother and child. Attention is directed instead to women's occupational engagement, West Indian women being seen as an immature and incapable labor force. Eggington wrote that West Indian women were 'slow, patient and content to stay in lower paid jobs,' while the more ambitious found that the nursing exams were 'far beyond them' (1957: 132). Patterson noted that West Indian women had little experience of 'routine work, industrial discipline, time-keeping and regular attendance at work regardless of minor ills or domestic troubles' (1965: 75). She reports that management found West Indian women to be 'slow,' 'lazy' and 'child-like' (Patterson ibid.: 99, 100). While it is acknowledged that not all West Indian women had men in England, economically independent female migrants were immediately pathologized where their circumstances and experiences were tied to the issue of motherhood and illegitimacy (Eggington 1957: 132–6; Patterson 1965: 292–3). The issues of employment, motherhood and domestic responsibility raised by these accounts, though later elaborated with considerations of class and race, were to become the essential and enduring baselines from which the position of African-Caribbean women in England was addressed.

In 'Women, Work and Migration' (1976), the anthropologist Nancy Foner draws upon migrant women's own interpretations and perceptions of their circumstances. Comparing migrant women to women in Jamaica, she argues that the position of migrant women has 'on balance' improved because they have greater independence and better relations with their husbands (ibid.: 85, 88).[3] Foner explains this improvement in terms of two 'new features' of migrant women's lives in England: superior wage-earning opportunities and the greater isolation of the nuclear family. While Foner is careful not to reproduce the dichotomy of no work/work which characterized earlier studies, she argues that the difference between irregular work and regular work is crucial.

3. See Lawrence (1982b) for criticisms of Foner's work.

Thus what it means to work and the value of women's previous work experience as nurses, teachers, secretaries, shop clerks, domestics, seamstresses and agricultural laborers in Jamaica is suppressed, while the increased opportunity for regular work and a regular wage in England is en-valued and read only as beneficial. In contrast, the greater isolation of the nuclear family is interpreted as a 'mixed blessing.' In spite of the fact that migrant women have to contend with an increased burden of childcare, they are seen as 'freer from family constraints' because the fact that they work means that men have had to shoulder some of the domestic burden (1976: 93, 86). Work also implies freedom from domestic constraints because it provides the financial wherewithal to leave male partners if necessary. Foner argues that the husband–wife relationship has changed because of the absence of female kin upon whom women could rely and because the presence of a 'normative stress' on joint husband and wife activities has meant that women look to men for support and companionship. It may be the case that among some couples there was a shift towards a more joint relationship between husband and wife; however, we cannot assume that this shift was the norm nor that it was indicative of assimilation to British society.[4]

There are few women's voices in the accounts offered by Eggington, Patterson and Foner, and the variety of women's circumstances can only be perceived through the prism of their conjugal relationships with men. What remains unclear are the circumstances which confronted single, widowed and divorced women and how the factors of race and class have a significant bearing on the experiences and perceptions of all Black women in Britain. Fiction affirms as well as repudiates some of the common-sense assumptions which guided early work. It provides valuable insights into the motivations behind female migration, the multiple circumstances West Indian women confronted in Britain and how they incorporated these experiences into their perceptions of self.

In *The Lonely Londoners* (Selvon 1993 [1956]), the characters of Ma, Tanty and Agnes challenge the stereotype of the economically dependent, isolated, backward 'wife-migrant.' Ma is 'sent for' not by a husband, but by her son, and Tanty, Agnes and Lewis decide to come along as well. This alerts us to the fact that the pattern of

---

4. Compare working-class British conjugal partnerships (Bott 1957; Young and Wilmott 1962).

female migration may be more complex than simply husbands sending for wives; other male kin – fathers, brothers, sons, etc. – may have provided part of the motivation to migrate. Margaret Prescod-Roberts also reminds us that single women, mothers and wives came to England to earn money and send remittances home (Prescod-Roberts and Steele 1980: 25). Ma is not economically dependent on her son. She is economically active, but the terms of her employment are structured by her gender and her 'race'; she is employed as an institutional domestic, cleaning dishes out of sight in the kitchen of a Lyons Corner House[5] (Selvon 1993: 81). It is unclear whether Agnes is economically active. When Lewis, her husband, begins to beat her she finds the strength to leave him not from a wage packet but from the support of her female kin (Selvon 1993: 72). It was never Tanty's intention to 'work' for wages in England: she arrives as an unexpected dependent. It is quite clear, however, that Tanty's job is the social reproduction of her kin so that she can enable them to go out and work (1993: 31). Although she is economically inactive, Tanty is the most visible and well-developed of Selvon's female characters. On the surface she is like Henry-Galahad, she appears knowledgeable about life in England and confident. If in reality she is scared or unsure, she does not show it. Tanty leads a circumscribed life within 'the colony' of Harrow Road, but she is also prepared to take on London and British society when necessary (Selvon 1993: 78–9, 81–3).

Joan Riley's story of Adella Johnson in *Waiting in the Twilight* (1987) demonstrates how the domestic circumstances of women change over time and exposes the personal feelings absent in other accounts of migrant women. Adella was 'sent for' by her husband Stanton, but upon arrival she is employed as a seamstress, utilizing economic skills she had used in Jamaica. Women may be 'sent for' as wives, but this does not preclude their becoming economically active in England. The institutional racism which undervalued their spouse's skills and legitimized low wages, together with the isolation of life in a boarding house, often led women to work.

Central to Adella's story is the acknowledgment that racism and discrimination intervene and restructure relationships between husband and wife and parent and child. Adella remembers a proud, responsible and respected Stanton in Jamaica. In Britain his skills go unrecognized, he is emasculated by society and feels

5. A chain of popular tea and coffee shops.

cuckolded by Adella. He adopts an external posture of acquiescence; he lacks authority and respect in society but grabs hollow
power and respect by beating Adella and the children. Finally, he
abandons a crippled Adella, their children and the mortgage.
Adella's domestic circumstances shift from being part of a couple
with small children in a bedsit, to being a family in a house of
their own with tenants, to being a single mother with boarders
and male friends who help her make ends meet, to living in a
council house with her daughter. Paralleling Adella's changing
domestic circumstances is a progression from hope and expectation
about her future and the future of her children to the erosion of
hope and expectation. England took away Stanton's pride and stole
Adella's expectations for herself and her children.

In her short story 'Let Them Call it Jazz' (1973), Jean Rhys'
character Selina Davis is the exception seized upon to confirm
racist stereotypes about Black women. She is a single Caribbean
woman who is economically inactive. She appears to lack family
and friends. She is isolated, living outside 'the colony' in a white
suburban neighborhood, where she is perceived as a threat and
as a prostitute. We witness her descent into feelings of misunder-
standing, persecution and worthlessness. This leads her to
depression and drink, and when she tries to cheer herself up by
singing she is called 'drunk and disorderly.' She hits rock bottom
when she is arrested and incarcerated in Holloway Prison. In
prison she slowly learns to sing again and reemerges back into
life in a migrant neighborhood, where she gets a job and makes
friends. Selina has made her accommodation with British society:
her strategy is to deal on the level of surface pleasantries, to talk
about the weather and to let them misread her blues for jazz.
Racism no longer affects her to the core, perhaps because like Ralph
Singh there is no core left.

Replacing earlier uncritical work, the 1980s witnessed a radical
shift in thinking about the experience of work for Black women.
During this period, attention focused on the articulation of race,
gender, class and migrant status in determining the position of
African-Caribbean women in the labor force. Research focused
squarely on the crucial issue of motherhood and work for Black
women, thus incorporating the issue of women's role in the
domestic sphere, which had been absent in the work of Patterson
(see Dex 1983; Phizacklea 1983; Phoenix 1988; Stone 1983). The
dominant ideological construction of women's gender in Britain

was that motherhood and work were mutually incompatible. The guiding premise in this work was that women occupy a segregated and subordinate position in the workforce determined by their position in the family, their reproductive role and patriarchal relations (Bradley 1989; Dex 1985). Given this starting premise, these studies examined the specific location of migrant women in the workforce relative to the indigenous female workforce. It was found that Black women occupied a subordinate position relative to White women (Phizacklea 1983; Stone 1983). Since the engagement of Black women in the workforce differed from that of their White counterparts, women's role in the family alone could not account for the subordinate position of Black female workers. Hence, in order to understand the position of Black women in the workforce, answers were sought in terms of race and class as well (i.e., Phizacklea 1983: 101).

Although these approaches acknowledged the complex articulation of race, class and gender in determining the engagement of Black women in the workforce, they failed to acknowledge the complex articulation of these issues, which results in a different construction of the family and of gender for Black women. If the position of Black women in the workforce is to be understood with reference to their role in the family, explanation must take into account the differences in the Black family and the specific construction of gender for Black women, which are evident in the fictional record. The Black feminist critique of White feminist theory draws our attention to the complexity of the Black family and the implications of different forms of patriarchy for understanding the subordinate position of Black women. Where the family is central to White feminist theory as the locus of women's oppression, the Black feminist critique challenges the way in which academics define the family and the role of Black women within it and the way in which this is seen to articulate with women's engagement in the labor force (Amos and Parmar 1984: 9; Carby 1982a). Although Amos and Parmar concede that White feminists do not accept the stereotyped representations of Black people unquestioningly, they suggest that White feminist scholars have nonetheless been influenced by them. Here White feminist theory works with the idea of the strong and dominant African-Caribbean woman as head of the household, who is nevertheless exploited by the sexism inherent in the relations between African-Caribbean men and women (Amos and Parmar 1984: 9). Other dominant conceptions of the family deal with the oppression of women in the family in their roles as mothers and wives, and Amos and Parmar feel that this conceptualization of the family cannot come to terms with the contradictions which surround the various roles of Black women in the family as sisters, aunts or daughters (1984: 10). In a slightly different vein, Hazel Carby questions the view that the nuclear family is somehow progressive and liberating for Black women, and that as such its absence can be used to measure the pathology of Black women (1982a: 217).

Carby (1982a) also notes that White feminist 'herstory' in Britain constructs work and marriage as inimical alternatives and cannot explain how Black women bridged this gap. The inherent contradiction between mother/wife and worker coalesced in the dominant perceptions of Black women. While the terms of White women's employment were dictated by the privileging of family life and their role as mothers, Carby notes that in fact Black women were recruited into the labor force in a manner which disregarded their family roles and the Black woman as mother. Instead, in Britain, the state reproduced common-sense notions of the Black family's inherent pathology: 'black women were seen to fail as mothers precisely because of their position as workers' (Carby 1982a: 219).

This work is indebted to the contribution to thinking about gender made by the Black feminist critique, but it also recognizes that this critique is of limited use in understanding the full complement of Black women's lives in Britain today. To concentrate on the domestic sphere is to work within a highly restricted and sterile view of women's lives, positing a norm of work and family life which does not characterize the lives of many women. Just as we have come to recognize the diversity of Black identities in Britain, we also need to recognize the varied experiences and circumstances of Black women and the plurality of Black female identities. Black women also live their lives in and through leisure activities and in voluntary associations like African-Caribbean churches, all of which can provide the commonality of experience necessary to act as point of reference in the construction of a Black identity.

Religion

The West Indian Pentecostal sects which provided a basis of association and identity during the 1950s and 1960s have not disappeared but have continued to grow. Among the diverse forms of African-Caribbean religious participation in Britain are Rastafarianism, the Church of the Cherubim and Seraphim, and a variety of non-conformist Black churches like the Pentecostal New Testament Church of God and some congregations of the Seventh Day Adventist church. Since religious participation remains a central feature of the lives of many African-Caribbean people in Britain, an understanding of the significance and nature of their religious participation remains crucial to our understanding of the construction of identity for older African-Caribbean women. While only ten percent of the total population in the UK attends church (CSO 1993: 153–4) by contrast it is estimated that twenty percent of the African-Caribbean population regularly attend,[6] with almost 70,000 attending African-Caribbean Churches (Brierly 1992–93: 216).[7] Rough estimates suggest that over two thirds of African-Caribbean church membership is female. The single largest African-Caribbean denomination is currently the Pentecostal New Testament Church of God, which has an estimated 6,507 members in 103 congregations and accounts for over nine percent of all members of African-Caribbean churches (Brierly 1992–93).

The view that Caribbean culture was a permutation of a more sophisticated British culture and the idiom of paternal colonialism affected the way in which African-Caribbean religious practice was interpreted during the period 1948 to 1965. During this period it was believed that English churches were the first place where integration and assimilation would occur (Hill 1963: 7; Patterson 1965: 226). There seemed to be good evidence to support this optimistic view. Since it was assumed that West Indians had inherited their 'culture' from the British, it was obvious that they

6. Bishop Kalilombe, Centre for Black and White Christian Partnership, Selly Oak College, personal communication; also Howard 1987.

7. While attendance in the Anglican, Methodist and Roman Catholic churches has fallen by one tenth, the Pentecostal and African-Caribbean churches have experienced an increase of eight and four percent respectively (CSO 1993: 153–4). Brierly 1992–93, records that African-Caribbean churches experienced a six percent increase in membership between 1985 and 1990.

shared the same cultural values, beliefs and behaviors exhibited in the same institutional forms, i.e., Christianity and churches. After all, hadn't it been English missionaries who had brought Christianity to the West Indies? Secondly, beyond the work shift, church services and activities provided a space for social interaction where favorable contact between migrants and their hosts would win out in the field of race relations (Patterson 1965: 226, 228).

However, it very quickly became clear that few Blacks could be found in the main English denominations. Although the various denominational synods and the more liberal clergy held favorable attitudes towards the newcomers, encouraging social integration premised upon the ideals of Christian universalism and brotherhood, lay members and many parochial clergy were reluctant to admit Blacks into their fellowship on equal terms. Blacks were actively discouraged from attending or participating in services (see Banton 1959: 122; Little 1947: 263–4 for illustrations). Banton and Little both noted that the discrepancy between the views of the synods and the laity was a 'galling' manifestation of the gap between a public policy of benevolence and equality and a private policy of antipathy and racism (Banton 1955: 222, 224; 1959: 121; Little 1947: 241, 257).[8] Either Blacks were perceived as heathens who had to be converted (Little 1947: 252; Patterson 1965: 227) or it was felt that one should maintain social distance in the field of religious expression (Banton 1959: 121).

Explanation for the absence of Blacks in the main denominations quickly moved from the responsibility of the hosts to the fault of the migrants. The idea that it was the English interpretation of Christianity that left something to be desired was replaced with the idea that because of the legacy of non-conformist Christianity in the Anglophone Caribbean, West Indians had a different interpretation of Christianity, one incompatible with English belief and practice. Stretching the idea that West Indians lack 'authentic culture' to its limits, Patterson argued that West Indian Christian belief and practices were based on a different set of behavior and attitudes, which were masked by the overall framework of

8. Deakin has outlined the reaction of the Church of England to New Commonwealth immigration and the race relations debate from the 1950s to 1982 and suggested that church policy has paralleled the political policies of the secular élite (1984–85). For criticisms of this work, see Leech 1985.

Christianity (1965: 204–5). It is in this vein that Eggington and Patterson transform recognizable Christianity into exotic religious expression, though they do so in different ways (Eggington 1957: 115*f*; Patterson 1965: 205–7).

In a prosaic account of a West Indian church in Brixton, Eggington exoticizes and de-normalizes West Indian Christianity by drawing contrasts with English orthodox Christianity *in absentia*. Although the Brixton church is a cold Victorian building adorned with Union Jacks and images of the Queen, the service is perceived as different. Eggington repeatedly refers to the length of the sermon delivered by a man who paraphrases the Bible and has 'a happy disregard for historical accuracy'; it is an emotional service where people actively respond to the message and carry musical instruments and where women wear 'strange hats' (1957: 117–18, 120). Eggington places this type of worship on a West Indian continuum of orthodox Anglicanism and the practices of Obeah and Pocomania reminiscent of 'ancient African tribal worship' (ibid.: 122). Although she concedes that this form of religious expression is a 'middle way,' she adds that Pocomania[9] is 'only a more primitive form of the worship [described for Brixton]' and that 'the line which divides them is thin' (ibid.: 123). For Eggington, then, the emphasis is upon cultural differences obscured by the common mask of Christianity.

Patterson, by contrast, emphasizes differences in function between the church in the West Indies and Britain. In the West Indies orthodox Christianity bound society together, but this function is no longer served by the churches in Britain (1965: 205). The orthodox Christian churches in the West Indies provided the individual with a sense of warmth and community with his fellow worshippers; when the migrant arrives in England he is subject to a rude awakening, and his reaction to this disappointment and disillusionment is his rejection of English Christianity (ibid.: 205). She writes that migrants 'gloss over the practical reasons' for not attending English churches and thus shift responsibility for their failure to attend church onto everybody else when rejection is rarely the fault of the minister or the congregation (ibid.: 227). For both Eggington and Patterson, the argument is that West Indians are unable to accept involvement in British institutions.

9. Pocomania is one of the numerous Afro-Christian syncretic cults which developed in Jamaica; see chapter 3.

For Patterson, this pattern is only a temporary one. Since Pentecostal sects connoted low economic and social status in the West Indies, as migrants' fortunes improve in Britain and as racial accommodation progresses, they will abandon their membership (ibid.: 305). However, she acknowledges that they are a form of protest and concedes that if the economic conditions of migrants were to worsen, there could be a rise in participation in cults like Rastafarianism. Given the secular nature of English society, however, it is more likely that migrants would turn to political associations (ibid.: 306).

It is certainly the case that membership of Black-led Pentecostal denominations was increasing at this time. It was originally carried to England by a handful of migrants who had been ministers and members in Jamaica and other parts of the Caribbean and also significantly originated within the context of life in Britain. Early commentators interpreted African-Caribbean Pentecostal expression within the framework of assimilation. The first comprehensive work on West Indian Pentecostal participation in England was conducted by the anthropologist Malcolm Calley (1965). His study, *God's People*, is rich in detail relating to doctrine, ritual, the processes of fission and fusion which aid or hinder the growth of congregations, and their internal organization. Although he differs from Patterson in some respects, Calley shares her view that the problems of assimilation rest with the migrant. In his analysis, the different functions of churches in British and West Indian society offer only a partial explanation for migrants' failure to attend English denominations and for the rise of West Indian Pentecostal sects. He suggests that even if the function of religion were the same in both societies, migrants would still participate in the sects because they do not want to identify with English society. Migrants are the ones who are rejecting English churches; racism and discrimination in English churches are reduced to a folk-myth charter which is cited as an excuse for migrants' failure to attend church (ibid.: 123). Because it is assumed that the individual's economic circumstances are improved by migration, Calley is led to posit discontinuity between the compensatory function of sectarianism in Jamaican society and its function in England. Instead, answers must be sought in the difficulty the migrant experiences in settling down (ibid.: 137). Although he mentions cultural differences, isolation, racism and discrimination, his explanation resonates with loud echoes of the hypersensitive migrant who does not want to adapt. Thus he argues that discrimination is a two-way street: the migrant has a discrimination 'neurosis' which provides a ready excuse for him to shun contact with English society and turn inwards to rely on the resources of the migrant community, notably the Pentecostal sects (ibid.: 140–1). Even if there were no racial discrimination, the sects would continue to exist; they are groups which exist for their own sake and function to increase ethnic group solidarity (ibid.: 142). Hence, sects are a stumbling block to assimilation because they provide a magico-religious refuge from the strains of settling down in a new country (ibid.: 144).

Unlike Calley, the minister and sociologist Clifford Hill offers a more consistent and equitable explanation for the growth of West Indian Pentecostal sects in Britain (1963, 1971a, 1971b, 1971c). He argues that no single causative factor can be identified and, like Calley, rejects the idea of economic deprivation. Unlike his predecessors, he argues that participation in the sects are symbolic of members' disillusionment and dissociation with a society that has rejected them (1971a: 13). However, his argument remains centered upon functionalist explanations where he proposes that, where the gradations of color, class and status have been obliterated by the crude dichotomy of Black and White which exists in Britain, the migrant experiences relative status deprivation. For Hill, the growth of African-Caribbean Pentecostal worship is directly correlated with status deprivation, and as long as this continues, membership in the sects will continue to grow. Like Calley, Hill recognizes that sectarianism among migrants in England differs from that in Jamaica, but he retains the idea that religion is a form of expression comparable to political expression in the West Indies. He suggests that in an atmosphere of partial assimilation and the migrants' desire for greater acceptance, religion can be understood as a second line of defense in the fight for recognition, where it lies between outright political activism and religions of despair which posit a complete withdrawal from the world and the overthrow of the status quo (1971b: 122).

In Hill's work, the only concession to the view that Pentecostal sects deter assimilation concerns the second generation. Hill suggests that if status deprivation were to continue and the second generation were to join their parents in this form of religious participation, it would increase the social distance between young Blacks and their White peers and result in a further deterioration of race relations (1971a: 19).

During the late 1970s, academic attention on African-Caribbean religious expression focused on Rastafarianism as a resource mobilized in the construction of Black identity among African-Caribbean youth. The work on Rastafarianism alerts us to the fact that African-Caribbean religiosity possesses a long history as a subverted form of political expression. Authors like Ernest Cashmore (1979), Ivor Morrish (1982) and to a lesser extent Ken Pryce (1979) trace the origins of Rastafarian political expression from the magico-religious practices of Obeah-Myal through non-conformist Christianity and African-Christian syncretisms like Revivalism. However, this historical insight is not extended to other current forms of African-Caribbean religious practice and participation, such as Pentecostalism, non-conformism and orthodox Christianity. In fact, during this period the study of African-Caribbean religiosity reproduced the biases of age and gender and the omissions of alternative strategies which characterized the dominant academic discourse regarding Black identity and gender.

The generation and gender gap is made explicit in Cashmore's work on Rastafarianism (1979). In Cashmore's analysis, the contrasting religious orientations provided by Rastafarianism and Christianity are a synonym of the disjuncture, rupture and tension between the first and second generations. He acknowledges that Christian parents and Rastafarian youth share the same lack of wealth, power and status in the British context and that the religious instruction of youth at the hands of their parents 'conveniently prepared the ground' for Rastafarianism (ibid.: 73). However, he argues the case for disjuncture by stressing the different interpretations of the Bible held by parents and youth. Parents who have a fundamentalist interpretation of the Bible are seen, in the words of his informants, as 'brainwashed' or 'misguided' and as not possessing consciousness of their true selves because they do not share in the tradition of critical Biblical exegesis (ibid.: 74). This argument rests on a literal interpretation of fundamentalism and an absence of history, ignoring the different uses and interpretations of the Bible throughout West Indian religious history and the hours of Bible study and discussion which constitute an element of fundamentalist worship. Although Black

Christians and Pentecostals find different meanings in the Bible from those of Rastafarians, this does not mean that they are not engaged in critically rethinking what the Bible means and how its message can be brought to bear on their own experiences. For Cashmore, the blind acceptance of Christianity is added to the migrant myth of return and different generational experiences as the cause of first-generation passivity (ibid.: 72). This seems a far cry from the earlier view that West Indian Pentecostal sects were a form of silent protest and resistance to assimilation. Further, by replacing matrifocality with a new dominant male identity, one of the issues Rastafarianism negates is the dominance of women in Jamaican society. Rastafarianism is 'men's property' and the few women in Rastafarianism 'graciously concede' its anti-feminist stance (Cashmore ibid.: 78, following Kitzinger 1969). It is unclear whether or not Rastafarianism provides a point of reference for the construction of a Black identity which has meaning for women in Britain.

In his study of the variety of African-Caribbean lifestyles in Bristol, Pryce (1979) reproduces the same divisions and omissions as Cashmore. It is significant that the strategies of 'saints'[10] (along with 'respectable proletarians' and 'mainliners') are seen not as 'expressive' but 'law-abiding.'[11] Here a generational divide and concomitant axis of acquiescence and resistance structures the text; the expressive strategies of youth are physically separated from the discussion of the passive protest of older people. Pryce's presentation and discussion leave little room for feedback or negotiation between youth and adults and the strategies they employ, only for conflict (ibid.: 167–8). He also reproduces the idea that women lack expressive strategies. In the first half of the book, women are portrayed as mothers, single mothers, aunts and willing and unwilling prostitutes, who by virtue of being on the receiving end can do little but complain and write letters to each other (ibid.: 80–94). In the second half, women predominate among the membership of un-expressive, stoic, politically apathetic, godfearing saints (ibid.: 185). Henry's findings remind us that there can be no easy division of the African-Caribbean population into first-generation 'quietists' and young radicals nor into male and

10. An emic term of self-reference for members of African-Caribbean churches.
11. Pearson, however, defines participation in African-Caribbean Pentecostalism as deviant non-respectable behavior (1976: 377).

female. We should also be wary of conflating age and gender divisions such that all women are passive and all men radicals.

Since the 1970s, there has been an increased sense of the continuing importance of Black Churches[12] in the lives of Britain's African-Caribbean population. Research has turned its attention to the role, actual or potential, of Black Churches in mediating the relationship between the African-Caribbean population and the state. In the context of multiculturalism, ethnic and religious institutions are seen as 'self-help' organizations through which state funds are channeled to ethnic minorities. Rex and Tomlinson (1979) were the first to recognize the potential role of Black Churches in multiculturalist policy. Due to their avowed withdrawal from the world, Black Churches provide a basis of passive resistance, self-segregation and solidarity. A church can therefore act as a 'Black self-help group' which can interface with ethnic social work and politics in a positive way (ibid.: 248). More recently, Johnson (1988) has examined how churches can address the 'challenges' and 'opportunities' of multiculturalist policy. Because of their 'legitimacy,' assets and members, Black Churches are uniquely qualified to articulate with the state and to renew the inner cities (ibid.: 91, 100). He argues that they are in a legitimate position of representation, not because of the theological justification for 'good works' which gives them a mandate to engage in social work, but because they possess 'street credibility': 'As community-based organizations with a membership drawn from those local communities, church groups can identify local needs and speak with the agencies and authorities of the state as something approaching equals. . .' (ibid.: 100). This perspective, however, neglects the nature of religious experience: churches are not simply Black self-help groups but are critically concerned with the questions of self, suffering, sin and salvation.

While Black academics were re-writing their own histories and becoming engaged in critically rethinking culture, race, class, gender and the implications of multiculturalism, the leadership and membership of Black Churches were also re-writing their own histories. It was clear to participants that the church was a vital resource for confronting the racism and discrimination which Black people face in Britain: 'Race issues should be tackled from a

12. The term 'Black Church' refers to denominations where the leadership and membership is predominantly Black.

Christian viewpoint, especially in a country that claims to be Christian' (Smith and Green 1989: 102).

However, African-Caribbean churches were also questioning the extent to which they could be defined as an ethnic community, as well as their religious mandate for ethnic self-help and articulation with the state (see Arnold 1992; Brooks 1982; Edwards 1991). The church leadership had to resolve the following dilemma: their theology advocated separation from the world and an inclusive Christian brotherhood which transcended race and culture, but participation in the ethnic politics of multiculturalism offered resources on the basis of an exclusive Black identity and involvement with the world. Although the theology of the church was founded upon meeting the spiritual needs of people, it did not encourage political activism and involvement in order to meet the social and economic needs of members. Yet the Gospel also justified social ministry: it would be easier to meet the spiritual needs of members if their social and economic needs were met. As early as the late 1960s and early 1970s, when the churches had been 'initiated' into the game of politics, they realized that if they defined themselves as 'Black Churches' and got organized they could harness the resources required to meet the needs of their members (Edwards 1991: 3). While it was relatively easy to organize themselves using their own administrative structures and by coming together in numerous African-Caribbean ecumenical groups, it was more difficult to define what constituency the church could claim to serve (ibid.). Even if the church was to compromise and call itself a 'Black Church,' what was meant by the community purportedly represented by the churches was uncertain. Leaders recognized the diversity of African-Caribbean cultures and the fact that membership in the church was not necessarily derived from a geographically bounded area which the church was supposed to service, but was assembled from different inner-city areas. To outsiders, the link between the church, the 'Black community' and certain kinds of social experience seemed clear. To church members, things seem much more complicated.

By questioning whether African-Caribbean Pentecostal churches should be understood as a means of self-expression and of articulation with society or as a compensatory stance based on withdrawal from society, all the approaches outlined above seek either/or answers while ignoring fundamental religious questions. For example: How does one become a member of such a church?

What is the nature of the religious community to which one belongs? What is the significance of belief for members? How does belief express the nature of society and one's place in it? Lastly, does belief resolve a problem of meaning regarding identity for adherents, and if so, how?

Outline of Study

The themes of identity, religion and gender structure the argument of this book. An understanding of the significance of African-Caribbean Pentecostalism and members' participation in this form of religious expression requires an understanding of members' circumstances and of how these circumstances are shaped by wider forces and by the grounding of the church in their lives. Hence, part 1 presents the setting of the denomination of the New Testament Church of God (NTCG) and the King Street congregation where research was conducted.

Chapter 1 examines the people who comprise the congregation. It locates the actors within the particular historical, social and economic situation of Birmingham in the early 1990s and within the city's African-Caribbean population. It proceeds to examine the nature of the local congregation and provides a profile of congregational membership.

Chapter 2 examines the setting of the NTCG as a denomination. It rejects the view that African-Caribbean Pentecostalism can be understood as a means of spiritual compensation for the economically disadvantaged. Instead it adopts the view that religious behavior (thought and practice) addresses questions of identity by providing people with a definition of the world as they experience it and of their place within it. Given the premise that religion provides a definition of the world and that this definition changes as experience changes, an understanding of religious behavior should adopt a historical perspective. Hence the chapter examines the changes in African-Caribbean religious practice during different social and historical moments, while recognizing that the parameters within which representations can be negotiated are also subject to change. Within the outline of changing social contexts, the chapter records the development of the NTCG and how it answers the question of identity by providing a metaphor of members' articulation with society.

In part 2, chapter 3 brings together the actors who were described in chapter 1 and the denomination as described in chapter 2 by examining the process of conversion which precedes membership, how the actors become members, and how members' belief is nourished and maintained through religious practice. This chapter is transitional, because in examining this process it moves the focus of the argument from a description of setting to the construction of representations. By examining the view of the world which members adopt in conversion and the adherence to this view as expressed and sustained in ritual, this chapter lays the foundation for an examination of how identity and gender are constructed within the idiom provided by the cosmology of the NTCG.

Part 3 examines the construction of representations by members of the church. Identity in general and African-Caribbean identity in particular is understood as resulting from the dynamic interplay between how others view you and how you view yourself. Hence the subjective ideologies and practices which are marshaled by those on either side of an identity boundary must be considered. This interplay is of relevance on two levels. First, it is necessary to understand how members perceive how they are viewed by others and how, in turn, they view themselves and position themselves with respect to the views of others. Secondly, within the broad identity of members which results from the interface of different ideologies and practices, there are profound consequences for the construction of gender for women of African-Caribbean origin in Britain.

Chapter 4 questions the premise that religious identity is tantamount to ethnic identity. It is suggested that this interpretation of members' identity may be forced upon them by others who have the power to determine the nature and placement of the boundaries of identity and the extent of group interaction. Before we can accept the view that religious identity is ethnic identity, we have to examine the meaning which members assign to religious identity. Following Barth (1969) and Anthony Cohen (1985a), identity is seen as an open category filled in by actors with symbols of their own choosing – that is, as culturally constructed difference. However, it is also suggested that the symbols which members manipulate in the construction of identity are chosen because they are those which are contested by others at the boundaries of group identity (Wallman 1978), and that the symbols which have particular social meaning for actors can change with each new social, economic and historical conjuncture (Abner Cohen 1980). The discussion examines the contested symbolic themes of nationality, status and material wealth, language, work, education and food which members manipulate in the construction of religious identity, as well as the models which members possess regarding the relationship between religious identity and ethnicity.

Chapter 5 examines the construction of gender in the church, where the themes of religion, identity and gender are brought together. Like identity, gender is understood as culturally constructed difference which cannot be approached from potentially biased constructions of culture/nature, public/domestic, individual/ person or power/inequality. Therefore the discussion examines imagery, social practice (Connell 1987) and issues of agency (Strathern 1980, 1981, 1987a, 1987b, 1988) in the social construction of members as persons and how the differences between people are organized through the idiom of gender.

Chapter 1

The Brethren of the King Street New Testament Church of God

Birmingham and its Residents

The King Street Congregation of the New Testament Church of God is located in an inner-city ward of Birmingham which is a traditional area of migrant settlement. Although the membership of King Street is drawn primarily from the ward in which the church is located, some members come from other city wards similar in nature. The road which forms the southern boundary of the church ward has an interesting mixture of state and volunteer resource centers, religious institutions, entertainment locations and businesses catering to Caribbean, Asian and English tastes. Interspersed among empty shops, abandoned houses and disused lots are numerous newsagents, Halal butchers, small Asian grocery stores supplying Caribbean and Asian foodstuffs, discount supermarkets, fabric and clothes stores, incongruous trade supply stores, an Asian resource center, a family-planning clinic, a Caribbean café, chip-shops,[1] an 'after-hours' drinking club, banks and post offices, a Caribbean-owned barber shop and beauty parlor, and numerous electrical supply and repair shops. Other main roads which border or traverse the research area present a similar variety of state services, religious institutions and ethnic entrepreneurship. While the research area is primarily residential, studded with retail shops and personal service firms, it is flanked by an industrial quarter on one side and a major hospital on another.

On main commercial streets, Asian music coaxes passers-by to enter shops, Asian sweetshops offer enticing delicacies, and greengrocers display a variety of produce like mangoes, yams,

---

1. Colloquial expression for fish and chip shops.

Plate 1 'A Main Road in the Study Area.' Source: Author

cassava, breadfruit, coconuts, plantains, pumpkins, christophene, ginger and sorrel. Elderly West Indian women run errands and stop to chat with acquaintances. Asian mothers ferry their children to and from school. The residential streets are quieter, and life is conducted indoors behind net curtains. When the social security checks are issued, the queues at sub-post offices reach the door. The sounds of children at play reveal schools tucked away among residential streets. In winter, the streets are gray and smoke rises from the few homes which still burn oil or coal; some households supplement their heating with bottled gas. In warmer weather, the front gardens of proud home-owners burst with roses and flower beds. Apart from small groups of young people congregating on the corners at dusk, Asian taxi-drivers waiting for a fare, people popping over the road to visit friends or neighbors or to get dinner from the chip shop, and people attending religious services, there is little activity on the streets in the evenings. Much later the 'after-hours' club opens for business. Amid this activity, stray dogs roam in and out of alleys and someone habitually feeds the pigeons.

Birmingham was a primarily industrial city focused on the manufacture of metal and engineering goods, with a sizable transport system and a large public health authority. During the post-war era, these sectors, faced with a shortage of labor, attracted thousands of male and female migrants from the colonial periphery.[2] Once in England, Caribbean migrants, along with other migrants, formed a corps of industrial labor.[3] They were overrepresented in certain industrial sectors like manufacturing and the health services, where they were engaged in low-status occupations, with poor conditions and low pay. Caribbean migrants were employed as unskilled and partly skilled manual labor or at best as intermediate non-manual workers in the health service.

The past two decades have seen a radical restructuring of the city's employment sector and the tenure of employment. Between 1971 and 1987, Birmingham experienced a significant decline in

2. See Banton 1955, Davison 1962, Glass 1960 and Peach 1968 for discussions of West Indian migration.

3. See Castles and Kosack 1981 [1972], 1973. For discussions of the economic and social conditions of West Indian migrants, see Banton 1955, Collins 1957, Eggington 1957, Glass 1960 and Patterson 1965.

the proportion of manufacturing jobs (a loss in absolute terms of 145,000 jobs) and only a moderate growth in the service sector. Despite this decline, the manufacturing sector still accounted for almost a third of the job market and remained significantly larger than that of the rest of the nation (BCC 1989). By 1991 'other services' had surpassed manufacturing as the main sector of employment (OPCS, Ten Percent Sample 1991b Part II: Table 73) and it was also clear that the other major employer in the city, the local health authority, would not escape the effects of the British recession. In early 1993, the government announced a restructuring of the local health authority, leading to redundancies and the closure of several hospitals.

These changes have had drastic consequences for the economic health of the city as a whole and for certain categories of people. In order to remain viable throughout the recession, many local firms altered their employment practices, relying on a greater use of part-time and temporary workers. This led to a growth in the 'secondary labor market' (including part-time workers, temporary workers, shift workers and homeworkers[4] including many school leavers, Blacks and women) characterized by low pay and insecure employment. On the basis of eligibility for Income Support and Standard Housing Benefit,[5] one third to one half of the city's population lived on the edge of poverty, which was primarily restricted to the inner-city area populated by New Commonwealth and Pakistani (NCWP) migrants and their descendants (BCC 1989). Among those most hard hit by the economic climate were the young, the elderly, the disabled, Blacks and women, all of whom are represented in the King Street congregation.

Population

The composition of Birmingham's population reflects the diversity of post-war economic immigration. In 1991, out of a population of over 950,000, 9.5 percent were either born in or claimed an ethnic identity originating in the NCWP, the majority originating in Pakistan, the Caribbean and India (OPCS, 1991b Part I: Table 5

---

4. Workers engaged in piecework production from home.
5. Government assistance programs.

and Table 7). Just under 45,000 residents, roughly 5 percent of the city's population, described themselves as being of African-Caribbean origin (OPCS, 1991a Part I: Table 6). Interestingly, the sex and age composition of the African-Caribbean population is comparable to the demographic profile of the city overall. Unlike other migrant groups, there is numerical parity between African-Caribbean men and women where women account for 52 percent of the city's African-Caribbean population (based on OPCS, 1991a Part I: Table 6). The proportion of African-Caribbean residents in the age groups under 24 and between 45 to 64 is similar to the remainder of the city's population; there are, however, significantly more African-Caribbean people in the age group 24 to 44 and significantly fewer elderly people (based on OPCS, 1991a Part I: Table 6). The percentage of African-Caribbean elderly (2.7 percent) is small, but growing. There is a realization that the specific needs of African-Caribbean and NCWP elderly cannot be met by basic government social services provision. This need has prompted a number of grass-roots organizations, religious institutions like King Street, and the local city council to sponsor daycare centers which cater specifically for their needs.

The rich cultural diversity of Birmingham's residents is not evenly distributed throughout the city. The divisions between Birmingham's residents, underscored by social, cultural and economic differences, are manifested in the allocation of space in the city. As various writers (Jones 1970, 1976; Rex and Moore 1967; Smith 1989) have argued, Birmingham's spatial order is affected by differential access to council housing as well as by differences in income. The migrant community was initially located primarily to the northwest (Lozells, Handsworth and Soho) and southeast (Moseley and Sparkbrook). In 1961, the distribution of NCWP migrants formed a discontinuous concentric belt surrounding the inner core of the city (Jones ibid.: 203), and today the ring of settlement has almost completely encircled the inner-city core.

Most of the wards from which the congregation's membership is drawn comprise a distinct inner-city area which has a much higher concentration of NCWP migrants and ethnic minority group members than anywhere else in the city. In 1981, a third of the total population of the church ward were born in the NCWP, and almost 60 percent lived in households where the head was born in the NCWP (in some sections, as much as three quarters of the population lived in such households).[6] Within the area, persons born in either the Caribbean or India comprised the majority of the NCWP-born population: just under 10 percent were from the Caribbean and over 14 percent from India (BCC 1987). The ward where King Street is located contains the highest concentration of the city's Caribbean-born population (approximately 2,600 persons), constituting 11 percent of the ward's total population and 34 percent of the ward's NCWP population (OPCS 1981a).

Unlike the age structure of the African-Caribbean population for the city as a whole, there was a higher proportion of elderly in the church ward (11 percent compared to 2.7 percent) and a lower proportion of people aged 45 to 64 (17 percent compared to 21 percent) (based on BCC 1987, 1988; OPCS 1981a). The fact that the research area was a primary area of migrant settlement may explain the higher proportion of elderly when compared to the African-Caribbean population overall. This is an area of aging African-Caribbean migrant settlement, since younger members of the African-Caribbean population are moving further afield.

Employment

There are stark contrasts in the patterns of economic activity for men and women and for different ethnic groups in the city. These patterns parallel national patterns.[7] In 1991, almost 60 percent of the city's total working-age population was economically active;[8] however, among the economically active population unemployment was around 14 percent (OPCS, 1991b Part I: Table 8). Those who were fortunate and had employment were concentrated first in other services (including local authorities, health, education), then the manufacture of metal and other goods, followed by distribution and catering (OPCS, Ten Percent Sample 1991b Part II: Table 73).

6. This is in contrast to the remainder of the inner city, where 43 percent of the population lived in households where the head was born in the NCWP.

7. See Brown 1984, Newnham 1986 and the *1984 Labour Force Survey*.

8. The working-age population encompasses people between the age of sixteen and retirement (60 for women and 65 for men). An economically active person is defined as one who is working or seeking work: it excludes the permanently sick or disabled, housewives and full time students.

Gender-based industrial and occupational segregation, reflective of general British patterns (Bradley 1989; Dex 1985), has significant consequences for rates of economic activity, unemployment, occupational status, tenure of employment and rates of pay. Manufacturing in the region is regarded as 'men's work' and services are seen as 'women's work.' In Birmingham and the West Midlands region, over 60 percent of female employees were engaged in the service sector and distribution, while only 15–17 percent were employed in manufacturing (OPCS, Ten Percent Sample 1991b Part II: Table 73). Birmingham men were more likely than women to be economically active (72 percent and 47 percent respectively); however, men were also twice as likely to be unemployed when compared to women (17 percent compared with 10 percent) (OPCS, 1991b Part I: Table 8).[9] A trenchant conception that men are responsible for bringing home the family wage while women are responsible for domestic tasks and social reproduction accounts for higher levels of male economic activity. Yet the erosion of Birmingham's manufacturing base has led to fewer traditional male jobs and high male unemployment, while the corresponding growth in the service sector implies increased job opportunities for women.

The fact that manufacturing is not regarded as women's work also explains why women are engaged primarily in jobs requiring fewer manual skills, but it cannot account for the lower occupat-ional status and pay of women (women comprise 74 percent of the skilled non-manual workforce, 58 percent of the unskilled workforce but only 12.6 percent of skilled manual labor). Male labor predominated in professional occupations (85 percent), at the managerial level (57 percent) and at the skilled manual and partly skilled levels (87 percent and 55 percent respectively) (OPCS, Ten Percent Sample 1991b Part II: Table 91). Further, manufacturing associated with men's work is ordinarily full time shift work, whereas in the female service sector employment is part time. Ninety-five percent of men worked full time compared with less than two-thirds of women (OPCS, 1991b Part I: Table 8). As a basic rule of thumb, women in full time work earn approx-imately three-quarters of the male wage (see Bradley 1989: 11);

9. Since married women and women who cohabit are not eligible to receive Income Support or Unemployment Benefit, the rate of unemployment among women may actually be higher (BCC 1989).

however, women in the West Midlands who worked full time only earned two-thirds of the male wage (CSO 1991: 166–7).

Among different ethnic groups, Birmingham's African-Caribbean population had the highest overall level of economic activity (Table 1.1), but it also had one of the highest levels of unemployment (OPCS, 1991b Part I: Table 9). Although the percentage of unemployed among the economically active African-Caribbean population (22 percent) was significantly greater than among the White or Indian population (12 percent and 17.5 percent respectively), it was considerably better than the percentage of unemployed in the Pakistani and Bangladeshi communities (37 percent and 42 percent respectively) (OPCS, 1991b Part I: Table 9).

A breakdown of economic activity by ethnic group and gender reveals striking differences between males and females in each group and across groups. These patterns are comparable with national patterns for the decade preceding the census (Lewis 1993; Phizacklea 1988; Westwood and Bhachu 1988).[10] The level of male African-Caribbean economic activity is similar to that of their White peers and they are engaged in similar sectors of employment. However, African-Caribbean men are more likely to be unemployed than their White peers, and even within these sectors

Table 1.1 Economic Activity as Percentage of Ethnic Group's Total Population

City	
All	59%
White	59%
African-Caribbean	71%
Indian	64%
Pakistani	47%
Bangladeshi	43%

(Source: OPCS, 1991b Part I: Table 9)

10. For detailed statistics on the employment of ethnic minorities in the national labor market, see *Ethnic Minorities in Britain* (CRE 1985), *Employment Gazette* (March 1988), the *Labour Force Survey* (OPCS 1981b) and Brown 1984. For information relating to Birmingham, see *1981 Household Survey* (Cross and Johnson, CRER; Warwick 1981) and *Last Among Equals* (WMCC 1988).

they are confined to lower status occupations and lower rates of pay. African-Caribbean female economic activity differs entirely from that of their White peers. Compared with women from other ethnic groups, women in the African-Caribbean population have significantly higher levels of economic activity, tending to work full time in the service sector, in equal or higher status occupations, this resulting in larger pay packets. Like the pattern for men and women in general, African-Caribbean women are less likely to be unemployed when compared to African-Caribbean men (16 percent and 27 percent respectively); however, the rate of unemployment for African-Caribbean women was significantly higher than for Birmingham women overall (OPCS, 1991b Part I: Table 9).

The 1991 census reveals the persistence of sharp disparities in the socio-economic group distribution of Birmingham's African-Caribbean population. In comparison with the White population and other NCWP groups, African-Caribbean people remain significantly under-represented at the professional and skilled non-manual levels. Compared with the White population, NCWP workers are over-represented at the level of partly skilled employment, except for African-Caribbean workers, who are appreciably under-represented at this level. It is significant that African-Caribbean employees remain over-represented at the level of unskilled work (Table 1.2). (OPCS, Ten Percent Sample 1991b Part II: Table 93.)

Table 1.2 Socio-Economic Group by Ethnic Group

	Total	White	Black Caribbean	Indian	Pakistani	Bangla-deshi
Professional	5%	5%	1%	6%	4%	4%
Intermediate	24%	24%	23%	21%	14%	11%
Skilled non-manual	23%	24%	17%	19%	15%	22.5%
Skilled manual	22%	22.5%	23%	19.5%	23%	22.5%
Partly Skilled	19%	17.5%	25%	27%	32%	29%
Unskilled	6%	6%	7.5%	3%	6%	4%
Other	1%	1%	3.5%	4.5%	6%	7%

(Source: OPCS, Ten Percent Sample 1991b Part II: Table 93)

The under-representation of African-Caribbean people at the level of higher occupational status is not due to lack of qualifications. *Labour Market Trends* (1996) reports that in the five years since the census the proportion of people with qualifications has been highest among African-Caribbean men and women. The increase in qualifications helps to account for the gains made by African-Caribbean workers at the intermediate level, where the percentage of African-Caribbean employees is almost comparable to the White population, but significantly greater than the remaining NCWP population. The large discrepancy between African-Caribbeans and others at the professional level serves as a reminder that having higher qualifications does not guarantee that an individual will be employed at a level appropriate to their training. A summary of surveys concerning school leavers conducted by the Runnymede Trust shows a greater tendency for young people from ethnic minority groups to enter higher education (Newnham 1986: 2). Young men of NCWP descent are more likely to pursue higher education than White males, but African-Caribbean males are less likely to pursue education. Young women of NCWP descent are less likely to be in higher education than their male counterparts, but African-Caribbean women outnumber both their African-Caribbean male and NCWP female peers in higher education. The decision to remain in school is determined by the lack of job opportunities and discrimination; however, while higher qualifications increase a young Black person's chance of finding a job, once in that job the qualified Black person faces a higher level of discrimination than less qualified Blacks (ibid.: 18).[11]

In addition to industrial and occupational concentration, there is evidence testifying to the low pay commanded by Black workers, and that among Black workers, low pay differs by ethnic origin and gender. According to the *1981 Household Survey*, African-Caribbean males in the West Midlands earned an average net weekly wage which was only three-quarters of the average White male wage (BCC 1989). The trend was reversed for African-Caribbean women. Figures cited by the West Midlands survey suggested that White women earned approximately half the average net weekly wage of their male counterparts (£43), while

11. For a comparison of West Indian and White female school-leavers, see Dex 1983: 61–2.

African-Caribbean women earned roughly 12 percent more than their White peers (£48) (Cross and Johnson 1981 in BCC 1989; also Brown 1984). Employment in the public sector and unionized work places with better rates of pay (Newnham 1986: 7), higher levels of full-time employment and longer hours accounts for the marginally higher earning levels among African-Caribbean women.

Housing

Housing in the area is mixed; rows of Victorian terraced working-men's homes alternate with large Edwardian town houses, twentieth-century semi-detached houses and modern red-brick bungalows and apartment blocks. One road may seem prosperous, but around the corner there may be a stretch of broken pavement with abandoned houses. Many of the larger houses, unaffordable for single families, have either been subdivided into flats or converted into community resource centers. In expectation of the future rise in the elderly population, the council and housing associations have invested in purpose-built sheltered accommodation.

The main difference in housing between the research area and the remainder of the city lies in the structure of tenancy and the availability of adequate council housing.[12] As of 1991, 60 percent of Birmingham's total population lived in their own home or were buying their own home, over a quarter lived in council housing, and only a small proportion of the population lived in privately rented accommodation or housing-association accommodation (OPCS, 1991b Part I: Table 49).[13] In the research area, however, there were fewer council properties and less owner occupation and conversely a higher level of housing-association and privately rented accommodation. Despite a large mixed-unit council estate in the area, the provision of council housing remains inadequate.[14] Compared to the research area, the church ward had a slightly

12. For an analysis of Birmingham's housing market, see Rex and Moore 1967.

13. Council housing is British public housing. Housing associations are organizations which provide affordable housing to community residents in lieu of the city council or private landlords.

14. The ward containing council housing has the lowest percentage of NCWP-born population in the research area (11 percent) (BCC 1987).

higher percentage of households in owner-occupied housing, significantly fewer households in council housing, an increase in households in privately rented accommodation and a sharp increase in households in housing-association accommodation (BCC 1987). However, in terms of tenancy structure, fewer African-Caribbeans own their own homes; only 44 percent own or are buying their own homes, while a significantly greater proportion rent from a private landlord, a housing association or the council (OPCS, 1991b Part I: Table 9).

The statistical facts reflect the circumstances of Birmingham's NCWP communities, the gains they have made over the past thirty-five to fifty years, and the legacy of overt and institutional racism. However, these facts do not offer a definitive picture of the African-Caribbean and NCWP populations and belie the unquantifiable activity and vitality of the research area's residents. A survey of recreation, leisure and community facilities in the area surrounding the church uncovered numerous facilities which provided a range of services that catered to the population as a whole and to the specific needs of different ethnic groups (BCC 1987). Myriad grass-roots organizations, community centers, ethnic resource centers and religious institutions offered sport facilities, health, music, dance and language courses, elderly clubs, youth clubs and crèche facilities. Speakers and preachers were often invited by grass-roots organizations and religious institutions to address issues of race and/or religion, and the area was the location for numerous fairs and events celebrating 'Black culture.'

From a variety of available activities, a major form of association for residents of the local area is institutionalized and non-institutionalized religious participation. There are a few community centers and a cultural shop run by Rastafarians. The institutional religious diversity of the area's residents is manifested in several Pentecostal, Baptist, Methodist and Anglican churches, as well as a Seventh Day Adventist church, an African Methodist Episcopal church, a United Reformed church, a Roman Catholic church, Hindu and Sikh temples and a mosque.[15] The proliferation of Christian denominations in the area and ward is represented along the road which forms the southern boundary of the research ward. Six churches sit on, or just off, the road. Of these, three are

15. There are no official statistics concerning religious participation in the city.

Pentecostal denominations, two are Methodist and one is Baptist. It is along this road that King Street congregation is located.

King Street Congregation

Congregational History

The administrative units of the NTCG are the basis for a network of interaction and communication where members are bound together by church and district-level activities. The denomination is divided into two national regions and twenty-two local districts. Each district is composed of a 'Mother Church' and several smaller 'Sister Churches' supervised by a 'district overseer,' who is usually the pastor of the 'Mother Church.' The city of Birmingham is similarly divided into two districts, roughly north and south, with seven congregations overall. King Street is the Mother Church for its district, which includes the Sister congregations of Queenspiece, Palace View and Eastleigh. King Street was founded in 1951 and in its early days the congregation held services in a rented school hall. The present building was purchased from the Methodists in 1953 and has been the permanent home of the congregation ever since.

The original King Street congregation and founding pastor came from Clarendon, Jamaica. Although there are only a few original members in the current congregation, there is still a strong presence of members from Clarendon, while a few are from the neighboring parishes of Manchester, St. Ann's and St. Elizabeth. Other members are from Portland and Westmoreland and the remaining parishes. The diversity of parishes in the congregation is representative of Birmingham's Jamaican population. Where once the parish accent was felt more strongly in provincial cities like Birmingham than in London, subsequent internal migration and the growth of the second generation has led to its attenuation. It has also faded in the congregation, as elderly converts from different parishes join and demographic composition shifts towards the 'second generation' of Jamaican-British.

The very early congregations in England reflected the demographics of initial West Indian migration (Hill 1971a). The majority of early members were devout middle-aged male migrants who had been converted to Pentecostalism in the West Indies: there were few women, families or children. As women began to migrate on their own or to follow partners, their presence in the congregations rapidly increased. King Street congregation has 269 members, of whom 68 percent (182) are women. The current preponderance of women in congregations in England is comparable to the pattern of religious participation among women in Jamaica during the 1970s (Hill ibid.) and differs from that of early UK congregations. Members account for the majority of female membership with reference to the belief that women are inherently more spiritual and more receptive to the Lord than men and by pointing out that there are generally more women in the world than men. However, the fact that 52 percent of Birmingham's African-Caribbean population is female suggests that women are truly over-represented, and the proportion of men and women among recent converts suggests that this pattern will continue. In a limited survey of the congregation, the three current members who had originally joined thirty-five years ago were all male; among the most recent converts, however, there was only one man compared to five women. In two of the four baptismal services which occurred from 1990 to 1991, only three of the twenty neophytes were male.

Since 1967, when he was appointed to King Street congregation, the current pastor has witnessed several changes in the composition of the congregation. Members who joined the congregation when they were young now constitute the aging segment of the African-Caribbean population and the congregation. However, the proportion of elderly in the congregation is rapidly decreasing; a decrease due not simply to death, but also to emigration. Between 1990 and 1991 five elderly members returned to Jamaica, five migrated to the US and Canada and four more were contemplating a future move to North America. Conversely, some of the elderly who have already 'left' England often resume their participation in the congregation when they return for prolonged visits and National Health Service medical care. Of current members, the pastor estimates that 40 percent of the congregation are under the age of thirty, 30 to 35 percent are middle aged and 10 to 15 percent are over sixty. Observation agrees with these rough estimates. Thus there are proportionately more elderly persons in the congregation than in the African-Caribbean population at large, but the church cannot simply be stereotyped as a preserve for the elderly. The elderly attend with apparently greater regularity, usually being present at Sunday morning services and weekday activities, but they are reluctant to attend evening services. However, there is a large proportion of young and active members who are employed and are more mobile, who may be at work or away lending support to other congregations in the city or in London.

Although there is a specified body of membership, the congregation which assembles for worship is fluid in nature.[16] It is rare for all members to attend a service or meeting, some may be attending services – 'giving support' – elsewhere, others may be abroad for extended visits, and others may be unable to attend due to illness or family or work commitments. Interaction among the members of different congregations is actively encouraged, as people are often exhorted to 'give support' by attending special services or programs at Sister churches in the district. The church calendar is filled with conventions, seminars and programs which celebrate different associations in the church and unite congregations at different administrative levels.[17] The majority of members may be away during national conventions, while the few who remain will attend services locally. Most members attend special services like baptism, convention, Bible School graduation, 'Infant Dedication' or 'Watch Night Service.'[18] During these special services, the pews and galleries groan with children, visitors, friends and members from other congregations as well as with regular members (see Appendix I).

A visitor may be a stranger who has wandered in from the street, a visiting relative, a former member who has returned to the area for a while, a member of a distant congregation, or a person who regularly attends services and is well known to the congregation but is not officially a member. The noting of occasional visitors is a regular inclusion in a Sunday Service; they are asked to rise and

16. Booth has also noted fluidity of membership in an Aladura congregation in Birmingham (1984: 113).

17. Pryce has noted a similar national church network (1979: 206).

18. Bible School is not equivalent to Sunday School but is a special course where members receive theological training, with a certificate at the end of two years. Watch Night is a service held on New Year's Eve, where members give thanks for the previous year and welcome in the New Year with a jamboree of music, addresses and sketches contributed by members of the district's congregations. Infant Dedication is not equivalent to Christening and does not confer membership.

greet the congregation with a few words of introduction and perhaps a testimony. The number of visitors varies according to the time of year and the type of service, but there are always a few in church on any given Sunday. While children are not officially members, they accompany parents, guardians or grand-parents to church and are said to be 'raised in the church.' However, children may also be sent to Sunday School by parents who are not members themselves.[19]

Membership

Although the church practices 'Infant Dedication,'[20] a person is not born into the church. A member is a person whose individual experiences have led to a growing sense of religious conviction and commitment, culminating in the experience of being saved or in a decision to 'convert' and join this specific denomination. When one converts, one accepts the Lord as one's personal Savior and is 'born again' as a 'Christian.' Although one may have been raised in a 'nominal'[21] church or have been religiously minded as an adult, this does not make one a 'Christian.' During the period leading up to conversion, one may experiment with other forms of Christian worship through participation in several denomin-ations.[22] This in turn strengthens a growing sense of conviction and may help people to 'make up their mind.' Often a visitor is

19. Participant observation and informal interviews were conducted at regular church services and meetings, district, regional and national conventions, church festivals and outings, and meetings of a women's auxiliary. Hence my status was one of a recurrent visitor to the church. As a visitor, I was able to participate in services by sharing in worship and I was occasionally asked to pray aloud, read from the Bible or offer a testimony. These were the agonizing moments of fieldwork. There was mutual respect concerning our religious affiliations and hence little concerted effort to make me convert. Members accepted my decision not to feign salvation. Towards the end of fieldwork I sensed an increased optimism among members that I would be saved. I interpreted their hopes for my future salvation as a valuable gift which a person wants to share with a friend.

20. For a description of 'Infant Dedication,' see chapter 3.

21. 'Nominal' is the term which members use to describe other Christian denominations, like the mainline Anglican, Roman Catholic or Methodist and Baptist non-conformist churches, which they feel are Christian only in name.

22. Gill has also noted religious mobility among Pentecostals in La Paz, Bolivia (1994: 136).

welcomed as such a person and is accordingly shown warmth, friendship and encouragement.

The diversity of previous religious experience is reflected in a limited survey of thirty-five members. Of the twenty-five members who were old enough to have had a history of previous religious affiliation in Jamaica, fourteen claimed membership in a Pentecostal denomination (NTCG or other denomination) and the remaining eleven had belonged to established denominations in the Protestant tradition (in decreasing order, Baptist, Presbyterian, Wesleyan Holiness, Anglican, Moravian, Methodist and Protestant Reformed). The remaining young members had no previous form of religious affiliation. Half the survey respondents had joined the church within the past twenty years, and four had been members for less than five years.

Since membership follows adult conversion, membership and kinship networks are not necessarily congruent. Out of thirty-four members, half had been introduced to the church by near or distant relatives (who were all church members), but the other half had found out about the church through friends, acquaintances or workmates, while one had heard of the congregation in Jamaica. The high incidence of relations as contacts can only be partially accounted for by young members who had been 'raised in the church' and had decided to become members when they came of age. In addition to these 'second-generation' members, others had come to the church through siblings, aunts or uncles, nieces or nephews or cousins. Among the variety of members' connections, there were discernible trends in the manner whereby men and women came to join the church. Male converts tended to be mostly young men who were 'raised in the church' and had become members when they came of age, or more exceptionally they were elderly men who had yielded to their wife's petitions to convert.[23] The age and circumstances surrounding female conversion varied much more widely. Young female converts were sometimes 'raised in the church,' but they might also have come to the church independently, while middle-aged and older women were likely to have joined independently.

23. See Brusco 1995.

Kinship

Given the individual circumstances surrounding conversion, there is a wide variation in the patterns of how individuals are connected to each other, the congregation and the denomination. Within the landscape of African Diaspora religious practice, variation in the church membership of family members is not unusual. As has been noted in the case of Jamaica: 'Husband and wife, children and parents, sibling and sibling may belong to different churches without conflict. . .' (Fischer 1974, II: 9). Brown notes that in a matrifocal Afro-Baptist church in rural Florida, recruitment is based on the principles of matrilineality and matrilocality, where a woman will attend her mother's church and a man will attend his wife's church (1994: 178). This practice maintains a family core and reinforces familial continuity within the church (ibid.: 176). However, she also notes that when a man from the community marries a woman from a different church, one of their children will attend the paternal grandmother's church, thus dividing parents and children and siblings in their pattern of church attendance (ibid.: 178).

Sometimes in the NTCG all the members of a family are members of the same congregation and the children are being 'raised in the church.' These are likely to be core members of the congregation and to be related to the pastor's family through marriage and kinship (Figure 1.1). For example, Brother and Sister Adler have been members of the congregation since they each arrived in England. All three of their children are members of the church and of the King Street congregation; their eldest son is married to one of the pastor's daughters and their children are in turn being 'raised in the church.' In yet other cases, spouses and offspring may be loyal to different congregations within the NTCG. In other families, members may belong to entirely different denominations or may not attend any church. Brother and Sister Clarence are both members of the NTCG; however, Brother Clarence is a member of King Street congregation, while his wife is a member of Riverlawn congregation in another district. Sister Adams is the only member of her family in the congregation; however, she has family in another congregation as well as in another African-Caribbean Pentecostal denomination. Sister Maguire is a member of the NTCG and King Street congregation, but her husband is a member of a Baptist church in a neighboring ward. Sister Windeatt and her daughter belong to King Street, but her husband and other children do not attend church. Finally there are many members, typically women who have come to the church independently, who have no family in the church or congregation. Although there is a solid nucleus of non-fictive kin which radiates outwards from the pastor's family, thus uniting certain families within King Street congregation, non-fictive kinship ties do not link the whole congregation together.

Though a person may join the church and the congregation as an individual, regardless of particular kinship ties and loyalties, once in the church members are enmeshed in a new network of fictive kin. The group the person enters is simultaneously regarded as the body of God and as a 'family.' A member's duties and obligations are derived from membership in both the body and the family: 'God calls us from different walks of life to make one little cell in that enormous body. We are his children' (Sermon, 14/4/91). In the spiritual body, God is the head and every member is a cell, a metaphorical ordering of positions that parallels that of the family metaphor where God is the head of the family and church members are his children. Though both metaphors reaffirm God's authority, they also reinforce the equality of undifferentiated membership. Though members may have different gifts and talents, all cells and all children are considered equal: all people can be 'saved' and 'adopted' into the family of God. Whatever the specific circumstances which tie a person to the congregation, church members are thought of as 'brethren' and regard each other as 'family.' Members refer to themselves and to others within this collective as 'saints,' and male and female saints are differentiated by the use of the kinship terms 'Brother' and 'Sister.'

In the NTCG the idiom of fictive kinship refers to two spheres of people which may intersect and overlap: sacred fictive kinship

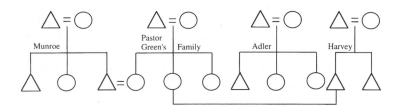

Figure 1.1 Nucleus of Non-Fictive Kin in Congregation

and secular fictive kinship. In the sphere of sacred fictive kinship, the terms 'Brother' and 'Sister' are regularly used to denote members of any age; since God is considered the Father of all saints and all saints are equal, then all saints must be siblings. 'Brother' and 'Sister' are terms of neutral hierarchical value signifying a wide category of people who can be relied upon for support. As one member testified, 'I feel closer to my church brethren than I do my own blood brothers.' Thus Sister Faulkner who attends the King Street elderly club (but is not a member of the congregation) commented in a general discussion that 'sometimes church people are better to you than your own family'; the other Sisters present agreed whole-heartedly. While the terms 'Brother' and 'Sister' are applied to members of one's own congregation and denomination, they can sometimes be extended to include members of other denominations. Thus members appeal to a universal kindred of Christian saints which extends beyond the immediate body of the congregation and with discretion beyond the denomination.

Although the congregation is a small face-to-face community, many members do not use or know each other's first names, being more accustomed to referring to each other by the term 'Brother' or 'Sister' followed by a surname. The use of sibling terms extends to spouses who are saints, but not usually to spouses outside the church.

Unlike the general terms 'Brother' and 'Sister,' the term 'Mother' not only denotes an older respected woman but refers to a specific status within the church. If sacred fictive kinship mobilizes the egalitarian kinship terms of 'Brother' and 'Sister' then the inclusion of the distinguishing term 'Mother' within the sphere of sacred fictive kinship may at first seem incongruous; however, there is an internal logic for its inclusion. The kinship terms applied to the different district congregations parallel the kinship terms used to refer to female congregation members. A congregation which is the head of a district is called a 'Mother church'; other congregations within the district are called 'Sister churches,' not daughter churches. Other than in the administrative schema, there is no hierarchical ordering between the congregations. A mother can have a sister who is like her and who can possibly be substituted for her in adoption or fostering. Similarly, as noted above, members can move around in space and attend services in different congregations. Within the category of sacred fictive kinship there is no corresponding term 'Father,' since this position is occupied by God. Although the term 'Mother' implies more status and respect than 'Brother' or 'Sister,' it does not denote a person with hierarchical authority. Within the model of the Christian family unit defined by the church, a mother is also a father's wife. Although a mother has authority over her children, as a wife she should defer to and show respect for her husband; hence a 'Mother of the Church' should defer to the pastor and the governing church council. This conceptualization of siblingship and motherhood has significant implications for the construction of gender roles in the church.

The use of fictive kinship terms within Black Churches has been noted by previous researchers (Booth 1984; Brown 1994; Calley 1965; Pryce 1979; Williams 1974). With the exception of Brown (1994), however, fictive kinship remains little analyzed. In the church where Brown conducted research, there was variety in the fictive kinship terms applied to women. Women were referred to as 'Aunt' and 'Cousin' as well as 'Mother' and 'Sister,' while men were only referred to as 'Brother' (ibid.: 180). On a general level, Brown interprets the use of kinship terms in the religious sphere as maintaining the distinct identity of the group. While the same can be said for many Black Churches as for the NTCG, in the NTCG the use of fictive kinship terms is not applied exclusively to denomination members. On a more specific note, Brown suggests that in this matrifocal church, the variety in female fictive kinship terms reflects the variety of female family roles and underscores the importance of women in 'maintaining inter-generational continuity of the family' in the church, especially where the role of 'Mother' ensures stability and family continuity (ibid.: 177, 180). In the NTCG the variety of secular non-fictive and fictive kinship roles of women is not incorporated into the sphere of fictive church kinship; only the terms 'Mother' and 'Sister' are used consistently. Paralleling the Afro-Baptist church, however, men are singularly referred to by the term 'Brother.' Since matrilineality and matrilocality play no determining role in recruitment to the NTCG, the difference between female kinship terms in the NTCG and the Afro-Baptist church may have more to do with the varied circumstances by which people become members of the NTCG, and less to do with a difference in the construction of gender in these two churches and the status and respect accorded to women.

The second sphere of fictive kinship which members draw upon is secular fictive kinship. While members do make clear distinctions between sacred fictive kinship and other ways of reckoning kinship, they do not necessarily make sharp distinctions between non-fictive and fictive secular kin. Secular fictive kinship is less clearly defined than sacred fictive kinship; it is constituted by the large catch-all of 'cousins, aunties and uncles' who cannot be directly traced.[24] The saying 'we know we are related somehow' legitimates the claim of kinship, provided that someone somewhere knows the connection. Unlike the sphere of sacred fictive kinship, in which membership is determined by membership within the body of God, the ties of secular fictive kinship and non-fictive kinship remain valid among people outside the church as well as within the body of brethren.

The complexity of non-fictive and fictive kinship ties and the lack of a sharp distinction between these two spheres is illustrated by the ways kinship connections are traced by the Burtons, Monroes and Adamses (Figure 1.2). The family of Brother and Sister Burton are related to the family of Brother and Sister Munroe because deceased Sister Burton was a half-sister to Brother Munroe; their children (not all of whom are depicted) call each other 'cousin.' The family of Brother and Sister Adler say they are related to the family of Brother and Sister Burton through deceased Sister Burton's father and full brother (although the exact relation-

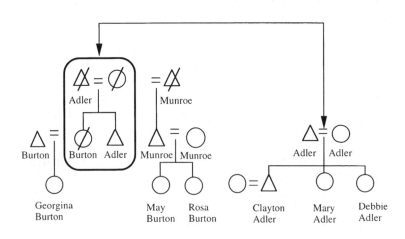

Figure 1.2 Secular Fictive Kinship

24. See Henriques 1953: 137; Stack 1974.

ship is unknown), and through them they claim kinship with the family of Brother and Sister Munroe. Brother Clayton Adler and Sisters Mary Adler and Debbie Adler call Brother Burton and Brother and Sister Munroe 'uncle' and 'auntie,' and they call Sisters Georgina Burton, May Munroe and Rosa Munroe 'cousin.' At the wedding of Sister Rosa Munroe, Sisters Mary and Debbie Adler were included in the wedding party, and Brother and Sister Adler also attended.

A church Member can rely on sacred fictive kinship, secular fictive kinship and non-fictive kinship for solidarity and support. The degree to which these spheres overlap and subsume each other varies from one member to the next. For some members, there is a tight congruence between all three spheres of kinship: for example, for the family of Brother and Sister Adler all three spheres of kinship operate within the congregation; they are related to the pastor and his family through non-fictive kinship; they are related to the family of Brother and Sister Munroe through secular fictive kinship; and they are related to all other members of the congregation, denomination and the body of saints through sacred fictive kinship. For other members, there is little congruence between the three spheres. For example, other than a niece in the congregation, Sister Queen has no secular fictive or non-fictive kin in the congregation or denomination. For Sister Queen there is little overlap between her spheres of non-fictive kinship, secular fictive kinship and sacred fictive kinship; her niece is the only point at which her spheres of sacred fictive kinship and non-fictive kinship intersect.

Sacred fictive kinship is a highly powerful idiom through which people can be organized, with the capacity to unite brethren not only across space, but through time as well (Figure 1.3). Due to the pattern of Caribbean migration, many individuals came as single independent economic actors or were sent for by family or friends; however, unlike the experience of some Asian communities in Britain, an extensive network of non-fictive kinship was not created to the same degree. The dependent elderly were not usually sent for, and often parents were unable to send for children either because they could not put together the necessary economic resources or because the child was approaching the age of sixteen and was too old to be considered a dependent. Where there are gaps between people created by the absence of non-fictive or secular fictive kinship, it is through a recourse to sacred fictive

Non-Fictive Kin

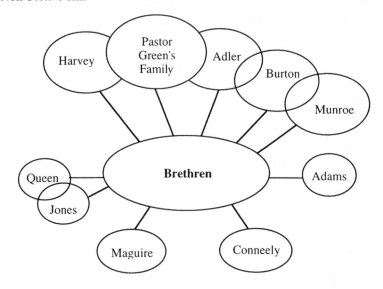

Fictive Kin

Figure 1.3 Local Sacred Fictive Kinship

kinship that brethren are united. Sacred fictive kinship serves as a safety net which encompasses members who cannot draw upon ties of non-fictive kinship or secular fictive kinship. Within a congregation such as King Street, the nucleus of the pastor's family and affines is related to other members through the use of the fictive terms 'Brother' and 'Sister.' It is the term 'Sister' which creates a bond between a woman like Sister Queen and women like Sisters Adler, Munroe, Harvey, etc.

Non-fictive kinship, secular fictive kinship and sacred fictive kinship unite different congregations across space: again, where there are no other ties of kinship, sacred fictive kinship will bind congregations together. It is sacred fictive kinship which unites members of a congregation in Birmingham with congregations in Brixton, Kingston, Miami, Toronto and other parts of the world.

In addition to engendering and strengthening connections between people across space, sacred fictive kinship establishes and affirms the connections between people through time. In *Natural Symbols*, Mary Douglas suggests that in anti-ritualistic Christianity there is a loss of articulation in the depth of past time; the historical continuity between the present-day sect and the primitive church of the Pentecost is traced by a 'thin line' where only a narrow range of historical experience and religious ancestors is recognized (1982: 19–20). In a similar vein, Calley has commented upon the general truncation of a sense of time among the members of a Pentecostal church:

> West Indian Pentecostal sects relive the early days of the church in a quite literal, almost self-conscious way. Members. . .are totally lacking in historical time-sense; the days of the Apostles to them are but yesterday and, as far as they are concerned, the two thousand intervening years of Christian history are irrelevant. (1965: 5)

The past is present in the present. Through the terms 'Brother' and 'Sister' current saints are related to all past saints who reside in heaven (Figure 1.4) in a manner which minimizes generational depth. Ties of non-fictive and secular fictive kinship are of little use in relating current saints to past saints if non-fictive and secular fictive kin were not saints themselves.

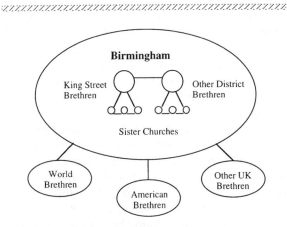

Heaven

Brethren

Birmingham

King Street Brethren

Other District Brethren

Sister Churches

World Brethren

American Brethren

Other UK Brethren

Figure 1.4 General Sacred Fictive Kinship

Women's Religious Participation

The diversity in previous religious affiliation, the manner of introduction to the church, recency of conversion and current ties with the church is illustrated by the stories of three elderly women members.

Sister Lorraine Jones   Lorraine is a jovial, strong woman in her sixties, who lives in a house rented from a housing association. She has four children, and dozens of family photos decorate her home. At the time I spoke with her, one of her daughters and her grandchildren were living with her while waiting for a council house. One of Lorraine's maternal aunts lives in a nursing home about a mile away, and Lorraine visits her weekly. Another maternal aunt lives several miles away in another city ward, but Lorraine and this aunt, Elma, see each other almost every day either at home or at church. In addition to her aunts, children and grandchildren, Lorraine has one uncle and 'cousins who can't be numbered' who also live in England. She keeps in touch with her relatives, who are scattered throughout the country, by phoning and writing every few weeks.

Lorraine was born in Clarendon, Jamaica, in the early 1930s, where she was raised as a Presbyterian in her grandmother's home. She moved to Kingston in her late teens. Here she later had her first child with Jake, her 'childhood sweetheart,' who was also from Clarendon. Although she was a member of the church, she says she was not a 'Christian' at the time. To her, being a 'Christian' means being born again, accepting the Lord as your savior and 'having a personal experience of Him.' Although she was a Presbyterian in Jamaica, two of her three children were 'blessed' by a Pentecostal minister and the third was christened in the Jamaican Anglican church.

Lorraine came to England in 1962, when Jake sent for her. She left each child with a different relative, two aunts and a cousin. Lorraine and Jake were married in an Anglican church in 1963. Jake died in 1966, leaving her to raise their children on her own. At this time, she only had one child in England. Lorraine had a very difficult time coming to terms with Jake's death, but she says her family in England rallied around her and supported her. When she recovered, she returned to work and began to send for her other children.

Lorraine was 'saved' in England while she was a member of a mixed Baptist congregation. In 1972, the Lord 'spoke' to her and informed her that she should be baptized. She became a deaconess in the Baptist congregation, the only Black woman in the post. Lorraine feels she was doing well in this church and the congregation showed her their appreciation, until she was filled with the Holy Spirit. She sensed that after this experience her brethren 'went funny' with her. They accused her of 'putting it on' and disturbing the service. Lorraine felt she had to leave, because in a 'nominal church' you cannot speak in tongues.

For a while Lorraine did not have any church to attend. She said she would stay at home on Sunday mornings and cry. One Sunday, around 1978, the Lord told her to get in touch with her husband's niece. This woman had a daughter who was attending King Street congregation at the time. Lorraine attended a service with her and knew from the first Sunday that this was the church the Lord wanted her to attend. The pastor interviewed her on her principles, and she was accepted into the congregation when she was in her late forties. Lorraine did not go through conversion again, nor did she need to be re-baptized. All she had to do was to regain her post as deaconess; since then, she has gained an equivalent post in the congregation.

Lorraine derives satisfaction from the church. She feels she is shown love and respect; she is occasionally invited to someone's home to share fellowship. She feels that since she has joined this church, there is more for her to do. She learns a lot from older Christians and has acquired physical and spiritual experience. She believes that there is a 'holy quietness' pervading the Baptist church which led them to turn against her and cover her mouth. She does not regret leaving the Baptist church; she feels that had she stayed with the Baptists, she would have eventually 'backslid.'[25] In the NTCG she feels that people are speaking the same language as her and that she is welcomed with open arms, so she has grown more in grace. In the Baptist church no one would invite her into their home on a Sunday to share fellowship. She feels this was because they were mostly White people. There was a 'selfishness going on' and she didn't 'feel free to worship.'

25. To 'backslide' is to sin and be obliged to leave the church.

Although her aunt Elma later became a member of King Street congregation, none of Lorraine's children are members of her church. Like many women in the church this is a source of anxiety; however, Lorraine feels sure that one day the Lord will 'save' her children and they will become members.

Lorraine's weekly schedule is structured by church activities. Because she holds a formal position in the church, she is involved to a greater degree than some other women. The rest of her week is filled with running errands, paying bills, shopping, visiting and sewing.

Sister Elma Queen   Elma is a woman of silent rectitude. She has three children, who all live in England. She lives alone in a house rented from a housing association. There are only a few photos in the front room; one which greets visitors is a photo of her baptism in the church. She is in regular contact with her sister, who lives in a nursing home, Lorraine (her niece), Lorraine's children and their children. She sees Lorraine almost every day. Elma has other relatives scattered throughout the country. Elma speaks reluctantly of her children or relatives. At the time of the interviews, she had limited contact with her sons in London; she kept in touch with them by phone and by visiting them periodically. Since then, they have had more frequent contact.

Elma was also born in Clarendon around 1923, where she was raised a Presbyterian (with Lorraine) in her parents' home. Like Lorraine, she feels she was not a 'Christian' then. She came to England in 1956 when her brother sent for her. She was married to a man from Barbados in an Anglican church, and her two sons, who were born in England, were christened in the Anglican church. Several years after they were married, Elma and her husband were separated.

In addition to relying on the Anglican church for the sacraments of marriage and christening, Elma has attended various English churches: two Baptist congregations, the Elim Pentecostal Church, the United Reformed Church and the Seventh Day Adventist Church. Since Elma's schedule as a nurse prevented regular religious participation, she was not a regular church member for over thirty years. She attended services opportunistically, when there was a wedding or a christening. The psychiatric hospital where she worked was Catholic, and one of her duties was to escort non-Catholic patients to Baptist or Anglican churches.

Elma was saved at an evangelist's tent meeting, and although she tried the evangelist's church, she wasn't 'settled down as a member.' She went from church to church, but always felt disappointed. She went back to the evangelist's meetings twice, but she 'didn't have the mind to go again.' Elma fell ill with the flu, and although her brethren had her name and address, no one came to visit her or bothered to find out how she was doing. She attributes this disappointment to the machinations of the devil. However, she did not loose the desire to become a committed Christian.

At this time, Seventh Day Adventists were actively evangelizing and would drop religious tracts through her letter box. Elma enrolled in their correspondence course and wrote to the Adventists requesting that someone visit her and pray. It was after such a visit that she decided to join the church. In 1986 she felt she had become a committed Christian. She attended the Seventh Day Adventist Church for approximately a year and was baptized there. She soon became discouraged and began to feel the enemy was turning against her and causing friction with her membership. One of the problems Elma perceived was a growing sense of isolation. After her initial visitor, people would not come around to visit her or share fellowship. She felt she needed support and a strong church. Elma wanted a church where people would come and pray for you, talk with you and give you support. She liked the idea of a Pentecostal church, because, unlike a 'nominal' church, 'a Pentecostal church has the Holy Spirit to warn you if things are going wrong and you can adjust yourself more easily.'

In 1987, Lorraine invited her to attend a King Street 'Building Program.'[26] After attending, Elma, then aged 65, decided to become a member almost immediately and was re-baptized the following year. Apart from her niece, Elma has no other relatives she can trace in the church. Elma does not hold a position in the church, but nonetheless her participation in services, meetings and activities structures her weekly round.

Sister Martha Adams   Martha, the daughter of a prosperous farmer, was born in St. Elizabeth around 1927. She was raised as a Methodist in her parents' home. Martha is a quintessential

---

26. A 'building program' is a fund-raising event to purchase or erect a building or to make improvements.

matriarch who holds her family together. She is respected and attracts people to her; sometimes sitting in her kitchen is like sitting in a train station, where the whole world eventually passes through. She has eight children and lives with her youngest daughter and husband. Two of her other daughters live within striking distance. Another daughter, who lives in another city with her husband and two daughters, visits frequently. The remaining daughter lives in the US with her husband and child. Her eldest son has recently married and moved to the US. Her second son alternates between living in London and Birmingham, and her youngest son lives in London. Martha's children and grand-children are always passing by. In addition to her immediate family, she has a niece, great nieces and nephews in a nearby city, whom she visits frequently. She keeps in touch with her relatives in London and her husband's relatives in Bristol. Martha speculates that when she is gone no one will keep the family together and they will each go their own way.

Martha came to England on her own in 1955 and met her husband two years later. Although they were not members of any church at the time of their wedding, they were married in an African-Caribbean Pentecostal church. They were married in the church because a friend had introduced her to the pastor and Martha did not feel it was right to be married in a registry office.

Like Elma, Martha always thought about going to church, but explained (as did Elma):

> At that time the English church didn't seem to accept us, you know. I didn't have that problem, but a lot of people claim they go to the church and the minister ask them not to come back, because he is going to lose his congregation. That didn't happen to me, because I never went to any church as such here. After I came here I stop going to church. You know the work and especially when I start having the children, I didn't bother.

Unable to attend church herself, Martha ensured that her children were 'brought up in the way they should go.' Three of Martha's children were born in Jamaica and were christened in the Method-ist church. Of the remaining five born in England, one was christened in a Methodist church, two were dedicated in the Pentecostal church where Martha was married and two children were christened in an Anglican church. She also ensured that her children received religious instruction by sending them to Sunday Schools. She sent three of her children to Sunday School at the Christadelphian church where her neighbor was a member, two to the Anglican church and one to King Street.

Occasionally she would attend a Christadelphian service, but she says she wasn't comfortable there and 'never saw much in it.' In the end her children played a significant part in her decision to become a church member. While she was sending one of her sons to the King Street Sunday School, he kept asking her why it was that he was being sent to church and she was not attending. In order to please him, she started attending the occasional Sunday service.

Martha became a member of King Street in 1982, when she was about fifty-five years old. She has no immediate traceable kin in the congregation; there is a family which she thinks is somehow related to her husband's people, but the connection is not known. One of her daughters and her son-in-law are active and prominent members of the denomination, but worship in a different congregation in another city. Another daughter and her husband are members of a different Pentecostal denomination. Martha also has a few former workmates who are members of the congregation.

Martha's week is structured around family and church commitments. When she is not at the church, she is at home or out running errands. She maintains limited contact with her church Sisters outside of church activities.

From the histories offered by Lorraine, Elma and Martha, it is clear that the experience of being a Christian woman does not stem from the simple act of church attendance; further, a person's career as a Christian does not follow a straightforward trajectory. It cannot be said that crises like bereavement or separation or monumental changes like migration, marriage or childbirth automatically lead to conversion. Instead religious experiences and actions intersect the narratives of these women, and of others, at random points; it is the cumulative effect of these experiences that results in conversion.

Congregational Employment

As with the profile of Birmingham's wider African-Caribbean population, most working-age members of the congregation are either economically active or seeking higher educational qualifications and training. Like their non-congregation African-Caribbean peers in the ward and the city, many of the younger members in the congregation are pursuing further education at college or university level. These are not only school leavers: many young people have left employment to return to education either to gain further qualifications in their field or to change occupations all together.

The occupation of employed members ranges from unskilled manual work to intermediate and professional occupations. The majority of members are employed in partly skilled, skilled and intermediate employment; the unskilled are under-represented in comparison to the local African-Caribbean population. On the whole, female members are more likely to be employed in 'other services' or the state sector, while male members are more likely to be employed in manufacturing and transport in the private sector (a national African-Caribbean pattern).[27] As with the local African-Caribbean population, there is a tendency for women to work full time and in partly skilled and skilled non-manual labor (OPCS 1981a:Table 52).

The employment of female members supports the findings of national surveys; however, there were significant differences between older and younger women. Among retired women, there was little diversity in occupation: women had either retired from the health authority as auxiliary nurses or domestic help (often having begun their careers in manufacturing) or they had retired from manufacturing in the private sector. For currently employed women, the largest employer was still the state sector. Currently employed women remained over-represented in nursing (where they have gained better qualifications than their mothers)[28] and auxiliary nursing; however, they are also obtaining employment in social work and other local authority positions. Economically active women in the private sector are no longer mainly employed in factory work: they have gained entrance to employment in distribution, catering and secretarial work.

27. See 1981 *Labour Force Survey*; Brown 1984; Newnham 1986.
28. African-Caribbean women who were recruited or later hired by the National Health Service were trained for inferior qualifications and junior positions. See Bryan, Dadzie and Scafe 1985: 38–50; Foner 1979: 142.

Although the occupation of male members appears to be more diversified when compared to that of female members, the occupational trends of male members support the findings of national surveys. Within private-sector work, men are still over-represented in manual factory employment and skilled transport. Other forms of male employment included work in engineering, social services, local-council work, security guards, a bakery assistant and an office clerk. It was more difficult to establish a relationship between age and occupation for male members. However, men over the age of forty-five were more likely to be in semi-skilled and skilled manual employment than their younger counterparts. Men under forty-five were more likely to be employed in white collar, non-manual desk jobs.

One issue which recurs through out the narratives of the first generation was the transition from a partial cash economy in the Caribbean to a totally cash-based economy in Britain. People found it very difficult to get by because everything had to be paid for; warm clothes, transportation, food and heat. Members of the African-Caribbean population have retained several economic strategies for making ends meet. In addition to waged work, many people meet their needs by participating in 'partners'[29] and providing necessary goods and services to family, friends and others in the community. Selling goods, tailoring, baking and decorating cakes, and catering for parties are alternative economic options available to women, while men sell produce (vegetables and herbs) grown on allotments,[30] do small repair jobs or drive chartered buses on weekend excursions.

Women's Work Experience

The work histories of Lorraine, Elma and Martha exhibit the nature of work for first-generation Jamaican women in Britain. Their stories highlight some of the issues involved in the conflicting ideological constructions of race and gender prevalent in Britain

29. A rotating credit scheme which provides a person with a cash sum which can be used to pay bills, finance a trip to Jamaica or make a capital investment like a downpayment on a house or car.

30. Garden plots made available to individuals by the city or town council. It is possible to eat a meal at a person's home where all the food, except the bread and meat, has been procured in this way.

– what is considered proper work for women and what is considered proper work for African-Caribbean women – while also highlighting some of the conflicts between work and religious participation:

Lorraine   When Lorraine was sixteen she left Clarendon to work in Kingston, where she worked as a domestic and did night-work in a restaurant. Lorraine's first job in England was piecework in a metal-goods factory, cleaning and polishing saucepans and kettles. She referred to the job as 'ghetto work,' since there was only one White woman in her section. She felt the working conditions in this job were the worst she had ever experienced; the chemicals damaged her skin, and she took the matter to the union. Despite the conditions, she had a good time with her work-mates. After the union intervened, she was transferred to packing with a reduction in wages. She later switched to testing and packing lamps.

   In 1963, Lorraine left work after the first trimester of her pregnancy because of illness. She returned to work nine months later, finishing hooks and eye-fasteners for the millinery trade. While Lorraine worked day-shifts in one factory, her husband worked night-shifts in another.

   After her job in the millinery trade, Lorraine worked for a jeweler for two years. She was then hired by another metal-goods manufacturer to clean trays and package trolleys. Lorraine believed this was a permanent position, but later discovered she had been hired temporarily to replace another woman who was on sick leave. When the woman returned, Lorraine was taken off packing and put onto cleaning and assembling the trolleys, which was 'hard work.' At this time, Lorraine was attending the Baptist church and she defined herself as a Christian; she remembers going into the washroom one day to ask the Lord if there wasn't some better work for her. Two weeks later, she approached a church Sister to ask if there were any vacancies at the hospital where the Sister worked. There was a place for a domestic assistant, and with the assistance of the Sister she filled out the application form and was called for an interview. Lorraine stressed that racism and discrimination had not influenced her decision to leave the factory job. She said there was no prejudice in the job, although she was the only Black woman in the department; it was just that the work was too much for her.

Lorraine worked at the hospital from 1979 until she retired in 1986. She found the work more satisfying because she could bring her experience of Christianity to the job. Lorraine feels that as a Christian, her work in the hospital was a privilege: she could witness to patients and pray for them, especially when they were dying. Her life was more complete because religion and work were no longer divorced from each other.

Lorraine said factory work was heavy work and Jamaican women were given the worst and heaviest jobs. Several employers had tried to put her on a power press, but she was terrified of it so she was put on a handpress. Lorraine feels that work conditions were bad for Jamaicans in the early 1960s, but that they have improved since then.

Working in a factory was an 'experience' for Lorraine for two reasons. First, it was the place where she first came into contact with 'White people, English people.' Secondly the nature of work was completely different. When she applied for a factory job in England, she told them she had no previous work experience. She felt the domestic work she had done in Kingston was not suitable experience for factory work. She said that in the factory you did finishing, packing and testing, which was an 'altogether different experience.' Lorraine also discounted her domestic experience as work experience when she applied for the hospital job:

> In the hospital, they show you how to do it. At home when you do domestic work you do the washing, the ironing, the cleaning and the cooking. In this country you do the washing in the kitchen, you don't do washing or ironing of clothes, unless it's in an old people's home or laundry. In the hospital, I washed the dishes, dried them, spread them on the table. I cleaned and polished the floor or tidied up the dressing table. It's a different domestic from home.

Elma   In Jamaica, Elma worked as a trained seamstress and as a nanny for a middle-class family. When she came to England, her first job was in an asylum, where her duties were to care for the everyday needs of patients. She bathed and dressed them, took them for walks and helped them to feed themselves. She enjoyed the work and feels it was 'fun.'

Like Lorraine, Elma feels that working in England was qualitatively different. She had to get used to a routine, whereas in Jamaica she could work as a seamstress at her own speed. She worked long hours for little pay in England; her shift was thirteen hours a day and she worked every Sunday for three years and ten months. Her time off was half a day on Thursday and all day Friday. If she wanted to attend a wedding, she would have to change her day off to a Saturday.

After living and working in Gloucester for three years, Elma moved to London in 1960. In London, she continued working as an auxiliary nurse in a psychiatric hospital until 1968. As an auxiliary nurse, Elma was often assigned to do the cleaning:

> You know sometimes if they don't have maids. . .well sometimes they will ask nicely and some will say that we are supposed to do it. We just do it, just to be quiet we do it, don't worry about it. We have it [prejudice], really it doesn't show up that bright, it never die out, it's always there, you know. You just go and take it. It was hard to do it, just ignore it and that's it.

Since Elma possessed practical experience with mental patients, she was offered a position on a training course to qualify as a state-enrolled nurse. While she was working, Elma began to put aside money to send for her daughter and made regular payments to a Jamaican travel agent. By 1962 she had paid the passage and her daughter arrived.

Elma was married in 1962. The couple had their first son in 1964 and a second son in 1968. Since Elma worked the day-shift at the hospital and her husband worked a night-shift for the postal service, they took turns looking after the children. Elma stated proudly that she never left her children in the care of a minder (baby-sitter).

In the early 1970s, Elma moved to Birmingham to be with her sister and one of her nieces while she worked at a specialist hospital. Elma later returned to London and worked in a geriatric hospital until 1974. After this, she returned to Birmingham where she worked as a state-enrolled nurse at a specialist hospital until her retirement in 1987. Elma values her work in the hospitals: she says it was a 'good experience.' She believes that had she stayed in Jamaica she would not have become a nurse.

Martha   The Tuesday following her arrival Martha went to the 'Labour Exchange'[31] and by Wednesday she was employed by a

---

31. The government's employment agency.

knife manufacturer. She was one of four Black women in her department. Martha was worried about the job and thought to herself: 'Oh my God, how am I ever going to work in this place, I never worked in a factory before!' Despite her reservations, she took the job, which paid £5 a week.

Her next adjustment to work in England was working on Good Friday. Martha had been brought up to believe that you should not work on Good Friday; she was upset and terrified, because she thought something terrible would happen to her. While she was at work that Friday the sky grew dark with an advancing thunderstorm, and Martha believed God was punishing her. She looked at the other Black women in the factory and noticed that they were not scared; she thought perhaps they had been raised differently.

Martha went to work in another knife factory, where she polished knives. There was only one other Black woman in her section. Martha felt that this was 'hard work' because it was piece-work: she had to fight for her fair share of work since the White women did not want her or the other Black woman to get any work. The knives came down a conveyor belt and the women would polish and box them. They were paid 1s and 6d (7½p) a box, so she tried to do ten boxes a day. The White women at the top of the belt would grab all the knives and place them on their laps. The foreman was aware of what was going on, so he used to rotate the seating arrangements daily. When Martha and her friend were at the top of the belt, they would let the excess knives pass down, but the following day the White girls would be at it again. One day, when Martha and her friend were at the bottom of the belt, her friend reached up towards the top and took up six knives and gave three to Martha. The other women threatened Martha and her friend and said they shouldn't bother coming to work the next day. Martha was outraged, she threw the knives on the belt and walked out.

Like Lorraine and Elma, Martha felt that work in England was qualitatively different from the work women did in Jamaica:

> I wasn't used to this working in this factory business, and to leave Jamaica from a store, where I used to clerk them, and to come here and my first job was working on a power press machine, it gets to me, man, I feel like walking back home. The first job that was offered to me was cleaning, and I resented it so much that I wouldn't take it.

I said when I was back home sometimes we have some girls come round and clean our house. And come here and gone to hospital to clean the floor – it gets to me stomach. I kind of thought I prefer go to the factory. But now when I look back at it now, I would be better off if I'd gone into the hospital and cleaned the floor.

When Martha moved to Birmingham, she accepted employment in a clothing factory. She left this job when she had her second son. Afterwards she returned to factory work making raincoats. When she had her fourth daughter, she was working in a metal-goods factory. After the birth of this daughter, she decided she had had enough of factory work, so she applied for a job at a specialist hospital and later switched to a general hospital. While she was working at the hospital and training she became pregnant with her last daughter. When her last daughter was over a year old, Martha began working at a local children's home. She did three nights at the hospital and then worked for four and a half hours at the nursery. She was going to leave the nursery job because she had no one to look after her youngest son, then only a baby. The nursery matron did not want Martha to leave, so she encouraged her to bring her son to work with her. Martha later took a job in the northeast of the US, where she worked as a nanny for a professional family. Since her son was still a young child she took him with her.

Her desire to train as a nurse was thwarted by her responsibilities as a wife and mother:

After I had Stephanie, I was working at [the hospital]. The matron call me one day and ask me if I would like to do my training, and I said yes. She didn't even give me any test. . .she tell me to come a couple weeks time to get me uniform so that I can start and I find myself pregnant with Monica so I didn't get to do it. Then after I had Monica, it was six years before I had Paul and I went to [___] to do a midwifery course and when I went for the test, before they call me, I find myself pregnant with Paul, but I didn't understand that I could go and do what I was doing and have maternity leave. I just didn't show up, you see, because I didn't understand. If I had gone to that job as a cleaner, I would be recognized from then. I wouldn't get married for a start and maybe I wouldn't have the children what I have now, I would be somewhere up the top, but you cannot look at life that kind of way. When you're not used to cleaning people's floor and you come here and they push a mop bucket and a broom in your hand, no sir, that turns me stomach.

Members' Residential Distribution and Housing

There is an extreme loyalty to the local congregation which transcends physical proximity. Most older members live scattered throughout the ward within a short car ride of the church. Many younger members have established their own households and live across town. There are a few roads in the ward and surrounding area where two or three church members are neighbors. Brethren help each other get to services and other church activities by offering lifts. The church owns a couple of vans whose drivers will collect or drop off anybody who needs a lift, no matter how great the distance. If a smaller meeting is held at a member's house, someone will volunteer to drive. In such cases the church building becomes the collection point, and at the end of the evening members will be dropped off at home.

Of members surveyed, 22 lived in homes which they or their parent(s) owned, five in council housing, five in other rented accommodation and three in housing-association accommodation. While these figures are not reliable indicators of the tenure of housing among members in general, they do point to their varied economic circumstances. Because of the shortage of council housing in the area adjacent to the church, members who live in council housing often live quite a distance from the church. One elderly couple who lived in council accommodation would travel across the city at least three times a week to attend activities and services, even though there was a smaller congregation of the NTCG directly across the road from their home. Rented accommodation and housing-association accommodation make it possible to remain in the area by filling in the shortfall in council housing provision. Access to rented accommodation can also be secured from among church members who are landlords or who take boarders.

Front rooms are always well furnished and maintained and tend to be used for visitors. Regular friends who drop by are entertained in the room where most domestic activities occur, i.e., the dining room or the kitchen. If several people drop in who are unconnected to each other except through members of the household, they will be entertained in different rooms by different members of the household. The back room, or the room in which living is done, is crowded with furniture; a glass cabinet displays china and valued gifts, a sideboard is usually piled with letters and bills, the walls are covered with photographs past and present of family near and far. There is little in the way of religious iconography, except for an occasional religious calendar, a picture of the Last Supper or seasonal greeting cards.

Summary and Conclusion

Why do some people choose to join the NTCG? Is there anything distinctive about the socio-economic circumstances of members which differentiates them from the wider African-Caribbean population and which can account for the appeal of African-Caribbean Pentecostalism and members' participation in the NTCG? Pentecostalism is usually understood either as compensating the socially, economically and politically disadvantaged members of society through spiritual provision, or as providing a balm for the adverse effects of uneven modernization which disrupts traditional values and social organization and displaces certain segments of the population. While such arguments may account for the rise and popular appeal of Pentecostalism elsewhere, their usefulness concerning African-Caribbean Pentecostalism in Britain is limited.

The legacy of overt and institutional racism and sexism which has structured the access of people of African-Caribbean origin and descent to education, housing and employment and which have placed African-Caribbean peoples in a marginal position in Britain cannot be denied. The experiences and circumstances of members of King Street congregation and the NTCG denomination fall well within the parameters of experience for Birmingham's, and Britain's, African-Caribbean populations. Hence, if an explanation for the appeal of Pentecostalism could simply be founded on a compensatory argument for the material effects of racism and discrimination, we would still need to ask why the remainder of Black British people are not to be found in Pentecostal churches. Further, we need to refine our understanding of what it means to be Black British. A neat statistical portrait of disadvantage may not necessarily offer the best insight into Black British experience. There have been changes in the composition and circumstances of the African-Caribbean population. Speaking demographically, members of the African-Caribbean population have more in common with the White population in terms of age structure and the ratio of men to women. There has also been a diversification in the socio-economic circumstances of Britain's African-Caribbean population.

The nature of employment for first and second generation church members is representative of the wider African-Caribbean population. Church members and others offer the observation that church membership for the second generation results in 'redemption and lift.' Members of the second generation who are also members of the church are understood to possess values compatible with success in British society, remaining in school, receiving qualifications and being employed in better jobs. The second generation has built upon the gains of the first, the nature of employment for sons and daughters being a progression from the employment of parents. In state-sector employment, younger women have gained higher qualifications in the health services than their mothers and have diversified into civil-service occupations where they work in local-authority offices and for the social services department. In the private sector, younger women have gained entry into the higher status occupations of traditional women's work, where they are engaged in distribution, catering and secretarial work. Younger men have proceeded to non-manual jobs with higher status than older men, as engineers and accountants. They have also joined young women in the civil service. It is difficult, however, to offer a clear correlation between socio-economic success and church membership. There are successful members of the second generation who are not church members and there are young church members who have not been successful.

While not clearly an overall 'success story' like members of the Indian community, where there is a higher percentage of professional workers and fewer unskilled workers, the African-Caribbean population is not as disadvantaged as members of the Pakistani and Bangladeshi communities. Yet it is important to bear in mind that members of the African-Caribbean community have the highest rate of economic activity, which suggests that they have had to work doubly hard to make modest gains. If there is indeed any socio-economic difference between members of the church and the wider African-Caribbean population, it is that they are less likely to be employed in unskilled manual labor. Any relatively modest success among members would again discount the utility of a compensatory argument.

Where church members differ from the wider African-Caribbean population is in the higher proportion of women and elderly in the church. Given the demographic composition of the African-Caribbean population, women and the elderly are over-represented in the church. While two-thirds of the congregation are female and ten to fifteen percent are aged over sixty, one-third of the congregation is male and over eighty percent are members of the second and third generations of Black British. The church is a cultural institution which offers a site of continuity between male and female and old and young, a community reflected in the subtle and complex use of fictive kinship terms.

In a congregation that has a higher than average proportion of women and the elderly and a fairly economically successful membership overall, it may seem a truism to state that what is absent are the characteristics of poverty and high unemployment which are commonly associated with the culture of disaffection adopted by some sections of urban Black youth. At the same time, these very characteristics – as well as the presence, albeit a not very significant presence, of young Black men – places a question mark beside the standard interpretation of African-Caribbean Pentecostalism as a 'culture of disinheritance' for the older generation (cf. Calley 1962, 1965; Henry 1982; Hill 1963, 1971a, 1971b, 1971c; Pryce 1979). This raises the issue of the actor's choice in the construction of identity. One can be relatively successful and still choose to participate in African-Caribbean Pentecostalism. One can be young, Black, alienated and unemployed, yet still not embrace the culture of disaffection. African-Caribbean Pentecostalism must therefore be understood as one choice among several open to African-Caribbeans in Britain.

If we cannot clearly differentiate between members of the church and the wider African-Caribbean population, except by the fact that they are members of the church and others are not, then we have to ask why they join the church. Following the narrative experiences of Lorraine, Elma and Martha, it is suggested that for the older generation, religious experience is a powerful idiom in which to construct identity. However, unlike other African-Caribbean identities of choice, there is no clear discontinuity between the way in which the first and second generations negotiate the terms of representation. Although the ethnographic focus is on the way in which the older generation constructs identity within the religious idiom and the implications this identity has for women, this form of religious expression is also an active identity choice for men, and for members of the second and subsequent generations. While members share with other African-Caribbeans the same external ideologies and practices which have placed Blacks in Britain in a marginal position, they differ significantly in the manner which they have chosen to address and redress their circumstances. Before considering this process in detail, the history of Pentecostalism in Jamaica is examined and another explanation for the development of African-Caribbean Pentecostalism in Britain is offered.

Chapter 2

'Moving up the King's Highway': African-Caribbean Pentecostalism in Jamaica and England

African-Caribbean Pentecostalism, in both Jamaica and England, is the result of migration processes. Pentecostalism had existed in Jamaica since the beginning of the twentieth century but did not flourish until the 1940s, when it was reintroduced by 'itinerant journeymen,'[1] men who migrated to the United States as seasonal farm-workers during the Second World War. However, as one author has emphasized: 'Pentecostalism was not transplanted fully grown from America to the Caribbean . . . North American and West Indian Pentecostalism developed hand in hand' (Calley 1965: 15). Or as another put it, Pentecostalism found its way to the Caribbean not as a fully developed movement, but as an idea (Booth 1984: 33), while Bryan Wilson reminds us that 'sects being exportable acquire differing cultural connotations in different societies' (1970: 231). Upon arrival in Jamaica the idea of Pentecostalism was modified and inserted into a pre-existing order of socio-religious status assertion, where it acquired cultural significance in the solution of the problem of an individual's social identity.

Similarly the idea of Jamaican Pentecostalism found its way to the inner cities of England as an idea carried by itinerant journeymen and women. In his discussion of the formation of Caribbean Pentecostal sects in England, Calley notes that 'West Indians have imported their preachers and their sects ready made; they have not joined sects they found already operating in England' (1962: 58). We cannot immediately assume, however, that the meaning of African-Caribbean Pentecostalism in England is the same as that

1. The phrase is adapted from Max Weber.

Plate 2 'A New Testament Church of God Hall' Source: Author

which adheres to Pentecostalism in Jamaica or even to indigenous English Pentecostalism.

At the same time, it would be equally misguided to treat African-Caribbean Pentecostalism solely as a product of the British context. Earlier attempts to account for the popularity of African-Caribbean Pentecostalism in Britain were influenced by theories which interpreted Black participation in African-American churches and sects as a means of economic and social compensation.[2] Yet they also sought to explain the Black church movement in England in terms of immigrant assimilation and integration (Calley 1965; Hill 1971a, 1971b, 1971c). For Calley, the West Indian Pentecostal sect represented a deliberate attempt to create an ethnic enclave, engender group solidarity and construct a refuge from the wider society. For Hill, its significance lay in the compensatory functions it offered to members suffering from racism and status deprivation in Britain. The interpretations offered by Calley and Hill are not wrong in contributing to an understanding of African-Caribbean Pentecostalism; however, history reveals facets which provide deeper understanding.

It may be true that African-Caribbean Pentecostalism in England emerged partly in response to the racism of the 1950s and 1960s. However, the view that Jamaicans in particular, and African-Caribbeans in general, first encountered racism when they docked at Southampton or landed at Heathrow is not totally accurate. To see African-Caribbean churches as a 'response' to racism in England overlooks the fact that Jamaica and the Caribbean possess a long history in which an indigenous system of racial differentiation governed society. There was racial discrimination in the Caribbean long before 'the problem' surfaced in England. Jamaican society possessed its own internal logic and strategies to deal with differentiation based upon race, class and color. Religion in the Caribbean reflected this logic and presented one such strategy.

The meanings of race, class and status, how they articulate with one another and how they signify the identity of an individual differ in Jamaican and British society. Further, the manner in which the social order is conceived and a person's place in that order conceptualized and expressed by religious belief is also structured

2. See Nelsen and Nelsen 1975 for a review of theories concerning the African-American church in the 1960s. See Lincoln and Mamiya 1990 for a contemporary approach to the study of the Black churches in the US.

differently in the two societies. By examining how the Jamaican construction and expression of social identity differs from that in Britain, it is possible to propose an alternative explanation for the development of the NTCG and the continuing significance of African-Caribbean Pentecostalism in Britain.

Jamaica[3]

Status and Identity in Post-war Jamaica

Identity is estimated by the self and others on the basis of criteria like race, class, and status. The definition of each criterion and its configuration in the estimation of identity will vary from culture to culture and society to society. In ascertaining an individual's social identity the configuration of race, class, and status will vary; in some instances these criteria may be tightly or loosely integrated and may be weighted and/or ranked hierarchically. In societies characterized by stratification, a specific configuration of indices may be used to locate individuals within different social strata.[4]

Since race, class and status are historically and culturally specific, what is the nature of difference in the estimation of social identity in Britain and Jamaica? Black identity in Britain was based on a tight integration of race, class and status such that each criterion served as a synonym for the others. Over time, however, the phenotypical and biological signifiers of race were replaced with a cultural conception of race that became synonymous with class and status. Only in the last decade has there been a conceptual loosening of race, class and status which permits a view of a heterogeneous African-Caribbean population. How were race,

3. The representation of Jamaican society portrayed here is a historical contextualization and does not portray the current social order of Jamaica.

4. Husband notes that individual actors' 'common-sense' theories of race may possess common elements but the unique pattern which each person holds is shaped by their individual situation and unique experiences (1982: 19). Further, the 'common-sense' notion of race held by any one group in society is not necessarily the same as that held by another group in society; hence, a particular concept of race may manifest itself as a status convention. Inasmuch as we can acknowledge the different concepts of race between individuals and groups, we should also acknowledge difference across societies; we should be cautious about drawing direct comparisons between concepts of race which are Jamaican and those which apply to British society.

class and status defined in Jamaican society and what was the
nature of their configuration, which resulted in a unique ideology,
or ideologies, of identity? Of critical concern is the estimation and
assertion of identity in Jamaica in the late 1950s. This period is
significant because it is the social, economic and historical juncture
in which first-generation migrants experienced their identity as
members of Jamaican society. Jamaica, past and present, is a
complex and heterogeneous society. Thus a conception of race as
a 'diffuse pattern of beliefs and images' specific to individuals and
perhaps overlapping in a group helps us to approach the meaning
of not only race, but of class and status as well (Husband 1982: 19;
Weber in Gerth and Wright-Mills 1991: 181–92).

The history of race, color, class, status and identity in Jamaica
is a long and complex one.[5] It is clear, however, that in the past
there was a powerful if not perfect concordance between race,
economic position and status at both the ideological and practical
level (R. T. Smith 1988: 89). The White planter class occupied the
highest echelons of the social order, free people of Color and free
Blacks formed the upper and lower middle class respectively, while
the at the base of the social pyramid lay the class upon whom the
whole social order depended – the Black and Colored slaves. This
three-tier system of color and status differentiation was produced
and reproduced by the eighteenth- and nineteenth-century pattern
of isogamic marriage for high-status White and Colored men
coupled with inter-racial concubinage between persons of unequal
status. The term 'Colored,' or 'Brown,' denoted a person of
evidently mixed western European and African ancestry, while
the term 'Black' denoted a person of predominantly African
ancestry (Henriques 1953: 43).

The intermediary status of the Colored middle-class person was
precarious and ambiguous. Members of this status therefore
sought to maintain their middle-class standing by asserting social
distance between themselves and Blacks and stressing social
proximity with the White upper class by adopting White attitudes
as their own (R. T. Smith 1988: 91–4; Curtin 1955: 174–5). If the
possibility of 'passing fe White' was precluded by skin color, there

---

5. See Braithwaite 1960; Brathwaite 1971; Broom 1954; Clarke 1966; Curtin
1955; Furnivall 1948; Henriques 1953; Kerr 1952; Kuper 1976; Lowenthal 1972;
Post 1978; Rubin 1960; Simey 1946; M. G. Smith 1965a, 1965b, 1965c, 1965d; R. T.
Smith 1987, 1988.

remained the conscious anxiety to appear White in behavior and ideals (Henriques 1953: 45). 'Color' did not simply mean gradations of skin pigmentation or phenotypical appearance, but more significantly the behavior which expressed the values and ideals of a status group. According to the ideology of 'White bias,' appearance and behavior which denoted European ancestry and conventions were accorded high status and were positively valued publicly. Conversely, appearance and behavior which denoted African ancestry and origins were publicly denigrated and assigned low status.[6] 'Color' provided an idiom for talking about race, economic occupation, class, lifestyle, attitudes and behavior, and as such it provided an index of the individual's or group's social status (M. G. Smith 1965b: 60–2).

The idealized schema of 'color' persisted into the mid-twentieth century, when it continued to serve as a yardstick against which all variations and progressions in social status were measured (R. T. Smith 1988: 89). However, by the twentieth century increased economic opportunities and political reform[7] had resulted in the loosening of the articulation between race, class and status. 'Color' was no longer an index, but an ambiguous symbol. The color-class system was not inviolate; there was ample room for maneuver.

Since color-class positioning incorporated values and behavior, the individual could negotiate status and respect by manipulating patterns of conjugal union and household composition,[8] and of religious participation, which were graded along the racial hierarchy from negative Black to positive White. One's choice of partner was suffused with status implications. The practice of choosing a wife fairer in complexion than oneself is called 'marrying light,' and having fair children 'raises' or 'lifts the colour' (Henriques 1953: 51). Having a fair wife and fair children had a reflexive effect on a man's status: 'the lighter complexion of his mate offsets the bad effects of his own colour in social terms . . . the practice of 'marrying light' brings prestige to him through the colour of his wife . . .'(ibid.: 50). As a strategy for assertion, the practice of 'marrying light' was an option only available to men. By default, a woman was prevented from 'marrying light' by men

6. See Henriques 1953: 47–9 for an assessment of appearance and behavior which denote 'color.'

7. See Henriques 1953: 51–2; Nettleford 1965: 62; Post 1978; M. G. Smith 1965a.

8. For discussions regarding the status implications of different household and conjugal forms, see Clarke 1966; Henriques 1953; R. T. Smith 1987.

who would not risk the loss of status involved in marrying a woman darker than themselves. However, a middle-class woman should be happy if she married a man in a secure economic position who was not too much darker than herself (ibid.: 51). A woman could not 'raise the color' by using the norm of legal marriage; she could only do so by becoming the mistress of a fairer man and having his children. A general pattern of color, status and marriage for the middle class emerges from this situation in which women married downwards but cohabited upwards, and men married upwards but cohabited downwards. The pattern was slightly different for the lower class. Men and women cohabited with status equals, and eventually married status equals, but a marriage, by definition, indicated a slightly elevated status. Lower class men and women both retained the possibility of 'raising the color.' Women could cohabit upwards and have fair children, while men could 'marry light.'

To pinpoint the dominant ideology concerning color, class and status at the end of the colonial period is difficult. The period is one of structural change in which the dominance of the external White ruling group was being contested and supplanted by the Colored population, who was claiming the right to govern themselves and the 'Black masses.' However, there were also voices among the 'Black masses' which contested the legitimacy of the Colored population's claim to leadership. Changes in the ideological biases which legitimated the status and right of a group to dominate and govern society were concomitant with structural change. Differing ideologies were held by different status groups but could not be directly correlated with class, so that despite similar economic circumstances, individuals could be divided in their loyalties to different ideologies.

While 'color' continued to serve as an idiom for race, class and status, it is unclear to what extent groups defined by reference to color remained fixed social categories. Parsonians and plural society theorists offer two models regarding the nature of social groups and their integration in post-war Jamaican society. Both models begin with a view of a society with three hierarchically ranked social strata symbolized by color. Where they differ is over the issue of culture (Kuper 1976: 52), the potential for social mobility and negotiating identity.

In *Family and Colour in Jamaica* (1953), the Parsonian Fernando Henriques depicts a single society divided into three social classes which are differentiated on the basis of color as it articulated with economic acquisition and occupational prestige. At this time a person's position in the labor market was becoming an increasingly important criterion of class. However, Henriques argued that economic position was less significant than social status. While a Black man could acquire high economic status and high public status, he would not be accepted as a member of the upper class and would not be able to mix intimately with members of this class. Thus, while color was not the sole determinant of social status, it remained the prevailing factor (ibid.: 42, 51–3).

The logic of 'White bias' helped mediate the discrepancies between color, economic position and social status. In this model everyone strove towards a modicum of acceptance by imitating the conventions of status superiors and by distancing themselves as far as possible from anything which would belie affinity with a lower status group (ibid.: 54, 51). By positing a value consensus of 'White bias' which forms the basis of behavior and the stereotypes upon which members of society interpret the status and identity of themselves and others, Henriques offers a fairly fluid picture of society where group membership and individual status is not necessarily fixed. The ideology of 'White bias' permitted status assertion and social mobility and provided the means to negotiate and resolve questions of identity.

The absence of competing ideologies and the contradictions between economic class and social status which arise in Henriques' model of Jamaican society form the point of departure for the plural society model as advocated by M. G. Smith (1965a). Smith suggests that the contradictions are indicative of ideological and institutional differentiation which characterize the different groups in society; hence Jamaican society is not a single culture inhabited by different color classes but a single society containing fundamentally different cultures (1965c: 58). Smith argues that the three groups which can be conveniently signified by color – White, Brown and Black – inhabit three distinct cultures (1965d: 163).[9] Each of these color sections possesses value systems which differ

9. Smith acknowledges that these color labels are heuristic, because they refer to the 'racial majority and cultural ancestry' of each section (1965d: 163). Absent from his analyses are people whose different phenotypical color makes them the anomalous minority in the color-status section to which they belong. Further, his model does not include the cultural differences of Jews, Syrians, Indians and Chinese, who were also significant members of Jamaican society.

in the modes of action and explanation which they employ (ibid.: 174). Smith sees the cultural institutions (i.e., marriage, family and religion) of the White upper class as those belonging to 'mid-twentieth-century Western European society,' while those of the intermediate Colored section are an admixture containing 'institutional syncretism' coexisting with institutional alternatives drawn from the upper and lower sections as well as institutional forms unique to the middle class (ibid.: 163, 164).[10] However, the cultural institutions of the Black 'lower class' differ from those of the 'upper and middle classes' because the elaboration of lower class institutions is derived from the problem of finding avenues of expression which are not denied by the wider society (1965c: 59).

In addition plural society theory, as elaborated by Smith, suggests that the culturally differentiated groups of White, Brown and Black are hierarchically ordered such that Whites have the highest social status and Blacks the lowest (ibid.: 62, 1965d: 163). If these are three different cultures with distinct value systems, how is consensus regarding the value assigned to each group arrived at? How is color tied to culture, culture to status and thus color to status? What determines the uncontested higher prestige ranking of one group's color over that of another? Rather than yield to the concept of 'White bias' and thus admit to a convergence of cultural worlds and integration, Smith suggests that different cultural sections are assigned value and integrated by a single political order (1965c: 67). The institutions of this political order are under the exclusive control of one of these culturally differentiated groups, which in turn seeks to maintain its dominant position by monopolizing ideal and material goods and services (ibid.; also Weber in Gerth and Wright-Mills 1991: 186–91). Unlike the consensus of 'White bias' in Henriques' account, here integration and the attribution of social value is achieved by power. Smith's model links the hierarchic relations of dominance and subordination with the stratification of the social order which are obscured in Henriques' description (Smith ibid.).

---

10. Madeline Kerr notes that the values embodied in the middle class were influenced by 'second-hand' conceptions of English and American culture, and while the culture of the upper class continued to develop along the same lines as provincial English culture, the English influences among the middle class were those of Victorian culture (1952: 93–4).

Smith's work is critical to an understanding of Jamaican society, because it underscores ideological differentiation and offers an alternative view concerning the nature of interaction between individuals. The different ideologies engender different modes of action, behavior and institutions, which in turn express and represent the diversity of society. Since members of each status section possess their own standard of value, their interpretation of events, patterns and behavior will differ significantly. In this atmosphere individuals must continuously redefine and reaffirm their status and social identity. For Smith, one's social identity is asserted by drawing a sharp contrast between the value systems and conventions of the status group to which one claims inclusion and the values and conventions of other status groups (1965d: 175). The necessary corollary of maintaining social distance between oneself and others is the assertion and maintenance of status affinity.

Unlike the fluidity inherent in Henriques' portrayal, Smith sees social mobility as clearly bounded by the status of the group. This means that it cannot be transcended by economic aggrandizement, with the result that contradictions of status remain within each group (1965c: 61, 72). Positive instances of social mobility, such as that implied in Smith's concept of 'associational color,' are negated (ibid.: 61). Individual exceptions and contradictions, like the fact that a person can simultaneously hold anti-White and anti-Black views (Kerr 1952: 96), or that the estimation of a person's 'class colour' may vary at different times in his life (Smith 1965c: 61, 71), are sacrificed in this model in the service of making clear connections between the criteria of color, culture and status. Hence, Smith renders a picture of Jamaican society where membership in groups is fixed and there is little room for social mobility and the negotiation of identity.

The pluralist approach raises an interesting question which has the potential to illuminate the nature of Jamaican society and the social identity of individuals. Despite differences in value systems, the White section and its conventions remain hegemonic in assigning value to status sections and in ordering the relations between different status sections and their members. How different might the nature of Jamaican society and the nature of individual's interaction appear if they were apprehended from a different vantage point and a different value system? If we assumed the vantage point of the Brown or Black sections, the exceptions and contradictions in the behavior of these groups could be seen as an indication of a very different perception of the nature of Jamaican society, a person's place in society and the interactions of individuals. Here it might not be the strict observance of status difference which characterizes society, but the fact that one can manipulate behavior so that status and a person's articulation with the social order appears negotiable.

Perhaps the exceptions and discontinuities which emerge from the foregoing accounts are not contradictions but, as Adam Kuper suggests, the very essence of society (1976). Writing in the early 1970s, Kuper argued that Jamaicans use numerous varied criteria to rank themselves and others and that the importance of each criterion for indicating status changed with different historical moments. He also suggested that the post-war period addressed by Henriques and Smith was a historical moment in which the weight of criteria was shifting, such that there was a disassociation of the hierarchical systems of culture, class position and social status. Economic position was challenging the previously dominant criterion of color, this being one reason why the concordance between race, economic position and status which obtained in the mythical past cannot be assumed. Kuper also suggested that the various criteria were no longer congruent with each other, but 'yield a complex and flexible series of social classifications.' In the context of Jamaica, what these criteria retained in common was an underlying notion that race is a fact of nature which stretches beyond appearance to include beliefs and behavior: as such, it divides people into unequal sets. The variability and ambiguity of status criteria and the variety of ascriptions which they produced were allowing Jamaicans to maximize the ambiguities of race, culture and class. In the 'extremely complex' and 'fluid situation' of Jamaican society the actors referred to different values in different situations. There were no clearly defined groups with social boundaries agreed upon by the actors, and therefore actors did not see themselves as consistent members of self-conscious and ranked categories (ibid.: 56, 61, 60).

The essence of Jamaican society, the ambiguity of 'color' coupled with the manipulation of actions, behaviors, values and institutions in the assertion and estimation of an individual's social status, is illustrated in the following folksong:[11]

11. The song dates from the late 1930s to early 1940s; the singer, an elderly Sister in King Street Congregation, was a schoolgirl when she learned it.

I met a White White girl drivin moto car.[12]
I met a Black girl do the same.
I met a poor Black girl drivin a donkey cart,
   but I'm [*sic*] drivin all the same,
all the same, my baby, all the same.
In simple living, living for a honeymoon.

I met a White White girl drivin aeroplane.
I met a (Black) Brown girl do the same.
I met a poor Black girl drivin a donkey cart,
   but she's drivin all the same,
all the same, my baby, all the same.
In simple earning, earning for a honeymoon.

Although the song explores the ambiguities of social status, it is informed by and contained within the parameters of the ideology of 'White bias.' While the 'White White girl' is placed unquestioningly at the top of the color-class hierarchy, the alternating color of the middle-class girl is ambiguous. Although the shift of color could be a result of confusion on the part of the singer, it is equally probable that the change in lyrics reflects the color composition of the middle class. In a stratified society characterized by social mobility, in which behavior can be simultaneously read as a reflection of the values and conventions of a status group and an assertion of status affiliation, we can assume that the Black and Brown girls are middle class because they 'do the same' as the 'White White girl' and distance themselves from the lower class. While the position of the 'poor Black girl' at the bottom of the color-class hierarchy is clearly stated, the song suggests an acceptance of middle- and upper-class status conventions. Despite the fact that she is not driving a car or flying a plane, she is 'drivin all the same.' The 'poor Black girl' sees the behavior of the other girls as worthy of approximation by driving her donkey cart all the same. The last line of each stanza would be a curious inclusion were it not for the fact that legal Christian marriage had high status value. Through hard work, economic security and the appropriation of middle- and upper-class domestic and conjugal forms, the 'poor Black girl' can assert a higher social status. The actions, behavior, institutions and values which are appropriate to a status

12. The repetition of 'White' is for emphasis and suggests that the girl is not only very fair but is most likely of English parentage and is to be distinguished from 'fair Colored' or Jamaican White.

section cut both ways. If they can be used to maintain status by indicating membership in that section, they can also be appropriated by others to negotiate a different status and hence a different articulation with the social order and a different social identity.

The Origins of Religious Differentiation

As with the differentiation of society itself and the diversity of institutional forms, the origins of religious differentiation lie in the development of Jamaican Creole society during the late eighteenth and nineteenth centuries.[13] Philip Curtin has described the religious landscape of nineteenth-century Jamaica as a 'spectrum showing a coloration from African to European' (1955: 32). The different forms of Jamaican magico-religious belief expressed different conceptions of the social order as held by different status groups and presented different solutions to the problem of meaning and identity for individuals in society.

From the eighteenth century until emancipation in 1834, the established Anglican church had remained the exclusive property of the planter class. There was little or no provision for the religious needs of slaves. The baptism of slaves required the payment of a fee on the part of the slave owner; slaves were not taught catechism, nor were they allowed to marry (Curtin 1955: 32). Slaves were not simply denied access to a particular form of religion as an instrument of domination and as a convention of the dominant ruling elite, they were denied access to a particular world view, and most importantly they were denied moral worth as humans. It was felt that the Christian gospel which preached human equality and love was potentially subversive to the interests of the ruling class (Simpson 1956: 335; Smith 1975: 313). It was not until 1815 that the Jamaican state assembly addressed the issue of religious instruction for slaves (Gardner 1873: 331).

At the other end of the spectrum of belief lay what was called the 'Obeah-Myal' complex of the slaves, which was a system of

13. For full accounts of religion during the eighteenth and nineteenth centuries see: Curtin 1955: 28–38, 162–77; Furley 1965; Gardner 1873: 175–91, 192–202, 329–92, 458–80; R. T. Smith 1976. For a discussion regarding the development of Obeah and Myalism, see Williams 1933: chapters 4 and 5.

'explanation, prediction and control' (Horton 1967) directed towards the regulation of social relations through the intervention of spirits. In the context of slave society as it developed in Jamaica, the West African pantheon of spirits, ancestors and deities was reduced to a general belief in good and evil spirits which could be manipulated for good or evil effects and a powerful belief in the shades of the dead or 'duppies' (Curtin 1955: 32).[14] The magic, incantations, charms, fetishes and poisons of the Obeah practitioner were used to cause illness or death, restore health and life, punish an enemy or win his favor, or detect a thief, murderer or adulterer (Simpson 1956: 389; Williams 1933). By the twentieth century the adversarial aspects of Obeah were being used to dispel evil spirits, injure enemies, ensure success in court cases, discover the identity of a thief and acquire one's proper share of an inheritance (Simpson ibid.).

Whereas Obeah was practiced individually in response to a particular need, Myalism developed as a cult aimed at counteracting the effects of evil and Obeah by using equal or superior magic.[15] The supernatural power of the Myal men allowed them to unearth the fetishes and charms which had been planted by the Obeah practitioner, to catch the duppies which the Obeah men used as their messengers and servants, and to release the shades of the living which had been captured by the Obeah man. Common to both practices are the West African practices of divination, healing, prophecy, spirit possession, sacrifice, dancing and drumming. Although the Obeah-Myal complex was not an organized religion and did not contain an ethic of redemption and salvation, it posed a threat to the hegemony of the planter class not only in the form of personal destruction, but by offering slaves a means of resistance and leaders from among their own ranks (Williams 1933: 145–8, see also Gardner 1873; Simpson 1956). Unlike the religious beliefs and practices of peasants, which regulate and control unpredictable natural processes, the Obeah-Myal complex addressed itself to the unpredictable in social

14. A duppy is the ghost of a dead person. Jamaican soul concepts are derived from West African beliefs regarding multiple souls (Kerr 1952: 131; Morrish 1982: 43–4; Simpson 1972: 9; Williams 1933: 151). Every person possesses a soul which is inseparable and a shadow (Kerr ibid.). It is believed that when a person dies, although their soul goes to God, their duppy may linger on earth.

15. Although it is difficult to pinpoint when Myalism emerged, it was in existence by the beginning of the nineteenth century.

relations. By addressing uncertainty and competition in human relations and the destructive power of others, Obeah-Myal reflected the lived experiences of Jamaica's African population.

The first attempt to proselytize and convert slaves to formal Christianity began with the arrival of the Moravian Brethren in 1754 (Gardner ibid.: 199). By 1767–1768 the Moravians were baptizing 260 converts annually (ibid.: 201). The success of the Moravian missionaries can be attributed to the fact that they worked from inside the system, only preaching to slaves at the invitation of plantation overseers. By contrast, the ideas of Baptist Christianity, introduced by the movement of slaves and ex-slaves from the American colonies from 1783 onwards, were spread from slave to slave (Curtin 1955: 32; Gardner ibid.: 343).[16] The Wesleyan Methodists arrived a little later, in 1790 (Gardner ibid.: 345), followed by the English Baptists in 1814 and the Presbyterian mission in 1818 (ibid.: 351, 337). While some missions like the Baptists and Moravians confined their proselytizing efforts to slaves, others like the Methodists and the Presbyterians sought to reach the White and Colored population as well (ibid.: 199, 337, 345, 351; Hall 1992a).

The initial success of missionary efforts was fueled by social change and the loosening of planter control in the early decades of the nineteenth century. Although the missionaries were initially careful to frame the message of salvation in terms of a deferred reward in heaven, by their very presence on the island they were the representatives of the English abolitionist movement (Curtin 1955: 35). Non-conformist missionaries asserted the 'human' status of slaves and individual integrity within the discourse of Christian rationalism accepted by their masters at the time (Hall 1992b). Missionary Christianity offered the slaves a religious ethic of redemption and salvation which was closely linked with Calvinist ideas of hard work and economic autonomy. Here action and work were connected to mid-nineteenth-century English middle-class

16. American planters shared the same misgivings as Jamaican planters concerning the proselytization of slaves, and American slaves were neither taught to read the Bible nor to write. There was, however, a greater degree of religious toleration, so slaves were given a rudimentary religious education by their masters or itinerant Black preachers (see Frazier 1964: chapters 1 and 2). Hence, many of the newly arrived American slaves were already converts to Christianity and became 'unofficial missionaries,' succeeding in spreading Christianity among Jamaican slaves (Curtin 1955: 32).

ideas of the individual, personhood and masculinity, where to be an individual and a Christian man was premised upon independence secured through action, and to be elevated as a Christian woman was to be subject to such a man, to carry out his action as his 'beautiful reflex' and helpmeet (Hall 1992a: 219, 237; 1992b: 266). Thus while we should be cautious about assuming that Christian conversion held the same meaning for slaves as for missionaries – the ideas of personhood and individuality ensconced in Christian missionary thought could be seen to share the same aims of Obeah-Myalism, namely freedom from dependence and subjection to the will of others – this was achieved by positing a different relationship to the world and others in it. In converting to Christianity, one escapes subjection to the will of others and redefines one's relationship to the world and one's personhood through subjection to the will of God (Cucchiari 1988: 433). Ideas of personhood and gender framed in this way are incorporated into African-Caribbean Pentecostalism, where they remain powerful but are also transformed.

With the cessation of the slave trade in 1808 and the abolition of slavery in 1834, the millennial hope of Christianity could no longer be presented as a story of deferred reward. Christianity was transformed into a potentially effective idiom of collective social and political expression, which would be able to assert the status of its followers and claim a change in the individual's relationship to the social order, if not an actual change in that order. Lastly, in so far as Whites, Coloreds and Blacks attended services together, the non-conformist Churches served as an integrative force in Creole society (Furley 1965).

It would appear that non-conformist Christianity was well positioned to emerge in nineteenth-century Jamaica as the middle-class form of religious expression. However, the popularity of non-conformist Christianity among the middle class proved to be limited: in 1866, one-third of all Jamaican church members were Anglican (Curtin 1955: 165–7). Prior to 1845, all the non-conformist churches witnessed an increase in their following, though from 1845 to 1865 they lost their following (ibid.: 168). Two main obstacles prevented the wholesale adoption of non-conformist Christianity among the Colored middle class (ibid.: 32–7, 162–8, 171). The first was the question of racial integration which arose in the Methodist church; during the period following emancipation, this resulted in schism and the development of the

Jamaican Wesleyan Methodist Association. Those members of the
Colored middle class who favored Jamaican nationalism left the
church and joined the Association, while those who aligned
themselves more closely with the Whites out of a desire for
assimilation and social acceptance joined the Anglican church
(ibid.: 166). Orthodox Christianity thus continued to represent the
acceptance of White values and a denial of African values, but no
single church emerged as the vehicle for middle-class expression.
The second problem was the potential for the incorporation of
devalued West African beliefs within non-conformist Christianity
(Booth 1984: 15f; Curtin 1955: 32–7; Gardner 1873: 343–4, 357–8).
Like the Methodists, the Baptist Church also experienced limited
middle-class popularity. Because of its association with the Native
Baptist movement, the Baptist church had moved closer to a
syncretistic position.

Among the influx of American Baptists following the American
Revolution was a freedman named George Lisle. Although Lisle
is credited with the founding of Native Baptism in Jamaica, it is
the personal interpretations and innovations brought to Baptist
doctrine by his followers which significantly contributed to its
eventual development in Jamaica (Curtin ibid.: 32). Two prominent
followers, Moses Baker and George Gibb, introduced the 'leader
system,' which divided church members into 'classes' for teaching
(ibid.: 33). The spiritual position of the class leader underwent a
series of transformations, which reintroduced into Christianity a
measure of charisma based upon supernatural power. Class
leaders were not simply the teachers of doctrine to new converts,
they were spiritual gurus and guides akin to the leaders of Myal
cult groups (ibid.: 33; Gardner 1873: 357) and had the authority to
deny membership by refusing baptism or expelling members
(Curtin ibid.; Gardner ibid.: 357–8;). Spirit possession, often
involving fasting and a vigil to induce possession and its manifestation in the dreams and visions of the prospective candidate,
who was vetted by the class leader, became the requirement
for membership (Curtin ibid.: 33, 34; Gardner ibid.: 357).[17] By

17. The fact that a dream should be the necessary medium whereby the spirit
descended upon the person is not simply premised upon the Christian belief
that 'old men shall dream dreams' but also demonstrates a concordance with
the belief that the duppies of the dead will attempt to communicate with the
living through dreams.

neglecting the written word and emphasizing spirit possession, Native Baptism provided a space in which certain aspects of African-Caribbean religious practices and orientations could be incorporated into Christian belief and practice (Curtin ibid.: 33).

Once the precedent for syncretism was established, it produced a seemingly endless series of variations which were themselves syncretisms of earlier syncretisms. After emancipation, Myalism experienced a period of resurgence (1841–1860) associated with the incorporation of an increasing number of Christian beliefs and practices. The most notable of these was the inclusion of a chiliastic millenarian promise.[18] The new Myal men declared the advent of the millennia and that God had sent them, in preparation, to uncover Obeah and catch the duppies (Reverend Banbury, in Williams 1933: 149). Other Christian elements included preaching, hymns, prophesying and the use of Biblical phraseology (Curtin ibid.: 170). Non-Christian elements incorporated in the new practice of Myalism were the sacrifice of fowl, extempore song with a choral response, ecstatic dancing, and utterances which were interpreted as divine revelation.[19]

There is evidence – although scant – which suggests that where African-Christian religious belief and practice tends to differ significantly from non-conformist Christianity is in the construction of gender. In the descriptions of Obeah-Myalism and later Revivalism, there are references to women as practitioners of Obeah, and to the Mothers, Mammies, Governesses, Leaderesses and Sheperdesses of Myalism, Pocomania and Revivalism (see Beckwith 1929; Gardner 1873: 358; Kerr 1952; Simpson 1956). While the structure of agency for women appears as diverse as the number of sects enumerated by these accounts, it is clear, following accounts of women's conversions, that these women felt themselves to be empowered by the spirits (cf. Beckwith 1929: 33–4; Kerr 1952: 128). It is also clear, following Kerr, that there existed an idea of complementarity between male and female religious leaders. She notes that in the African-Christian syncretism of Pocomania the male leader or 'Shepherd' needed

18. The Christian belief that Christ will return to the earth and rule for a thousand years, during which time the current unjust and social order will be replaced by a good and equitable order (see Hobsbawm 1959).

19. See Curtin 1955: 170 and Williams 1933: 154–6 for descriptions of nineteenth-century Myalism.

to have 'Mothers', and female 'Leaders' needed the help of men (ibid.: 127). The complementarity between male and female religious leaders appears as a continuation of Christian non-conformist ideas about gender, while the autonomous agency of women empowered directly from the spirit appears as a radical departure from non-conformist ideas of gender and personhood. These ideas are later incorporated into the Pentecostalism of the NTCG.

In 1861 the Moravian mission mounted a Christian revival which was picked up by other missions as well as the Native Baptists and Myalists. The result of the Revival was twofold. First, it firmly and forcibly established Jamaica as a Christian society. William James Gardner, an observer at the time, recounts with satisfaction that the evil habits of society were forsaken. People abandoned the rum shops for membership in one of the numerous congregations and flocked to the churches to be married. Despite a high level of illiteracy, 37,000 copies of the Bible were sold (1873: 466). Secondly, as more and more people were converted to Christianity, the pace of syncretism also quickened.

The new practice of 'Revivalism' was the result of the syncretism of Myalism and Christianity during this period. At its inception, Revivalism was characterized by the emotional display of belief; new converts were struck prostrate or were given to oral confessions, dreaming, trances, prophesying, spirit possession and dancing in the spirit. This emotionalism was not tolerated by the missionaries and the 'Revivalists' were disowned, but Revivalism did become a permanent addition to the range of Jamaican African Christian cults (Curtin 1955: 171; Gardner 1873: 465–6). It underwent numerous modifications, such as the re-invention of a spirit pantheon coupled with saints, an emphasis on healing, and the use of balmyards.[20] By the twentieth-century Revivalism was a well established phenomena; there were various sects throughout the island, each possessing its own form of organization and syncretism (Beckwith 1923, 1929; Simpson 1956).

Each variation of African-Christian syncretism enlisted a different form of religious expression which could be utilized in the negotiation and construction of identity. In its swing from

20. The ritual yard of a leader of an African Christian religious sect used for worship and healing. The leader is often associated with Myal practice and as such may remove Obeah curses or may also be a practitioner of Obeah. See Beckwith 1929: 137; Cassidy and LePage 1967: 22; Kerr 1952: 137.

Obeah to orthodox Christianity, the pendulum of syncretism continued to offer up new syncretic forms such as Convince, Pocomania and Bedwardism. The particular mix of Obeah or Christianity depended upon where the pendulum was halted in its swing.[21] While each new form of African-Christian practice integrated traditional Christianity with West African beliefs and thus reflected the diversity of Jamaican society, their adherents were the poor Black members of society. Hence, these forms acquired meaning as a convention of lower class status. By contrast the Anglican church and its members had high status value as a convention of the upper class. While no single non-conformist church was the church of the middle class, participation in any one of the non-conformist churches indicated an acceptance of middle-class values and attitudes and an assertion of middle-class status.

Religious Differentiation in Post-war Jamaica

By 1943 the spectrum of faith ranged from the established denominations (Anglican, Baptist, Methodist, Presbyterian, Roman Catholic, Moravian and Congregationalists) through the sects (Society of Friends, Salvation Army, Seventh Day Adventist, Christian Scientist, Bedwardites, Jehovah's Witnesses, the Church of God and other Pentecostals) to cults (Convince, Pocomania, Rastafari and Revivalists) (Table 2.1).[22]

The incipient religious-color spectrum described by Curtin for the nineteenth century had crystallized. At one end of the spectrum was decorous Christianity associated with White values and respectability. At the other end lay emotional religious beliefs or practices, like Obeah, Convince, Pocomania and Revivalism. African-Christian cults, like traditional African belief systems, sought to explain and control a complex and disordered universe

21. See Hogg 1960 for a description of the Convince cult, Beckwith 1923, 1929 for a discussion of Pocomania, Revivalism and Bedwardism in the early twentieth century, Simpson 1972 for a discussion of Afro-Christian syncretism in the Caribbean and Simpson 1956 for an ethnographic account of Revivalism.

22. In addition to Christianity, Judaism, Hinduism and Confucianism were still practiced. Judaism had entered the island with the arrival of the Spanish and Portuguese Jews, prior to the conquest of the island by the English in 1655 (Gardner 1873: 196–8). Hinduism and Confucianism were introduced following emancipation, with the arrival of indentured labor from India and China.

Table 2.1 Jamaican Religious Affiliation in 1943[23]

Religious Affiliation	Percent of Population
Anglican	28%
Baptist	26%
Methodists	9%
Roman Catholic	7%
Moravian	4%
Church of God	3%
Pentecostal	0.4%
Pocomania	0.3%

(Source: Jamaican Census 1943; cf. Henriques 1953: 77; Simpson 1956: 338)

with reference to spirits and duppies which could be manipulated and controlled. Since they connoted African origins, the beliefs and practices of cults were publicly negatively valued. The logic of ambiguity which had engendered and ordered the racial hierarchy and permitted movement within it had also engendered and ordered the religious hierarchy and permitted the use of religion as a basis for status assertion.

By the 1950s, the local church had assumed, a major if not dominant role in structuring local social life. Almost every village or town had one, if not several, churches (Fischer 1974). Where there was no official denomination, there was at least a local Revival cult (Simpson 1956). Church activities structured the round of daily and weekly life (Frazier 1964; Gardner 1873: 202, 369). Church attendance was a family affair. Children were sent to Sunday School and were accompanied by their parents (or guardians) to services. The members of the family would walk or ride to church together, wearing their 'Sunday best' (Fischer 1974, I: 31–2; Henriques 1953: 78; Kerr 1952: 116). In the evenings there was often family worship, known as 'family altar.' Children were expected to study their Bible and say their prayers under the supervision of their mother or a female guardian. Orthodox Christianity not only promoted middle-class values and ideals by

23. Official figures for religious affiliation in Jamaica should be regarded with reservation. Since religious expression is a means of value assertion where denominations are ranked on a hierarchy of social status, it behove a person to name the affiliation which they felt best expressed their view of their social status, or which expressed the social status they wanted others to believe they possessed.

structuring the daily activities of the family, it also structured the form of the family itself by prescribing legal marriage and patriarchal authority.

Different forms of Christian expression varied directly with social status group; the more restrained and orthodox the higher the class status, the more emotional and spiritual the lower the class status. Kerr writes that the Anglican church possessed 'snob value' for the ambitious social climber, and the more prosperous members of her community were Jehovah's Witnesses or Congregationalists (1952: 116–18). While the Anglican and Roman Catholic churches possessed definite prestige value (Henriques 1953: 78), the social status value of the other denominations would have been determined by local history and would have varied from region to region. At the bottom of the religious value hierarchy lay the emotive Revivalist sects and demonstrative cults of the lower class (Henriques ibid.: 77; Kerr ibid.: 116, 118; Simpson 1956: 408, 413). For most commentators, these churches were understood entirely in functionalist terms: 'The cult groups provide the means of temporary escape from the tedium of everyday life' (Henriques ibid.: 78). While they address the use-value of religion as a means for the assertion of status or escape, they fail to consider the religious in the religious; there is a lack of insight into ideas of personhood, coming to terms with suffering and the management of experience.[24] Although the sects and cults had little social prestige, they met the emotional and spiritual needs of people. African-Christian sects not only offered explanations of suffering but also provided an otherwise un-empowered people with a system of practice through which they might seek to control the unpredictable and make reparations for perceived injustices.

In the early twentieth century it was common for a person to participate in two religious spheres: membership in a main denomination gave social benefits and prestige to the individual, while participation in ecstatic cultism 'topped up' the individual by giving him greater emotional satisfaction (Kerr 1952: 120; Wedenoja 1980: 36). The onus of integrating issues of suffering and asserting social status in the religious spectrum rested on the individual actor. In the mornings people would attend a 'high

---

24. Simpson comes close to addressing religious questions when he veers towards issues of world view and answers to the problems of everyday life (1956: 412).

church,' an established denomination, and in the evenings, or on other days of the week, they would attend a 'low church' such as the open-air meeting of a revival cult. While no self-respecting middle-class Jamaican would admit to attending a Revivalist meeting, persons who regularly attended Revivalist meetings would also attend orthodox services (Hogg 1960: 18; Kerr ibid.: 116). Some of the elderly Sisters in King Street congregation recounted how they used to sneak out of the house to attend a meeting ('any little jump up') or would linger to listen to an itinerant preacher at an open-air service when dispatched on an errand. It is in this context that Pentecostalism developed.

The Development of the Church of God

Around 1918, Pentecostalism as embodied in the Church of God (COG) was inserted into the pre-existing order of Jamaican socio-religious expression. As Pentecostalism developed, it acquired new meaning from the context of Jamaican society. Like Native Baptism, Revivalism and Bedwardism, which had syncretised the emotion-alism and thaumaturgical spiritualism of African belief systems with the practices of Christianity, Pentecostalism also proved capable of syncretism. Pentecostalism removed the burden of the religious integration of status and suffering from the individual by providing a form of religious expression which combined the highly valued behavior of regular church attendance of denominational Christianity with the devalued emotionalism and spiritualism of the African-Christian cults and sects.

The Church of God in the United States

The NTCG is an affiliate of the COG of Cleveland, Tennessee, a Holiness Pentecostal denomination with roots in the religious fervor of the late nineteenth century. The COG began in 1886 as the idea of R. G. Spurling, an ex-Baptist minister who lived in Barney Creek, Tennessee (Conn 1955: 5–7). Spurling's original intention was not to establish a new denomination, but to organize a 'body' which would revive original Christianity and 'extend across, enrich and revive other churches' (ibid.: 7–11; Hollenweger 1972: 48; Jones 1983: 271).

Thus this group, which came to be known as the 'Christian Union,' began as an ecumenical endeavor set against the background of the Holiness schism in the Methodist church.[25] The Holiness movement held that sanctification began when one repented of one's sins and was complete when one was baptized by the Holy Spirit, as evidenced in the gifts of tongues, interpretation of tongues, healing, discernment and prophecy. Holiness dissenters felt that the Methodist church had departed from Wesley's teachings and had allowed worldliness to enter the church. Hence, they seceded from the Methodist church, and between 1880 and 1926 twenty-six Holiness and Pentecostal churches were established (Conn 1955: 11).

Although the Wesleyan doctrine was not part of Spurling's original message and contrasted with his Calvinist origins as a Baptist, Spurling taught the doctrine of rebirth and followed the Arminian theology of Justification. Spurling was later joined by a Methodist and two Baptists, who traveled as lay evangelists throughout the remote rural region of the Tennessee and North Carolina border, spreading the Gospel and the Wesleyan doctrine of sanctification and urging their audiences to seek the spiritual experience of sanctification by emulating Christ's perfection in their everyday lives (ibid.: 15–17, 23).

Anyone wishing to join the Christian Union was simply admitted and extended the 'hand of fellowship.' According to official church history, by the end of 1896 a hundred followers had manifested baptism by the Holy Ghost by speaking in tongues. At first the behavior of the Christian Union attracted little serious opposition, but followers – initially rural, White and poor – were derided due to the emotionalism which characterized their services, and they became the object of threats and verbal abuse. Baptism by the Holy Ghost differentiated members of the Christian Union from their brethren in the local Methodist and Baptist congregations. Followers were accused of heresy and were excommunicated from their churches and subjected to physical violence (ibid.: 14, 24–5, 30–3, 35, 39, 60).

25. Wesley had preached an Arminian doctrine of repentance and salvation for all, in contradiction to the Calvinist theology of predestination and salvation for the elect few. For Wesley, salvation was attainable for all through a commitment to Christ and a life of Holiness and sanctification.

The need for a more formal organizational structure became apparent by the turn of the century. In 1902 the church, now known as the Holiness Church, established an administrative system, ordained its ministers and appointed Spurling as its pastor (ibid.: 44–5). A former Quaker and colporteur, A. J. Tomlinson was appointed pastor a year later (ibid.: 52) and under his leadership the group moved into association with the Pentecostal movement (Jones 1983: 271). The Pentecostal movement arose out of the Azusa Street revival, led by a Black ex-Baptist preacher, W. J. Seymour.[26] Pentecostals also believed in sanctification, though they did not accept that sanctification and baptism by the Holy Spirit were the same thing. This new movement distinguished between sanctification, which purified the heart, and subsequent baptism by the Holy Spirit, manifested in glossolalia, which empowered people for service.

In 1907 the church moved to Cleveland, Tennessee, and adopted its current name from the scriptures (I Corinthians 1:2 and Acts 20:28). By 1916 what had started as a tiny backwoods revival in one of the poorest and most remote regions had 202 churches and 7,784 members; by 1955 the number of churches had grown to 2,750, with a membership of 138,349 (Bloch-Hoell 1964: 58), mainly scattered throughout sparsely populated regions of the South. Today, however, the COG is an international denomination with congregations in over a hundred countries.

The first Black congregations were established in Florida prior to 1909, but initial popularity for the COG among Blacks in the United States was limited (Jones 1987: 92–3). In 1912 a Bahamian called Edmund Barr, who had converted to the COG at a camp meeting in Florida, was ordained as the first Black minister (ibid.: 83). In 1915, Barr was appointed as the first Black overseer of the Florida congregations, but two years later these congregations were reincorporated into the church's general assembly and placed under the authority of a White overseer (Conn 1955: 133). By the early 1920s the question of race and administrative independence had become a potentially divisive issue (see Brooks 1982: 6). Some Black congregations felt that their own forms of cultural worship and the needs of their members would be better served if they

26. For the development of the Pentecostal movement and the COG, see Bloch-Hoell 1964; Hollenweger 1972; Anderson 1979; C. E. Jones 1983. For the specific history of the COG, see Conn 1955.

had a separate leadership and Black assembly (Brooks ibid.; Conn ibid.: 201). Various organizational strategies were tested, the final result being an optional arrangement whereby each congregation could decide whether it wanted to participate in the Black assembly, the general assembly or both (Conn ibid.: 202; Jones 1987: 92–3).

Optional segregation continued until the mid-1960s, when Black congregations were placed under the direct supervision of state overseers. In 1964 the COG passed a resolution on human rights declaring that 'no American be deprived of his rights to worship, vote, rest, eat, sleep, be educated, live and work on the same basis as other citizens' (Brooks 1982: 8). Brooks records that in 1965, five percent of the Black population were Pentecostals compared to only two percent of the White population. In 1966 the church removed all references to color from its official minutes and records (ibid.). Jones records that in 1976, 180 of the 4,615 congregations were dominated by Black members or had a majority of Black members; this had increased to 203 congregations by 1978 (1983: 271). In 1988 the Church of God had 17,202 churches and claimed a total international membership of 1,813,004 (COG 1988: 5).

The Church of God in Jamaica

In 1988, 307 of the COG's foreign churches, which had a membership of 39,058, were found in Jamaica (COG 1988: 14). The early history of Pentecostalism and the COG in Jamaica and the Caribbean is poorly documented. Contemporary accounts of religious expression between the 1920s and 1950s have tended to focus on Pocomania, Convince, Revivalism and Rastafarianism (see Beckwith 1923, 1929; Hogg 1960; Kerr 1952; Simpson 1955, 1956), while Pentecostalism, Seventh Day Adventism and the Salvation Army are only mentioned briefly in the literature (e.g., Simpson 1956: 409, 439). The relative silence concerning Pentecostalism indicates that it did not prosper immediately; this is further supported by official church history.

Having only just begun to organize itself, and still concentrating its evangelical efforts on its home territory, the first missionary efforts reached the Caribbean accidentally, when Barr returned to the Bahamas in 1909. Unlike the missionary efforts of the non-conformist churches during the eighteenth and nineteenth centuries, the COG lacked an official missionary program. The Pentecostal message was not immediately tolerated and members were persecuted (Conn 1955: 113).

By 1917 it appears that the Pentecostal message of the COG had reached Jamaica, where there were reported to be four churches and eighty members (ibid.: 144). Brooks records that a man called Mundle, a native of Clarendon Parish and a Revivalist, preached the Gospel and established the first contact with the COG in the US (1982: 2). This first contact appears to have lapsed, and it was a follower of Mundle who later re-established contact with the COG (ibid.). In 1918 a man called Llewelyn was sent from the US to Jamaica, where he organized a church of seven members in Kingston (ibid.: 3). By 1920 there were reported to be 232 members in seven churches. The West Indian missions were incorporated into the general administration of the church and a separate overseer for the West Indies was appointed (Conn 1955: 145). However, in 1924 when E. E. Simmons, the newly appointed overseer for Jamaica, arrived in Kingston, he could not find a single local congregation (ibid.: 193). Many members had left to join the newly founded Church of God of Prophecy.[27] In Borrowbridge, Simmons discovered 62 believers, whom he organized into a church; this is cited as the birthplace of the COG in Jamaica (Brooks 1982: 3; Conn 1955: 193). By 1935 there were reportedly 52 congregations with an average of thirty members each (ibid.: 220).

It was not until the period 1950 to 1970 that Pentecostalism began to prosper in Jamaica, as support for the main denominations (Anglican, Roman Catholic, Methodist, Baptist, Presbyterian, Wesleyan, Congregationalist and Moravian) fell away (Wedenoja 1980: 30, 33; see Table 2.2).

In 1976, William Wedenoja conducted a survey of church attendance and church establishment in a northern region of Manchester Parish. He found that 50 percent of the population attended small churches and that 59 percent of the churches in the survey area had been founded between 1946 and 1976. Pentecostal churches accounted for 39 percent of the newly founded churches in the area (ibid.: 32).

Wedenoja notes that although Pentecostal missionaries from both the United States and England were responsible for the

27. The Church of God of Prophecy was founded in 1923 by A. J. Tomlinson after his dismissal from the leadership of the COG for financial impropriety.

Table 2.2 Growth of Pentecostalism in Jamaica: Claimed Religious
Affiliation as Percentage of Population

	Pentecostalism	Main Denominations
1943	3%	82%
1960	13%	63%
1970	20%	55%

(Source: Wedenoja 1980: 30)

introduction of the religion to the island, it was the repatriation of
Jamaican men from US farm work which was the most influential
factor in its renewed prosperity (ibid.: 34, also Calley 1965: 10).
For many of the men, this was their first experience of temporary
migration. Migrants returned from the US not only with money,
but as converts and ministers to a new faith with new values,
elevated prestige and influence, which enabled them to establish
churches in Jamaica (ibid.: 35).

In the early period, the insistence that members live lives of
'Holiness' probably rendered Pentecostalism relatively unappeal-
ing in the Jamaican context (see Conn 1955: 220). What was it about
the prevailing social conditions of Jamaica during the post-war
period that proved to be fertile ground for Pentecostalism when it
was later reintroduced by return migrants? Between 1940 and 1962,
Jamaica had one of the highest economic growth rates in the world
(Wedenoja 1980: 34; Peach 1968: 27). The economy was transformed from one based on agriculture to one based on industry
(Wedenoja ibid.: 32–5). Wage labor replaced subsistence labor, and
as was noted earlier, economic achievement replaced personal ties
and other criteria as a basis for prestige (ibid.: 34). In Jamaica this
process resulted in an increased emphasis upon individual
achievement and decreased communal and familial co-operation,
a division of labor by skill rather than by age, sex and kinship,
and in the undermining of traditional patterns of authority. There
was conflict over goods, resources, traditional norms and increased
personal and economic insecurity (ibid.). These changes overlaid
an already socially and economically stratified society in which
identity was negotiable, membership in social categories question-
able and issues of race tinged with questions of social and moral
worth. Here was a stage fully set with the props of potential social
and economic disorganization for a play about anomie.

For Wedenoja and Calley, modernization provides a plausible explanation for the success of Pentecostalism at this time. However, they differ in their estimation of modernization and hence of the significance of Pentecostalism. For Wedenoja, Pentecostalism resolved a mass identity crisis: being a Christian provided the individual with new social reference points (ibid.: 39–40). Where traditional patterns of authority and co-operation had been disrupted, the Pentecostal sect provided the individual with an immediate network of fictive kin. In addition, Pentecostalism 'assuage[d] the pain of modernization' by equipping the individual with 'psychological traits and patterns of behavior which are conducive to success in a capitalist economy,' such as gratification deferral, thrift, self-denial, self-discipline and achievement motivation (ibid.: 40–1).

Modernization and social change, however, have a differential effect upon different regions and segments of the population. It is significant that this was a period of massive out-migration from remote areas, as people sought employment elsewhere, in Jamaica and abroad. Hence, the effect of modernization in remote areas was not the introduction of an industrial economy, but increased economic marginality and the disruption of familial and social relationships. Wedenoja's concern with the independent variable of modernization, although appropriate, is not a sufficient explanation by itself for the popularity of Pentecostalism. Significantly the Pentecostal movement was not evenly spread throughout the island, but was at its strongest in the poorer and more remote parts of the island which previously lacked any form of organized religion other than a Revival cult (ibid.: 32).[28] In contrast, Calley has argued that in the face of modernization and increasing marginalization, Jamaican Pentecostalism offered members new values and new self-respect. Where the church encouraged a general inversion of society's dominant values, a member's disadvantage in the wider society became an advantage in the society of saints (1965: 136).

Religious innovation and expression have consistently attended social and economic changes throughout Jamaican history, so the innovation represented by Pentecostalism is not as novel as

28. The heart of Jamaica's Pentecostal movement is located in the border area between Clarendon and Manchester parishes.

arguments premised upon modernization suggest.[29] Pentecostalism and Rastafarianism are both religious innovations. They share the same stage sets, their plots – the critique of the social order and the resolution of a meaningful identity – are the same and their audiences are drawn from the same constituency. However, they diverge in their executions of the play. Yet the particular appeal of Pentecostalism remains unexplained.

A more fruitful and specific explanation of the popularity of Pentecostalism focuses on the process of indigenization: how Pentecostalism acquired a different cultural connotation in the context of Jamaica. Wedenoja (1980) and Austin-Broos (1987) both examine this process and suggest that what made Pentecostalism successful was its ability to combine aspects of Jamaican folk beliefs, of African belief systems and of Christianity. In his discussion of Jamaica's 'ecology of religion,' Wedenoja notes that prior to the reintroduction of Pentecostalism, the traditional pattern of religious participation for the lower class was dual religious affiliation in an established denomination and a Revival cult. Denominational affiliation was associated with the *status quo*: participation in this sphere demonstrated at least a superficial commitment to the values of the dominant section of society and conferred status benefits on the person, whereas Revivalism was never part of the acceptable mainstream *status quo* and was denigrated as being superstitious, backward and lower class. Revivalism, however, emphasized group participation, divination, healing, spiritual protection and possession, all of which met the spiritual needs of the individual, but were incapable of securing status benefits for the individual. In its emphasis upon the Christian pantheon of God, Christ, Angels, Satan and a legion of evil spirits, Pentecostalism echoed the Revivalist pantheon of good and evil spirits and saints. Pentecostal religious expression also encompassed group participation, healing, spiritual recompense and possession. Wedenoja summarizes the significance of Jamaican Pentecostalism as follows:

> it offers the appealing features of both denomination and cult; it is a successful syncretism of two opposing religious traditions in Jamaican culture. It has emerged as a religion which is neither foreign like the

29. See Barrett 1977; Cashmore 1979; Gardner 1873; Hogg 1960; Morrish 1982; Nettleford 1972; Post 1978; Simpson 1955, 1956.

denominations nor indigenous like the revival cults, but both indigenous and international. It is a religion for every man regardless of race or class, and it offers both respectable status and popular enthusiasm. Thus it reflects an increasing unification of disparate trends in Jamaican culture, and acts to further integration of a pluralistic culture and stratified society. (ibid.: 37)

In her comparative work on Pentecostalism and Rastafarianism (1987), Austin-Broos reaffirms this insight and underscores Pentecostalism's dimensions of social critique and assertion of moral worth. For Austin-Broos, Pentecostalism in contemporary Jamaica is 'not an African derived religion' but a 'folk religion' associated with the poor (ibid.: 3). Pentecostalism shares with Rastafarianism the fact that it serves as an alternative to established religion, but as an alternative, Pentecostalism has a very different ethos. Unlike Rastafarianism, Pentecostalism is a 'conservative force': it does not aim to invert or topple the existing order but seeks to redefine the social hierarchy and claim integration within it such that adherents can aspire towards upward mobility (Austin-Broos ibid.: 2; 1991–1992: 308). Pentecostalism has taken over from the Revivalism of preceding decades, offering the lower class a 'vehicle for folk beliefs highly critical of Jamaica's religious establishment' and possessing a 'theological critique of Jamaican society' (1987: 6, 7). Inherent in this critique is an assertion of the moral worth of Blacks, which had been previously denied to the slaves in the eighteenth and nineteenth centuries.

Religious belief and practice became a dense, three-dimensional symbol of the Jamaican social order. Situated within a religious hierarchy that corresponded with the social hierarchy, any single form of religious expression was symbolic of the whole religious order and the entire social order. Not only did the part reflect the whole, but any single part (any action, behavior or institution) became an instrument of social identification. Like the status markers of color and form of conjugal union, religious practice could be manipulated to express one's relationship to the social order and to signal status by demonstrating adherence to the religious conventions of a particular status group. As a convention of status group, religious participation could be read many ways: it could be used to express identity to the self and to others, to maintain affinity and membership with a particular status group and to maintain status group distance. In this way, religious practices integrated the individual with the social order and thus provided the individual with meaningful identity. However, religious practices remained disparate. Forms of religious expression which were highly valued could be used for asserting a higher status or a different relationship to the social order, while forms with low-status value could only offer answers to painful existential questions. By inheriting the earlier integrative aspects of Jamaican religious practice and bringing together questions of status and suffering, Pentecostalism became the most compact religious symbol of Jamaican society.

England: The Growth of African-Caribbean Pentecostalism and its Interpretations

When migrants began to arrive in England, it was quickly noted that they were not joining the established churches. In 1963 Hill noted that 54 percent of Jamaican migrants and 69 percent of all Caribbean migrants had attended the equivalent of the English churches in the Caribbean (1963: 7). Migrants only attended church on special occasions such as weddings, christenings and funerals, and only 4 percent of the migrant population in Greater London regularly attended an established English church (ibid.: 22).

One explanation for the drop in church attendance is the 'rejectionist view.' This view posits that racism had caused the migrant community to reject the main White Christian denominations (Anglican, Baptist, Congregationalist, Methodist, Presbyterian and Roman Catholic). Hill (1971a), an early proponent of the rejectionist view, accepted that most of 'the blame' lay with the churches in England, which were not prepared to face the issue of racism within themselves and despite a liberal clergy had a less than welcoming membership. The migrants' rejection of the churches was due to a basic failure of the Christian mission, which was willing to evangelize to Blacks in their homelands but unwilling to accept them as equal status members in their own churches (Hill ibid.: 14; Patterson 1965: 226–33). A second factor, of lesser significance, was the failure of the churches to satisfy the religious needs of migrants due to inherently different doctrinal beliefs, pattern of worship and atmosphere (Hill ibid.: 15). Had doctrinal difference and not racism been the salient reason for the almost wholesale rejection of the English churches, Hill argues, we would have expected to find migrants joining English Pentecostal denominations, but this was not the case (ibid.).

Although migrants lost faith in the established denominations, they did not lose their belief in Christianity. While migrants were not found warming the pews of the Anglican church or of English Pentecostal churches, their membership in African-Caribbean Pentecostal sects was growing. Why did African-Caribbean Pentecostalism become the dominant form of Caribbean religious expression in England?

Since migration had improved the financial circumstances of most migrants, Calley felt that the growth of West Indian Pentecostal sects could not be understood as a means of compensating for economic deprivation (1965: 137). Therefore, he suggests that continuity is a cause of the development of Caribbean Pentecostalism in England: 'West Indian migrants have transplanted a familiar form of group organization, and to some extent the development of sects amounts to a recreation of the Caribbean in England' (ibid.: 28). While the argument of the familiar is beguiling, the history and diversity of religious expression in Jamaica and the fairly recent conversion of some elderly NTCG members discredits this assumption. Working within an assimilationist/race-relations paradigm, Calley shifts some of the responsibility for racism and discrimination from the 'host society' onto 'the migrant,' making the problem of assimilation the fault of the migrant:

> he gives up trying to associate with white people and comes to depend increasingly on the social resources of his own community . . .. Prominent among these are the Pentecostal sects. (ibid.: 141)

> . . .these sects are a stumbling block to the assimilation of Britain's West Indian minority. . .. Saints are much farther from assimilation than non-Pentecostal West Indians, because they erect cultural barriers to assimilation additional to those which the migrant must encounter anyway. (ibid.: 144)

Do ethnic churches hinder assimilation? In a study of Korean ethnic churches in the United States, Won Moo Hurh and Kwang Chung Kim (1990) found no evidence to suggest that membership of an ethnic church either promoted or hindered assimilation.

Compared to West Indian migrants in Britain, the authors found that only 3 percent of Korean immigrants attended American Christian churches. Meanwhile for Protestant Koreans membership in Protestant Korean churches jumped from 21 percent prior to emigration to almost 77 percent following immigration (ibid.: 20). It cannot be denied that part of the attractiveness of Korean ethnic churches is that they meet specific social and psychological needs, namely, acting as a social center and an ethnic educational resource for the instruction of Korean language and history, and also serving as brokers between the congregation and the bureaucracy of American society (ibid.: 21). However, the primary reason for Korean ethnic church participation as cited by members was that the church met their religious needs; the social and psychological needs of the church were cited as secondary and tertiary reasons for attending. As with African-Caribbeans in Britain, the length of residence in the US could not be correlated with church attendance or frequency of attendance (ibid.: 25). Thus, the ethnic church cannot be understood as a temporary cultural institution which buffers the culture shock of immigration.

Although the reasons for the popularity of Korean ethnic churches offered by the authors differ from that proposed here, there are similarities between the experiences of Koreans in the United States and African-Caribbeans in Britain. The authors note that in the United States, Korean immigrants experience involuntary ethnic containment – they constitute an ethnic minority which experiences segmentation and disadvantage in the labor market (ibid.: 31). Where Korean and African-Caribbean experience diverges is in how each wider society deals with the question of ethnic diversity. In the US racial and ethnic segregation is not officially encouraged while religious pluralism is; therefore the Korean church becomes an effective mechanism for preserving ethnic status (ibid.: 32). Religious pluralism also exists in Britain, but racial and ethnic segregation is given greater implicit acceptance. The problem which West Indian migrants and people of African-Caribbean origin confront in Britain is not the maintenance of a discrete ethnic identity through religious participation but one of attenuating racial and ethnic distinctiveness.

Hill does not share the 'stumbling-block' view proposed by others. Compared to Won Moo Hurh and Kwang Chung Kim he suggests that the growth of sects can be attributed to the social deprivation of West Indians as a recognizable ethnic and status group in Britain (1971a: 16). Hill tests the validity of this correlation by examining the growth rate of the NTCG. Prior to 1964, the growth rate was small but steady, but when race became a political issue in the 1964 British general election, the growth rate accelerated (ibid.: 17). Before concluding that a worsening racial climate by itself led to the growth of the sect, he examines several other variables. One alternative variable is sex. In Jamaica, 70 percent of the NTCG membership was female, in England 40 to 60 percent of the pre-1964 membership was male (ibid.: 18). Hill points out that by 1962 more than half the annual inflow of migrants from the West Indies were women and children. He thus dismisses sex as an important variable, because the accelerated growth rate should have started in 1962, if not before (ibid.: 18). He then turns to a compensatory approach and suggests that there is a direct correlation between felt social deprivation and growth in sect membership. The compensatory view of Black churches suggests that they provide an alternate, or compensatory, means of attaining the goals of power, authority and status which are denied to members in the wider society. In an article later the same year (1971c), Hill refined what he meant by status deprivation. He agreed with earlier writers like Calley that West Indian immigrants were not suffering from economic deprivation, but argued that they were experiencing ethnic and status deprivation:

> This is particularly true of the light brown and fair-skinned West Indian who had high status in the Caribbean colour-graded system of social differentiation but who is simply classed as 'coloured' in Britain. No distinction is made by the British between Blacks and fair coloured; all are low status. (1971c: 188–9)

This represents one of the most insightful comments concerning Caribbean immigration and the resulting position of the migrant in the British status hierarchy.

The 'rejectionist view' is also central to the story of the foundation and development of the NTCG as recorded by two of its ministers, Reverend I. V. Brooks (1982) and Reverend S. E. Arnold (1992). In 1951 O. A. Lyseight, a former Methodist who had been converted to Pentecostalism in Jamaica and who had served as a Pentecostal pastor in St. Ann's Parish, arrived in Wolverhampton (Brooks 1982: 11). Because he could not locate his Pentecostal brethren from home, he shared in fellowship with a

Methodist congregation and later joined an English Pentecostal congregation. Lyseight and other migrant ministers were seldom asked to preach in Pentecostal congregations because indigenous Pentecostalists found their style of service too emotional and noisy (ibid.: 12; Arnold 1992: 17–18). Other migrants sought worship in the established churches they had known at home, but were 'shocked' by English attitudes towards religion as a whole and Sunday worship and attendance in particular (Arnold ibid.: 17; also Eggington 1957: 115*f*).

There were two conditions which made the British religious landscape inhospitable to West Indian migrants. The first concerns the tenor and place of religion in British society, the second the different articulation of British social class, form of religious expression and religious participation. In *Religion in Britain Since 1945: Believing without Belonging*, Grace Davie aptly describes Britain's religiosity as 'understated' (1994: 37). In comparison with Jamaica, Britain was and remains a more secular society (Argyle and Beit-Hallahmi 1975; Davie 1994). Religion does not assume a central role in the structure of society or in public or political debates,[30] but it does continue to conduct sacraments. Amid the increasing secularization of the twentieth century, there has been a decrease in church membership, particularly since World War II, but more so among non-conformists than the Church of England (Argyle and Beit-Hallahmi 1975; Davie 1994: 18–24). Davie describes the period from 1945 to 1960 as one of post-war reconstruction, during which the church tried to rebuild itself physically, revive flagging attendance and participation and reconstruct the pre-war social order (ibid.: 30–2). Despite moderate success throughout the 1950s, when it bestowed sacramental grace on Queen Elizabeth II, the church was ultimately unsuccessful. In an effort to combat indifference in the 1960s, the church became increasingly secular, a move which shifted the nature of British religion further away from West Indian migrants, despite an ecumenical campaign (ibid.: 33–5).

In addition to possessing a different tenor, the socio-religious order also differed in the qualitative nature of religious practice. Argyle and Beit-Hallahmi refer to an earlier study, which demon-

30. Although, during the premiership of Margaret Thatcher and the increase in privatization, the church became a vocal contributor to public debates (Davie 1994: 39).

strates that previously a distinction could be made between social class and denominational affiliation, such that the upper and middle classes attended the Church of England while the lower classes participated in the non-conformist churches. The nature of religious expression and rates of attendance also varied with social class: formal religious expression was associated with a higher social status, and an emotive and spontaneous form of religious expression was associated with a lower social status. Although church attendance was on the decline, a higher percentage of persons from the upper and upper-middle classes attended church (82 percent to 62 percent) than the lower-middle and working classes (47 percent to 33 percent) (Argyle and Beit-Hallahmi 1975: 28). However, the authors note that by 1964 social class differences in forms of religious participation had been blurred; there was no longer a clear difference in the form of religious expression and attendance of the upper, middle and lower classes (ibid.: 169). The religious environment of Britain was at odds with Caribbean experience, religion was not pervasive, did not reflect the social order and could not be used to assert a higher social status. There were lower rates of attendance, and compared with the African-Caribbean working class, the indigenous working class found more meaning in social and political movements than in religion (ibid.: 25–8).

The experience of encountering a religious environment which on the surface of naive realism appears the same but in the depth of cultural meaning is qualitatively different is not unique to West Indian migrants. Fitzpatrick (1987) and Poblete and O'Dea (1960) have examined a similar experience among Puerto Rican immigrants in the United States who converted from Catholicism to Puerto Rican Pentecostal sects. Fitzpatrick argues that Catholicism in Latin America differs significantly from the Anglo-Saxon Catholicism prevalent in the US (ibid.). In Latin America, Catholicism was integral to the definition of the community (*pueblo*) – which was structured by a pattern of personal relationships (*padrino*) with saints and people – from which the individual derived meaning and identity (ibid.: 119–22). In the US the Catholic church lacked the qualities of *pueblo* and *padrino*. This fact, coupled with a dispersed Puerto Rican migrant population and the decision of the Catholic diocese to favor the integration of religious participation over a former policy of 'national' (ethnic) churches, imparted an unfamiliar quality to Catholicism (ibid.: 128).

Although there was an attempt to provide religious services in Spanish and to incorporate Puerto Rican culture and folk beliefs into the Catholic church, integrated congregations did not represent a community which equipped the individual with identity (ibid.: 129).

Why did Korean, Puerto Rican and West Indian migrants not join indigenous Protestant and Pentecostal denominations? For Won Moo Hurh and Kwang Chung Kim (1990) and Poblete and O'Dea (1960), indigenous congregations could not fulfil migrants' religious needs nor address issues of identity or community. Bryan Wilson's (1961) work on the British Elim Foursquare Gospel Church suggests that there were few if any doctrinal differences between Jamaican Pentecostalism and English Pentecostalism. While by no means a large denomination, the Elim Church was fairly widespread by the time of Commonwealth immigration. Wilson records that in contrast to other churches, the Elim Church experienced moderate growth after the war: by 1954 there were 250 congregations, 14 in Birmingham (ibid.: 99). Members were drawn primarily from the poor working class, factory workers and laborers, who had previously been non-conformists. Thus the Elim would appear to be a perfect form of religious expression for West Indian migrants, yet their absence seems to give credibility to the idea of a racially divided working class and to the rejectionist view. However, the absence of West Indians may also originate in the relationship of English Pentecostalism to the social order. In the post-war period, the increasingly secular nature of British society and the attenuation of a religious hierarchy articulated with the social hierarchy, it is doubtful whether Pentecostalism or any form of British religious experience could be symbolic of the social order. Religion could not integrate the socio-religious order or fasten the individual to society, nor could it be used as an instrument of social identification and status assertion.

It was left to the Black community to develop its own religious forms. Migrants discarded their old religious differences and in the 'need for consolidation' accepted the Pentecostal message (Arnold 1992: 17; Brooks 1982: 13). It is only in this sense that it can be argued that the new churches were a form of refuge where migrants sought to preserve their spiritual life until they returned to the Caribbean (Arnold ibid.: 18).

In 1953, Lyseight rented a local YMCA hall in Wolverhampton, where he formed a prayer group with seven members (Brooks ibid.: 13; also Hill 1971a: 4; 1971b: 115; 1971c: 187). Meanwhile in London, brethren were also organizing meetings in rented halls and people's homes (Brooks ibid.: 14). The church developed centrifugally, one local group giving rise to other smaller groups in the region. In 1955 a missionary official from the COG in the US arrived in the West Midlands, where he was received by 65 members (ibid.: 16). The representative established two churches in the West Midlands, one of which was King Street congregation. In 1956 Lyseight was appointed national overseer unifying the dispersed members in the south and the West Midlands (ibid.). By 1958 there were twelve congregations with a membership of 373 (ibid.: 21) and the first building was purchased in Hammersmith in 1959 (Hill 1971a: 4). By 1963 there were twenty three congregations, and the national administrative network was based in Birmingham (ibid.: 4; 1971b: 115; 1971c: 187, see Table 2.3).

When Jamaicans arrived in England, it is clear that they were shocked by the secular nature of society and the racism and discrimination they encountered (see Banton 1955: 189–206; Little 1947: chapter 10; also Eggington 1957; Glass 1960; Patterson 1965). We have to question, however, whether they were shocked by the fact that racism and discrimination existed or by the fact that it was grounded in a different logic and possessed a different nature, which could not be resolved with an appeal to exactly the same logic and strategies which had been effective in Jamaica.

Table 2.3 Growth of The New Testament Church of God in England

	Number of Churches	Total Membership
1967	65	3,000
1971	78	3,963
1988	102	6,504

(Sources: Brooks 1982: 45, 47; COG Minutes of the General Assembly, 1988: 15)

Conclusion

For a sizable proportion of Britain's African-Caribbean population there has been a growth in intra-group religious activity, which concerns not only the first generation but also the second and third generations. However, for these new generations the form of religious participation and expression is not simply a matter of cultural continuity. How can we continue to speak of modernization, culture shock, assimilation and the church as a barrier when the first generation of members has lived in England for over thirty years and many have only recently joined the church, or when many second generation members were born or raised in England? Equally the church has not taken the route of active political protest after the model of the African-American church.

In the light of history and the continued growth and popularity of Pentecostalism as a dominant form of religious expression among Blacks in Britain, it is necessary to offer an alternative explanation for the significance of African-Caribbean Pentecostalism in Britain. To a limited degree African-Caribbean Pentecostal churches are a form of continuity from the Caribbean. Their significance is partly derived from the meaning they acquired in Jamaican society. Although Pentecostalism had only existed in Jamaica for a short while prior to immigration and its subsequent exportation, it had acquired enough meaning to make it a candidate for resolving the problem of social identity for Caribbean migrants in British society. In Jamaica, where there were few firm boundaries around the categories of social life, the possibility existed for the individual to negotiate his or her status and identity. Pentecostalism flourished in this specific context because it combined issues of suffering and status and therefore integrated diverse trends in the religious order. Pentecostalism synthesized dual religious participation; it offered the prestige benefits associated with attendance in a main denomination while at the same time offering emotional satisfaction without relying on African-Christian syncretism. Thus Pentecostalism could mediate a problem of identity where an individual's articulation with the social order and status could not be accurately expressed by participation in either denominational Christianity or African-Christian sects.

In Britain, African-Caribbean Pentecostalism is also capable of mediating a problem of identity, but in a very different context and with a very different meaning. It continues to address both questions of status and suffering, but it is significant that it does so in a racially divided society where segregation, not integration, stands at the center of African-Caribbean experience. The social context of Britain in the 1950s and 1960s was characterized by firm categories of race, class and status which confounded individual negotiation. Due to the different nature of English religious life, participation in English churches, unlike Jamaican churches, could not be used to make claims about status or to resolve a problem of identity for migrants. As in Jamaica, African-Caribbean Pentecostalism presented itself as an alternative to existing forms of religious participation: however, in Britain it has developed in a context of segregation, where it continues to resolve questions of suffering but cannot successfully unify diverse trends in the religious order or make the same links between religious participation and status. Despite attempts at ecumenism and Black and White Christian partnership by religious leaders and organizations, African-Caribbean Pentecostalism has had to sidestep issues of racial and religious integration; the issue of race in defining the NTCG and other African-Caribbean churches is problematic. Given these circumstances, African-Caribbean Pentecostalism continues to mediate the problem of identity, but in Britain the mediation of identity is believed rather than actual.

It is clear from King Street Congregation that the NTCG attracts not only those concerned with questions of suffering and disadvantage but also younger, successful African-Caribbeans. It seems plausible to suggest that the continuing appeal of African-Caribbean Pentecostalism for both old and young, economically advantaged and disadvantaged African-Caribbean people in Britain is not only that it offers a framework for the explanation and transcendence of questions of suffering, status and identity, but that it also privileges values like thrift, discipline and individual conscience which are compatible with the wider value system and with life in Britain.

Chapter 3

'Born Of The Water, The Spirit And The Blood': The Individual and the Collective

Religion is a system of meaning whose belief and practices represent and explain the nature of the universe and provide its followers with the means to construct a satisfying identity based upon that representation. Describing the varied social and economic circumstances of King Street members and locating the social space in which the NTCG developed provides a necessarily partial insight into the significance of British African-Caribbean Pentecostalism. By understanding the process whereby an individual becomes a member of the church, how social reality is expressed through belief and how belief is sustained through religious ritual, we can understand how Pentecostalism expresses the social reality of Britain to its followers and constructs a satisfying identity. Conversion and the rituals which sustain belief and a converted state are central to this process.

People and religious forms in the African Diaspora have been put together by emphasizing the functional purposes of religious rituals: religious expression attaches the individual to a moral community, raises the collective consciousness, and periodically affirms and expresses the unity of the collective. This approach is clearly based upon Emile Durkheim's proposition that 'religion is a unified system of beliefs and practices ... which unite into a single moral community, called a "church", all those who adhere to them' (Durkheim, in Giddens 1972: 224). In this vein Calley argued that members of West Indian Pentecostal sects in Britain did not distinguish between belief and ritual and asserted that religious rituals were 'performed for their own sake' as 'expressions of the solidarity of the church, a celebration of togetherness' (1965: 72, ix–x). If African-Caribbean Pentecostal churches are

Plate 3 'The Baptism of a Female Saint'. Source: Author

perceived primarily as 'ethnic churches' which function to maintain ethnic identity in the face of assimilationist encroachment, then this interpretation of religious practice is sufficient.

If by 'ritual', however, we mean actions and beliefs in the symbolic order without reference to the religious commitment of the actors (Douglas 1982: 2), then the religious practices in the NTCG originate in 'anti-ritualist' thought:

> Salvation is not church membership. Salvation is not dressing up and coming to church Sunday morning and don't come no other time. Salvation is not a family thing passed down from generation to generation. Salvation is not religious duties, cooking dinners and serving them to the bishop[1] and thinking you're gonna make it that way. You must be born again, you cannot enter again your mother's womb, but you must be born by the spirit and the blood. (Sermon, 6/10/90)

As the above makes clear, religious worship extends beyond ritual and demands belief, a belief which begins with spiritual rebirth. The Holiness Pentecostal tradition emphasizes individual conversion, and belief is the internalization of the symbol of Christ and the 'moods and motivations' characteristic of Christ (cf. Geertz 1973a). Since recruitment into the church is on an individual basis, upon conversion the individual becomes a member of a diffuse moral community whose unity is realized through sacred fictive kinship. A narrow reading of Durkheim's thesis can overlook the nature of the collective whose solidarity and primacy rituals assert, fail to address the nature of belief and, by placing the collective before the individual, ignore questions of personhood.

To assess the relationship between ritual and belief held by individuals and its implications for the collective and a person's identity, a wider reading of Durkheim is required. A more productive approach would stress two themes: first, a god is a symbolic expression of the collective (society) to which the individual belongs (Durkheim 1915; 1995: 351), and secondly, there is a duality inherent in the relationship between the individual and the collective (society) (Goody 1961: 146).

---

1. A term for the church's overseers.

> ... there are two sorts of social sentiments. The first bind each individual to the person of his fellow-citizens . . . .. The second are those which bind me to the social entity as a whole . . . .. The first leave my anatomy and personality almost intact. No doubt they tie me to others, but without taking much of my independence from me. When I act under the influence of the second, by contrast, I am simply a part of the whole, whose actions I follow, and whose influence I am subject to. (Durkheim, in Giddens 1972: 219–20)

For Durkheim, it is this latter interpretation of the relationship between the individual and the collective (society) that gives rise to and is reinforced by religious sentiment (Durkheim, in Giddens 1972: 220 and Goody 1961: 146). Here the collective symbolized by a god is internalized within the individual:

> ... the collective is not entirely outside us, and does not act upon us wholly from without; but rather, since society cannot exist except in and through individual consciousness, this force must also penetrate us and organize itself within us. It thus becomes an integral part of our being. . . .. (Durkheim, in Giddens 1972: 230)

In Durkheim's work the bonding between the individual and his god, and therefore with the collective to which he belongs, occurs within the soul which is acted upon by the emotional, sentimental and moral influences of religious ritual. Ritual has a 'profound influence over the souls of worshippers'; by virtue of moral efficacy, rituals possess the capacity to remake the moral nature of the individual such that egocentric impulses are yielded to the authority of the collective whose continued existence is thus assured (1915, 1971: 359, 209). The justification for religious practices does not rest on claims for their physical efficacy or purported ends, but on the invisible actions they have in our minds and the effects they have on our mental state (1915, 1971: 360).

We might emphasize the idea that rituals bind the individual to a collective or, alternatively, focus on the process by which religious rituals transform the individual and place the collective sentiment within him. Because of the diverse manifestations of the collective figured in NTCG belief (the local congregations of Mother and Sister churches, regions, the national denomination, the international COG, other Pentecostal Christians, other Christians, terrestrial and celestial saints) a singular focus on either the individual or the collective is inadequate. Hence, conversion and maintaining a converted state mediates between the individual and the collective.

Born of the Blood: Conversion and Belief

Members distinguish themselves and their faith from other Christians and Christian faiths by calling themselves 'Pentecostal.' The church, however, is described as a 'Holiness church,' and members adhere to a 'Holy life.' The beliefs and principles to which members adhere is encoded in the New Testament and a 'Declaration of Faith' (see Appendix II). The crucial diacritics of members' faith are: adult full water baptism in the name of the Father, the Son and the Holy Ghost; a life of Holiness and ongoing growth in sanctification; the conviction that baptism by the Holy Spirit, as described in Acts 2, is as applicable to contemporary Christians as it was to Christians at the day of the Pentecost; that baptism by the Holy Spirit is subsequent to a clean heart; divine healing; and the practice of the 'Lord's Supper' (communion) and the 'washing of the saints' feet.'[2]

The internalization of the collective and the symbol of God which results in the religious sentiment of 'Holiness' necessitates a radical transformation in the consciousness of the individual (Durkheim, in Giddens 1972: 233). This transformation is achieved by the process of conversion. Although there are clear universals in the process of religious conversion, there also exist specific circumstances within each instance of conversion which render the decision to convert personal and meaningful. Further, while conversion is gradual and chronic, it is also characterized by intense periodic spiritual moments which are necessary for perpetuating and maintaining conversion.

The church teaches that all people have sinned and have fallen short of the glory of God. Sin is a pervasive internal state which

2. The COG and the NTCG are distinguished from other Pentecostal denominations by the practice of baptizing converts in the name of the Trinity instead of the name of Jesus alone, and by making a distinction between sanctification and baptism by the Holy Ghost. For a discussion of doctrinal developments and strains in Pentecostalism, see chapter 2 note 26; also Bloch-Hoell 1964; Hollenweger 1972.

cannot easily be read off the external appearances and actions of others:

> Sin is an act of disobedience towards God and because the first created human beings disobeyed God, humanity has suffered . . . .. It is an inherited condition because according to the scriptures we are all 'Born in sin and shapen in iniquity.' . . . There are those who believe they are not sinners because of their good deeds but good deeds is not proof that sin is non-existent in an individual's life because sin is a fact and everyone needs to repent of sin. (Sister Dwire)

Since mankind is understood to be made in God's image, a transgression against fellow humans is a transgression against God. According to Sister Elma: 'Sin is when we do bad things, wrong things, think bad things of others, it all leads to disobedience and this is not obeying the ten commandments of God.' In the NTCG the correction of a sinful nature and re-establishment of communication with God requires the individual to repent, experience new birth, be baptized and lead a holy or sanctified life. In practical terms members speak of 'getting convicted,' 'getting saved,' 'accepting God's will,' conversion, being 'born of the water, the spirit and the blood,'[3] being 'born again' and being a 'Christian.' Repentance and conversion are the turning point in a process whereby a person gains conviction, accepts Jesus as his or her personal savior, and commits his or her life to Jesus as a 'Christian.'

Given the close relationship between the representation of society in religious thought and practice on the one hand and society (as experienced by the individual or group) on the other, when the nature of society or of one's experience of it changes, one must amend one's system of representation, and conversion may become necessary (Douglas 1982: 144; Wallace 1970, 1956). What precipitates the sense that a religion no longer offers a satisfactory account of the universe and of identity? Is there a single transformative experience or a gradual realization?

Following Ernesto DeMartino, George Saunders (1995) proposes that a 'crisis of presence' precedes conversion. To understand the meaning of 'presence,' it is important to distinguish between the 'individual' as 'the indivisible subject of mankind' (a particular

---

3. A popular chorus.

person) who possesses 'speech, thought and will' and an 'interior-ized conscience [with] feelings, goals, motivations and aspirations' (Louis Dumont, in Strathern 1981: 168; also Fajans 1985: 370); the 'self' as a personal identity (Howard 1985: 413; Lutz 1985: 71n.6) and the 'person' as a 'culturally constituted moral entity, one defined by its potential autonomy and independence from others like it' (Dumont ibid.; Strathern 1981: 12–15). The concept of the person with the capacity for independence, like the concept of the individual, implies the possession of interests, motivations, choices and actions. However, because the person, unlike the individual, is a culturally constructed moral entity, there also exists a cultural idea of morality or ethics which decrees what are the correct interests, motivations, choices and actions that the person must possess.

Presence is a sense of self where persons are conscious of their own autonomy and instrumentality, where they can perceive themselves to be the authors of their intentions, actions and definitions of self. A crisis of presence arises when the person is 'absorbed by the world' and becomes subject to the will of others, such that they lose self-consciousness, cease to be the author of their own thoughts and actions, and are hence rendered passive and ineffectual (Saunders 1995: 332). A crisis of presence can be overcome through rituals whereby the person is integrated into the world and regains a consciousness of self and ability to act in the world (ibid.: 333). By transforming the consciousness of the individual, realigning his or her relationship to society and creating new social relationships with others in society, the ritual process of conversion provides the individual with the resources to construct a new sense of personhood and identity (Cucchiari 1988: 418; Gill 1990: 709–11; Saunders 1995: 324). As Cucchiari notes, however, it is a paradox that the greater personal autonomy and moral responsibility achieved by the person through conversion is accomplished by substituting subjection to the will of others with subjection to the will of God (ibid.).

The view that a 'crisis of presence' precipitates conversion applies to members of the NTCG. A re-reading of the circumstances which led Lorraine, Elma and Martha to become members of the church after many years in England clearly illustrates that they found themselves in a continuous process in which the meaning of their social identity was continuously being redefined and debated. In the politics of representation, these women and other

African-Caribbeans in Britain were not the authors of their social identities: they experienced ineffectual engagement with society and other religious institutions which might have provided a resolution of their crises. Curiously, however, with the possible exception of Lorraine, the emphasis on this pre-existing state of suffering means that in the construction of their narratives, less emphasis is placed on single transformative crises, such as illness, death, bereavement, rancor, or racial victimization, which are characteristic of other Pentecostal conversion narratives (see Cucchiari ibid.; Saunders ibid.).

Although a 'crisis of presence' may be universal and members' conversion testimonies are highly stylized (Cucchiari ibid.; Lawless 1991; Saunders ibid.), there is ample room for personalization in the construction of testimonies (Saunders ibid.: 326). It is the unique in a conversion experience which renders it a compelling and logical option for the individual. Because conversion and salvation are perceived as highly personal experiences, members of the NTCG have difficulty in generalizing what it feels like to be saved.

> I cannot describe it . . . well I experience that, but is for you to really experience it for yourself, you can't tell nobody what it is all about and you feel . . . if you could just take out your heart and put it into someone else you would. To experience the joy and happiness that you have, if it was a thing you could split your stomach and take out your heart and put it into you that you could have the same feeling, you would. (Martha)

However, members can vividly describe their own experience of salvation, recalling the date, the circumstances, how they felt and reacted.

Before conversion, not all members' lives were devoid of religion. From a post-conversion perspective, members describe themselves as having been 'Christian in a loose sense of the word'; they believed in God, in going to church and in prayer. As one woman put it, 'You have the religious mind, but you're not committed, you're still doing wrong.' Gaining conviction usually begins with an intensely spiritual, physical and emotional episode, a 'vision,' in which it is understood that the Lord is speaking to the person. 'The Prayers of the Saints' in James Baldwin's *Go Tell It on the Mountain* (1953), illustrate the alternating dynamics between a general religious disposition and the moment of being saved which results in a strengthening of conviction. Although the character of Gabriel Grimes was raised in a Christian household and was exposed to the exhortations of his mother and the saints, his salvation required 'a vision':

> Then, in a moment, there was silence, only silence, everywhere – the very birds had ceased to sing, and no dogs barked, and no rooster crowed for day. And he felt that this silence was God's judgment; that all creation had been stilled before the just and awful wrath of God, and waited now to see the sinner – he was the sinner – cut down and banished from the presence of the Lord [. . .] and he cried: [. . .] "Oh, Lord, have mercy on me!" (Baldwin 1953: 96)

It is just such an episode which members usually refer to as the time when they 'got saved.'

> From I accept the Lord . . . the 5th of March, half past eleven, 1975 – I got saved in my bed . . . I remember this night . . . Thomas [her son] was going out with the White girl . . . but I always worried about him because sometimes he don't come in until twelve o'clock in the night . . . and there were skinheads on street those days raging like lion . . . This Thursday night I couldn't sleep...so I just says, "Oh let me just lie on my back and rest my back a little" and I heard when he came in . . . He went in the kitchen make his coffee and toast his bread, I just – I lie down on me back and quick flash . . . I saw this demon from hell, he was a man – a White man, underneath the window in me bedroom . . . and he was so daring and he was so fierce, and he had on a suit the like the color of this material [orange], and he had his mustache from here to here (neatly cut), and he had on a felt hat and his suit matched the color of his mustache, and he was just chewing up his mouth. Oh my God, and he had some teeth in his mouth (long) longer than the lens of me glasses, and Oh my God I tell you the Holy Spirit anoint me and I remember I just throw off the covering and I said, "In the name of Jesus" and I run him [the demon] out of the room and he went in the front room . . . 'cos the front room door was shut and I took my hands and give the door one hit and the door flew open and he went in Thomas' room . . . and I went in there after him . . . and I chase him down the fire escape and he went away . . . and when I went back upstairs, I go in the kitchen and I says to him [Thomas], I said, "I've been telling you about your late coming in and you won't listen to me, you see what could have happened to you tonight?" and he didn't say anything. And that night I went to my bed and I sleep as a baby, but there was one thing about it, when

I was waking out of my sleep in the morning I feel as if I was coming from heaven; there was a big, big place with just green pastures (it was ever so big, it was the biggest place I have ever seen) and just sweet melodious music. I can't remember the sound of the music, but it was beautiful, and the green pastures and the glorious light and that is what changed my life until this very day. (Lorraine)

They have this evangelist he always come and keep his meeting in [the] park and I usually go, until he had built a church now in Aylesbury Road, I usually go. At that time I wasn't settled down as a member of the church. I went there one evening, I was either praying or singing or something, I can't now remember what. I just find myself, I just see – I didn't know I wasn't really among the people – I just see this light and I was – feel light as a feather. I don't know if I was doing the action or anything you know, but I just say, "Oh Lord this is me, forgive your all" and I feel so glad and so good and light, and then all and [sic] a sudden I just feel like I snap and kick back down to myself you know . . .. They were having communion and he [the Pastor] say who feel like having communion to have it, but I said, "No, I'm not a Christian I can't have it." But all those time [sic] I never realized, now I realize you know, that is the devil telling you these things. That when you making up your mind, they always tell you [you hear], "Oh no, you're not this and you're not that." And is that [sic] the time they [people] say, "Talk and let the devil feel ashamed," because he always there saying, "Put it off, put it off," and that is the time you should react to the call. (Elma)

I was here watching the telly . . . before that I was working nights, is late and I woke up and the whole room was lit as if I had the light burning and I pull the switch over the bed and the light came on, because I thought I had left the light on and go to sleep. I pull the switch and the light come on and I thought that was strange. So anyway I was there wondering, but then I didn't feel right you know and I got out of bed and I knelt down and I pray, because I feel like I want to pray. After that I thought, "I wonder if Brother Grundy at home?" and I ring him, because to me I feel as if I wanted to talk to somebody. So anyway I went to work and the next morning I went down to him and said, "Is there meeting up church?" and he said, "Yes" and I went up this Monday night. I was in there watching the telly, and I can't tell you if the telly had a short or what, and I was watching this program and the telly went off and I just get up and turn it and it go off all together. So I thought what's going on, and I just switch off it [sic] and quickly get dressed and was going up to the church . . ..

The following Sunday I went to church and I went up to the altar
and I come home, and the Monday again I went to the prayer meeting
. . . before that I went one Monday evening and I couldn't go in the
church, I stood out by the gate, it was like I was frightened to go in, I
was so afraid, I don't know what it was, and this little girl came up
to me and she said, "Do you want to go in Miss?" and I said, "Yes,"
and she push the door and I follow her. And that night I stood there
and they were singing this song about "sing the wondrous story of
Jesus . . . " and I stood there with the book and I was really enjoying
the song and all of a sudden I just felt as if somebody push a spoon
down in me stomach and make a big turn. And I feel like I want to be
sick and I hold the book to catch the sick, and the book drop, and I
don't know – I didn't hear any sound come out of my mouth, the
person beside me . . . said, "Do you want to go up to the altar?" I
said, "No, I'm all right." She picked up the book and put it back in
my hand, then we finish singing the song. By the time it was near to
the end of service, I was up at the altar and I knelt down there and
they prayed for me . . . and then from I come home I don't feel the
same and I just start going to church every Sunday. I just feel different,
I felt as if I came out of that place that night, I was stepping that high
[she raised her hand two feet above the floor], I was so light and all
[sic] my feet when I step down I miss me step, because I lift me foot
up that high. I went back to Pastor [he] ask me if I want to baptize
and I said, "No" . . . before I went to the prayer meeting, after I woke
up and saw that light and rang Brother Grundy, I said I was going to
ring Pastor. I ring him and said I would like to talk to him. He said,
"Do you want me to come to your house?" so I said, "No". I was
frightened for him to come, I don't know why, on top of that I was
ashamed to see a pastor coming into my house. Now I understand
that it was the devil trying to fight against the spirit so that I give up,
that I don't accept Christ. So that is why, I was fighting the devil. I
want to accept Jesus and the devil didn't want me to. All the fear and
thing what I was experiencing he was causing it. So when Pastor said,
"I come down to your house", I said, "No, no, no I don't want you
come down." He said, "Well, I make an appointment and you come
up the church." I went up the church to see him. I remember going in
the office and he said to me, "What can I do for you?" I said, "Pastor,
I don't know, and moreover I don't know why I come here." I start
telling him I used to go to a Methodist church and all that and then I
said to him, "I don't know what to tell you, for I don't know for what
reason I come, but I just felt as though I wanted somebody to talk
to." Then I start telling him all the bits and pieces. And he said well
he used to go to a nominal church as well and how he got saved and
after that he prayed for me and I came out. And is like somebody

was speaking to me and saying, "What you go in there and tell that man all that for ?" And then the other voice come back to me and said, "Well he will be your pastor." And I start going to church a few Sundays after that and they ask me if I want to get baptized . . . so that's how I start going to the church. (Martha)

While the different circumstances of conversion are meaningful for the person, all circumstances are equally valid provided they result in conversion. As the foregoing indicates, the spiritual episode can occur at home, at work or during a church service. When people 'meet the Lord' at home or at work, they tend to seek out people whom they know are members of the church, in order to confess and have that person pray for them. If the episode occurs during a church service, the person may respond to an 'altar call.'[4] Not all people have 'a vision': some people simply make a self-conscious decision to accept the Lord and the life of a 'Christian.' A self-conscious decision is not considered less of a commitment to God; some people, however, speculated that it might be harder for such a person to remain with God. Once an individual has had a vision, conversion may not be instantaneous: instead, the individual may undergo a period of gaining in conviction and testing God's will:

The Lord speak to me at work and I didn't know what it is, I just was so like something was pressing me and I just start to cry and losing me energy and something was pulling me, pulling me . . . and I go to Sister Ramsey . . . and I went to her and I was confessing what I feel to her and she said it was "the conviction you getting, getting the conviction of the Lord." (Sister Ashe)

People do not choose God: He chooses them, but they must come to accept God's calling. The process of repentance, gaining conviction and confession culminate in conversion. Conversion is 'a birth of the blood' and 'a birth of the spirit.' It is a birth of the blood because it is in the act of repentance and confession that a

4. During an altar call the preacher entreats the unsaved or weak to come forward and kneel in prayer at the altar. Not everyone who approaches the altar is seeking salvation – some are members who may be having difficulty and want to renew their strength – nor is an altar call a prerequisite for salvation and conversion. The officers of the church, sometimes the Mothers of the Church, and the preacher will come and kneel beside them, speak with them, help them to pray and may lay on hands.

person is 'cleansed by the blood of Jesus.' The verbal symbol of blood is pervasive. Blood has the power to cleanse, protect, and identify the person as a 'Christian.' Sins are as red as crimson, but only the 'blood of Jesus' can wash a person 'clean as snow.' 'The blood is our ticket to heaven' (Sermon, 16/12/90), and people with 'blood on their hearts' are 'Christians.' Blood is the source of physical and spiritual well-being or discord; a person who sins, is of ill nature or backbites is someone whose 'blood is not in order' or is 'contaminated.' At conversion a person is given new blood, but the individual must safeguard this gift by obeying God's instructions:

> How important it is for the blood to be in order . . . when blood goes wrong, you need a transfusion . . . bad blood taken, good blood pumped in . . . but it must be the right blood, what kind of blood? Blood is pure. The Holy Ghost transfer pure blood, but some of our blood is impure. When your blood is wrong you act funny, you are miserable, bad tempered . . . when blood is right, storm and wind can blow . . . where spiritual blood is wrong, backslide, go back to the world. (Sermon, 16/12/90)

Jesus' blood not only has cleansing properties in conversion, but also restorative properties for persons who are weakening. A person who is spiritually weak can 'go back to Calvary' or 'back to Bethel' to renew their commitment and resolve and to receive a new injection of blood. Blood is protective; it defends 'Christians' against Satan, demons and evil spirits. When people are in danger or trouble, they are told to 'cover themselves in the blood.' 'Problems at home with . . . husband, when you go home go to your husband's favorite chair, sit in it and rub the Holy Ghost's blood all over the chair' (Sermon: 16/12/90). The parable of the first Passover in Exodus 12 tells of the identifying and protective properties of the 'blood of the Lamb.' It is not enough, however, simply to daub blood over the doorway or on your heart; it is imperative that one 'eats' or internalizes God's message fully.

Conversion is a spiritual rebirth; it is said that the spirit appears to the person and speaks to him. 'When the spirit speaks to me with my whole heart I'll agree and my answer will be "Yes Lord, yes."'[5] It is believed that the individual emerges from conversion as a new person with a new nature. However, the gains made by

5. A chorus lyric.

conversion are not necessarily permanent and can easily be lost. The maintenance of a converted state requires believers to assess their internal intentions, motivations and actions continuously in light of the expectations of the moral community. To avoid relapsing into their old ways and maintain the new nature they received in conversion, it is said that the 'Christian' must 'die every day' and 'pray without ceasing.'

The change in the person's internal state, effected by the cleansing properties of the blood and the presence of the spirit, may be manifested by external appearance:

> Some people going about wearing button on their clothes and identifying things on their clothes for people to see that they are a Christian. I don't wear those things on my clothes, because you see, by the fruit you shall know them. (Lorraine)

Some members recalled the changes that occurred in their countenance and the countenance of others who were saved. Others spoke of feeling nauseated or sick; they felt cold, they lacked control over their bodies, they could not walk or talk properly, or they simply collapsed.

> ... head thrown back, eyes closed, sweat standing on his brow, he sat at the piano, singing and playing; and then, like a great, black cat in trouble in the jungle, he stiffened and trembled, and cried out. *Jesus, Jesus, oh Lord Jesus!* He struck the piano one last, wild note, and threw up his hands, palms upward, stretched wide apart . . .. Then he was on his feet, turning, blind, his face congested, contorted with this rage, and the muscles leaping and swelling in his long, dark neck. It seemed that he could not breathe, that his body could not contain this passion . . .. (Baldwin 1953: 15–16, original emphasis)

While on the one hand salvation and conversion may be experienced as bodily dissociation and/or lack of control, the change which occurs at conversion must also be reaffirmed and sustained by the strict control of the body in appearance and behavior. The body is described as a 'vessel' which should be kept clean and pure through steadfast commitment and the observance of prayer and fasting, so that it may become an instrument of the Lord.

Conversion marks a radical shift in the ethos, moral standard and behavior of members. After conversion, members call themselves 'Christians' and distinguish between a time when they simply went to church and their present religious state. The referent for behavior and judgment ceases to be the wider world; instead, Christ and the laws encoded in the New Testament become the basis of belief and the referent for behavior and judgment.

To be 'Christian' means to accept and internalize the qualities members believe are characteristic of Christ, being obedient and humble; pure and without sin; kind, loving, nurturing and just. To be 'Christian' means to 'lead a Godly and sober life' and to 'walk in the spirit.' For the anthropologist Clifford Geertz, religion is a cultural pattern composed of a set of symbols 'whose relations to one another "model" relations among entities, processes [etc.] in physical, organic, social, or psychological systems by "paralleling", "imitating", or "simulating" them' (1973a: 93). These religious symbols induce 'in the worshipper a certain distinctive set of dispositions which lend a chronic character to the flow of his activity and the quality of his experience' (ibid.: 95). The dominant Pentecostal symbol of Christ, as part of the cultural pattern of religion, can be seen in Geertz's terms as both a 'model of' and a 'model for' human existence in this world (ibid.). As a 'model of' existence, Christ is the manipulation of symbolic structures (the embodiment of God) which brings God into parallel with the pre-established non-symbolic social system-relations between people. As a 'model for' existence, Christ is the manipulation of non-symbolic systems in terms of relationships expressed in the symbolic. Members can lead a life that is 'Christ-like' precisely because Christ was corporeal and therefore enmeshed in physical and social relationships which are understood by members to have approximated the ideal relationships expressed by their religious thought. By shaping himself to the social and psychological reality and by shaping it to himself, Christ, like other symbols and cultural patterns, possesses an intrinsic 'double meaning.' For members Christ is a model under whose guidance physical and social relationships are organized. The 'models of' and 'models for,' inherent in members' belief, mediate questions of suffering and status by simultaneously addressing and remaking the nature of the individual, the group to which he or she belongs and the nature of social interaction.

According to Geertz, sacred symbols work because they synthesize ethos and world view (ibid.: 89). Ethos is 'the tone, character, and quality of [a people's] life, its moral and aesthetic style and mood; it is the underlying attitude towards themselves and their world that life reflects' (1973b: 127). The ethos of members of the NTCG is encapsulated in the idea of sanctification, other-worldly orientation and the emulation of Christ. World view is defined as 'their picture of the way things in sheer actuality are, their concept of nature, of self, of society . . . ' (ibid.). The Pentecostal view is that the world is the domain of the devil. The world is unjust, the unworthy succeed while the righteous fail. Sin and evil are not simply part of the nature of the surrounding world but part of the intrinsic nature of mankind. To succeed in the world is to be in league with the devil; materialism and a preoccupation with success in the world is a mark of impurity. God and goodness will reign in the world only when everyone has heard the call of the Lord and has been given the opportunity to convert. After the second coming of Christ, God will purify and remake the earth and restore it to His rightful sons.

For members, this view of the world is undoubtedly inflected and reinforced by their experience of racism, discrimination and social disinheritance. One does not need to be the direct victim of discrimination, it is enough to have heard the experiences of other victims – whether they are African-Caribbean, Asian or Irish. The church provides an arena for the dissemination of personal experience through sermons, the testimonies of members, informal discussions at auxiliary meetings, and prayer and fasting: religious practice provides the means to address experience. Thus, within the church, experiences can be generalized from the individual to the collective, thus reinforcing the appropriateness of members' world view as framed by religious belief.

The 'cluster of sacred symbols' which constitute the religious system 'woven into some sort of ordered whole' supports ideas of proper conduct (the ought) by picturing a world (the factual it) in which such behavior is only common sense (Geertz 1973b: 129). For Geertz, the nature of the counterpoint between the view of the world as it is and the style of life which sacred symbols formulate will vary from culture to culture (ibid.: 130) and likewise from religious system to religious system. Pentecostalism posits an inverse relationship between style of life and view of the reality of the world. It proposes that 'this world is not our home': rather, a properly ordered, rational and just heaven is home. The only way to rise above this world and get to that properly ordered place is by being 'Christian' and leading a sanctified life: 'God lives and reigns in heaven and it is a holy place; when we live a

Christian life we will go there after death' (Elma). One lives a sanctified life, a life of holiness, not because the world demands it but because it is a prerequisite for heaven.

Unlike the image of the secular world framed by religious belief, the images of heaven and hell are ordered differently. While there is no understandable logic governing individual success and failure in the world, there is an apprehensible moral logic which determines the destiny of men. It is believed that after death, a person will go to a place of rest until the day of judgment. The souls of those who have heeded God's call and have been found worthy will enter heaven; where the soul will receive a new body and enjoy eternal happiness. It is stressed that one cannot work towards heaven, nor can one buy one's way into heaven. The only sufficient payment is to offer one's life to God. Thus the impersonal and amoral forces which govern individual success and result in the differences and inequalities between people in the world are denied final validity. For those who reject God's calling, the result is eternity in hell:

> Hell is real and not imaginary and I firmly believe all those who reject Jesus will spend eternity there. Even now it is occupied by those who have rejected the love that God offers and has [sic] died without hope. According to the scriptures it is a place of torment, and I believe just that. (Sister Dwire)

Born of the Water: Ritual

For members of the NTCG, to emulate Christ and be a 'Christian' involves what the church calls 'practical commitments', i.e. ritual.[6] In his interpretation of ritual, Geertz describes religious rituals as 'enactments, materializations, realizations' of a particular religious perspective (1973a: 114). Rituals generate the conviction 'that religious conceptions are veridical and that religious directives are sound,' because it is through religious ceremonies 'that the moods and motivations which sacred symbols induce in men and the general conceptions of the order of existence which they formulate for men meet and reinforce one another' (ibid.: 112).

Members constantly strive for 'sanctification,' setting themselves apart from the things of the world in order to maintain the

---

6. Symbolic action with reference to the belief of actors.

new nature received in conversion. Where one's inner state is 'clean' and 'pure,' there is dialogue with God and the possibility of being effective in the service of God. The ethos and aesthetic of sanctification are reinforced by behavioral commitments. Members abstain from habit-forming or mood-altering substances (alcohol, tobacco and marijuana) and show restraint in sexuality (i.e., avoiding provocative dress and sexual relations outside marriage). They engage in activities which glorify God and which Christ is known to have undertaken, such as prayer, praising, worship, preaching, meditation, fasting and confession. They re-enact the activities of baptism, 'Lord's Supper,' 'washing of the saints' feet' and the 'dedication of infants.'

It would be inaccurate to describe the behavioral commitments that re-enact the actions of Christ simply as 'rites of passage' or as practices that unite and celebrate a single moral community called the church. Not all these acts mark changes in a person's status and not all of them are performed exclusively for members of the congregation or church: some of them are collective acts, while others are conducted by the individual alone. The common denominator in all of them is the person, saved or un-saved, and his or her moral nature and relationship to the moral community and hence to the wider society. To focus solely on the collective denies the saliency and importance of the person and ignores the distinctive nature of Holiness Pentecostal belief.

Adopting Durkheim's interpretation of ritual requires a concomitant examination of the nature of the group which is united and sustained through ritual activity. Kinship links in King Street congregation (see chapter 1) reveal that the body to which the individual is united – through the capacity of ritual to demonstrate the collective consciousness by expressing, making and remaking the kinship of saints (Durkheim 1915, 1971: 358) – is not a neatly bound group. In the NTCG a belief in extended sacred kinship has unique implications for the way in which ritual demonstrates the unity of the group to the individual believer. The collective symbolized by God is diffuse, extending across space and time, hence its unity can never be visibly demonstrated through rituals enacted by members in assembly, i. e., at services, seminars and conventions. At most, what can be asserted and visibly demonstrated is the unity of the local congregation and the denomination, which in turn stands as a sign for the whole. The unity of the wider collective of saints and one's relationship to it is achieved through the capacity of rituals to influence the mind and soul of every saint; it is through belief and worship that the wider collective of saints is imagined.

The 'practical commitments' of the NTCG are at once 'imitative' and 'commemorative' (following Durkheim 1915, 1971); they are indeterminate and they conflate any distinction between physical and moral efficacy. Hence, the patterns that constitute rituals can be altered or substituted to varying degrees. Rituals are effective on several levels simultaneously: First, at the level of the person, the moral efficacy of rituals continuously engenders and affirms belief. Secondly, it is through rituals that saints make manifest their internal state to others and thus demonstrate that they are a member of the same moral community. Finally, rituals address a collective whose boundaries are not clearly demarcated. Given its diffuse nature, the Christian community can only be prefigured and represented to the imagination through the symbol of God. Yet there are also ostensibly social rituals which draw upon the principles of universal brotherhood and fellowship to express membership and unity within the congregation and which mark the increase and decrease of localized membership. Where rituals possess the capacity to operate on all these levels at once, it becomes necessary for the actors to delineate the level that the ritual purportedly addresses. In the case of commemorative rituals this is achieved by clearly underscoring a single ritual aim. Since rituals bespeak the consciousness of a diffuse collective as well as a concrete group, a saint can conduct rituals privately, with the assistance of others, or as a solitary act conducted in the presence of others.

The Bible

In the COG, the Bible is taken literally as the inspired word of God, and the New Testament represents the only legitimate rule of government and discipline for the church. If a form of organization or practice is not found in the Bible or if the Bible expressly forbids certain practices, these will not be condoned by the church. Belief and practice are supported with reference to relevant scriptural passages and Biblical citation.

At a more immediate and personal level, the Bible is a tangible instrument of faith. Saints have a direct and interactive relationship with God and the Bible, as the word of God, is one manifestation of this relationship. Most saints have a thorough and fluent knowledge of the contents and physical organization of the Bible: they read the King James version and use a concordance and amplified Bible.[7] When asked to explain a religious concept or when illustrating a story, saints may cite a text or relate Biblical parables. Bibles are always carried to services and meetings. The pages are annotated and highlighted and often interleaved with notes on scriptural references and themes presented in sermons or seminars. Bible quizzes and drills are a common form of entertainment and learning, often held at weekly 'Family Training Hour' or less frequently at the elderly club. Saints are asked to cite scriptural quotations beginning with the first letter of their surname or to complete quotations; children participate in simpler versions of these exercises.

A saint should spend part of each day in reading, studying and meditating upon the Bible, either alone or with others. This discipline is part of a saint's spiritual commitment to Christ. Since the Bible is the inspired word of God, it is one way in which God is seen to have a conversation directly with a saint. It is through reading His word that God is revealed to saints: through reading the Bible a saint learns from God, is given inspiration by God, and is even reproached by God. 'The word' is a source of nourishment, influence and correction, offering the principles and practical instruction upon which saints model their interaction with God and society.

Most gatherings, whether extremely public as in the case of Sunday Services or private like meetings held in members' homes, will include a Bible reading which confirms the fellowship as an act of worship that is dedicated to God. By sharing the reading of the Bible with others, saints demonstrate the belief by which they define themselves and demonstrate to each other that they are all members of the same moral community.

The passage chosen for private study or devotion in services, prayer meetings, Bible study meetings or auxiliary meetings usually sets the theme for the sermon or the ensuing discussion. The passage may be chosen because it was revealed to a saint

---

7. A concordance is an index to the Bible, useful for locating parables, allegories and events. An amplified Bible is an annotated Bible. Some members prefer to use the Good News Bible.

within the context of a dream; it may be one a member has difficulty understanding; it may be a personal favorite or one that has particular relevance for the member's circumstances; it may be set for the next Sunday School Lesson; or it may be cited in 'Everyday with Jesus'[8] as the passage for the day. In meditating upon and trying to understand difficult or obtuse passages in the Bible, members will pray for enlightenment; thus, scriptural interpretation is a direct revelation from God (Calley 1965: 61). Every Saint, male or female, has the right to interpret scripture by the power of the Holy Spirit (ibid.: 62). In meetings where members engage in Bible study, they may break up into groups to discuss and answer a specific question about the text. Every person's opinion is included in the discussion, as all have the right to interpret scripture through the power of the Holy Spirit.

The reading of a lesson from the Bible constitutes that part of the service which is referred to as 'devotion.' The scripture reading, led by a moderator for the service, is usually taken from the New Testament, but it can also be taken from the Old Testament (Exodus or Psalms). Since the preacher who delivers the sermon is not always the moderator, the passage read in the devotion may or may not be expounded upon in the sermon. When the lesson is related to the sermon, preachers are likely to focus on one verse in the reading whose repetition underscores or summarizes the point of the sermon (cf. ibid.: 86).

There is no strictly patterned behavior for the reading of the lesson; several different styles may be adopted, 'for a change.' A call-and-response style is the most common way of reading the lesson: the moderator will lead with a verse, and members will follow with the next verse, continuing until they reach the final verse, which is read in unison. In another form of call and response, the moderator may ask male and female saints to read alternate verses, again ending in unison. It is unusual for the moderator to read the entire lesson aloud; when this is done, saints will follow along with their own Bibles.[9] On special occasions, when the service focuses on the young, the moderator may ask a child to

8. An annual booklet, which sets out daily readings from the Bible and a thought for every day of the year.

9. Visitors are given a copy of the Bible to use in the service and members are eager to help others find the relevant passage. People are always willing to share if there are not enough Bibles to go round.

read the lesson in whole or in part, or may ask several youths to read different verses.

Prayer

Prayer in the NTCG is non-liturgical; other than the 'Lord's Prayer'[10] there are few formulas or rules. Prayer is seen as an opportunity to talk to God extemporaneously:

> Prayer is a relationship with God not a ritual . . . prayer is com-munication with God. You are talking to God . . . change your views about prayer. It's not called liturgy. It's not fancy words in church. It's talking with the Master, examine our language in prayer . . . not thee-ing and thou-ing . . .. (Sermon, 5/10/91)

While the form of prayer is not standardized, prayers also vary in the apparent aims to which they are directed. At the beginning of a service, the moderator will ask a member of the congregation to 'take us to the throne of grace' (see Appendix III). The purpose of this 'intercessory prayer' is to request that God help people to 'seek Him.' In the 'throne of grace,' the saint intercedes on behalf of others by asking God to help them be receptive to His message so that His words will 'not fall on deaf ears,' that a 'heart of stone be replaced with a heart of flesh' and that the 'scales may fall off their eyes.' To lead a congregation in prayer to the 'throne of grace' is to put them in an 'attitude of worship.'

By contrast, a 'pastoral prayer' is a request to the Lord to give a pastor strength and guidance so that he may be able to hear from the Lord. Communication from the Lord to a pastor, through visions and revelations, will aid the pastor in righteously guiding the saints. A 'prayer for the sick' is usually an intercessory request for healing, which may be accompanied by the laying on of hands and anointing with consecrated olive oil. During a service, the moderator may ask if there is anyone who is in need of prayer or healing. Those in need may approach the altar rail or may remain seated in their pew with their hands raised; the moderator then asks the ministers to pray for them. Any saint may be called upon

---

10. This prayer follows the Anglican formula. A reading from the scripture usually ends with a simple 'Amen'; occasionally it will be followed by the 'Glory be.'

to offer these prayers according to 'how well they put over the prayer'; the only exception is the 'dedicatory prayer,' which must be offered by an exhorter[11] or a minister. In another example of intercessory prayer, at the end of 'Ladies' fasting meeting' women place folded slips of paper with their prayer requests in a collection bowl. One woman is asked to pray for the collection and the remainder offer intercessory prayers for the unseen and unknown requests.

As with the reading of the Bible, members may pray alone or in the presence of others; neither manner of praying is considered more or less efficacious. The manner in which the prayer is rendered is open to variation; a prayer may be offered silently or aloud, it may be offered by one person for all, by all for one, or all may offer individual prayers simultaneously. During a service or a meeting, saints usually stand to pray; however, prayer may be offered standing up, sitting down, kneeling or prostrate, with arms out-stretched or at one's side. Although to kneel in prayer is an act of extreme submission that adds to the sense of earnestness, it is not felt that a prayer rendered standing is any less significant, heartfelt or effective. It is the content of prayer that is important, not the form it takes:

> I don't think whatever position you are don't make any difference, it's your heart . . . if it's genuinely coming from your heart it doesn't matter what position you are . . . pray while I'm walking, you should pray without ceasing . . . kneeling a way of humbleness or humility, because if you go to the King or the Queen you have to bow and she's only human, so what about God almighty, you should have some respect isn't it?! (Martha)

Intercessory prayer, whether offered in solitary privacy, in unison in the presence of others, or alone before others, prefigures the body of saints and instills in the worshipper a sense of collective consciousness. Since the unity of the body of saints is imagined beforehand, intercessory prayer can demonstrate and affirm the community without the presence of an assembly of saints. For example, Calley noted that his saints performed a 'Band of Prayer' in which each day, at a specified hour, every member was to cease what they were doing and pray: 'it was felt that such concerted

---

11. An exhorter is a person who has begun ministerial training. See chapter 5.

prayer . . . stood a better chance of capturing the attention of God than did the individual prayers of members at different times' (1965: 82). Calley interpreted the 'Band of Prayer' as a 'ritual of solidarity' that reaffirmed and demonstrated loyalty to group values (ibid.: 82). In a similar manner at King Street, saints would sometimes organize a 'prayer cycle': each member was asked to sign up for a different time in a twenty-four hour prayer cycle at which they would offer prayers. Likewise, at the prayer meetings of a young women's auxiliary, members were asked to choose 'prayer partners' whom they would remember in their private prayers.

Testimonies

Unlike prayer, testimonies are not a form of communication with God but a stylized form of extended praise and thanks in which the speaker gives an account or 'testifies' about the work of God in his or her life (see Appendix III). Calley (ibid.: 77) and Lawless (1991: 56) have described testimonies as a strictly patterned expression of 'what God has done for me.' Epithets such as 'Hallelujah!' 'Glory!' 'Praise the Lord!' and 'Thank you Jesus!' are also expressions of praise. Testimonies and epithets convey the 'moods' and emotions which belief engenders in the saint. Unlike sermons, which may be spiced with the inclusion of Patois and colloquialisms, the language of testimonies is stylized, combining everyday speech with the language of worship and quotations from the King James Bible. A testimony does not need to be spoken: it may also take the form of music or a song which conveys the saint's feelings more eloquently or appropriately (see Plates in chapters 4 and 5).

Testimonies are infrequent in the Sunday morning services but are a regular part of the evening service. They are normally given by regular members of the congregation. The moderator rarely asks a specific person to give a testimony, but rather specifies how many should testify, for example, asking for three testimonies from men, three from women and two from young people. A member usually testifies by standing at his or her place in the congregation. If it is an important testimony, the saint will move to the front of the hall and face the congregation.

For members of King Street, the testimony of a saint is more than just an opportunity to express thanks and praise, it is also an opportunity to say something about oneself to others and to convey news. A testimony presents an opportunity to express the fact that one's internal state is such that God can be seen to be working in the saint's life and thus to confirm that one possesses the same beliefs as others in the group. If a member has been away for an extended time, such as a visit to Jamaica, or has undergone a personal ordeal such as illness or bereavement, he or she is given a special opportunity to testify. The most common testimonial theme consists in thanking God for recovery from an illness or commenting on the service at hand. Often a person will testify about the day he or she was saved or will give news of a person who has been saved; Sister Conneely, for example, always testified on Easter Sunday because it was the day she was saved.

Baptism and Commemorative Rituals

Baptism, the 'Lord's Supper' and the 'washing of the saints' feet' are 'representative' or 'commemorative' rituals (Durkheim 1915, 1971). For Durkheim, representative rites are a 'social affair of the first order' whose purpose is periodically to renew the sentiment that the group has of itself and its unity and to strengthen the social natures of individuals (1915, 1971: 371, 375). Among King Street members commemorative rites are not justified primarily on the basis of desired ends, but by an appeal to tradition – 'because our ancestors did it this way' (Durkheim ibid.: 371). The NTCG belief that rituals of baptism, the 'Lord's Supper' and the 'washing of feet' are representations of the way Christ and his disciples did things accounts for their less variable form. Because the emphasis in ritual practice is the remaking of the moral nature of the person, the physical efficacy of the water in baptism to cleanse the body of either dirt or sin, of the wafer and wine in the 'Lord's Supper' to offer nutriment and of cleansing in the 'washing of feet' are played down.

However, the manner in which these rites celebrate the primacy of the group and assert the moral authority of the group over the individual differs for baptism and 'reception of members' on the one hand, and the 'Lord's Supper' and 'washing of feet' on the other. The accent in baptism and reception of members is placed on confirming and expressing the already remade moral nature of the person to others and asserting the primacy of the collective. In the 'Lord's Supper,' by contrast, the accent is on expressing belief to the self. Although baptism and the 'Lord's Supper' differ in this respect, they both highlight membership in the body of saints; where the former demonstrates one's membership to others by stating, 'I am like you,' the latter demonstrates the collective to the individual by asking, 'Am I like you?' Where reading the Bible and praying are instrumental in re-forging the nature of the person and can prefigure the collective, these rituals are conducted in the presence of others and require the assistance of others for their satisfactory completion, further demonstrating the collective indicated by them.

Baptism

The church teaches that all who repent and are converted should be baptized as soon as possible by full water immersion. It is felt that Satan will try his hardest to interfere and prevent a newly converted person from being committed; therefore to delay baptism is to risk interference from Satan. Prior to baptism, a new convert may enroll in a series of classes. Religious instruction is not absolutely mandatory, but the candidate must demonstrate faith and commitment to the pastor. Baptism must be a personally willed act: the youngest candidates for baptism are adolescents, usually members of nuclear and core church families.

Exegesis in sermons before baptism justifies the form which baptism takes and defines baptism as a 'symbol' of public obedience and public acknowledgment. The strict form in which the act of immersion is conducted is justified by an appeal to the way John baptized Jesus. Sermons speak of immersion and sprinkling in the Old Testament, but these forms are dismissed as 'mere ritual' or 'religious ceremony'; Christ's own full water immersion in the river Jordan is interpreted as an endorsement by God, the Holy Spirit and Christ that full water immersion in the name of the Trinity is the only true and proper form of baptism. To be baptized is described as being 'born of the water' but since the candidate has already been 'cleansed by the blood', baptism is not considered to 'wash away sin' nor is it considered a prerequisite for salvation. 'Whether we baptize them tonight or not, they have booked their ticket to heaven' (Sermon, 30/12/90).

Members often point out that baptism cannot 'wash away sin' because Christ was without sin when He was baptized.

The meaning of baptism in the NTCG thus differs significantly from the meaning attributed to baptism in other Christian faiths, like Catholicism. To be baptized in this manner is one visible and public way of imitating Christ; it acknowledges the re-forged social nature of persons whose egocentric impulses have yielded to the authority of God. In this act of obedience individuals publicly express, in word (through testimonies) and deed (by submitting to immersion), their acceptance of salvation and their acknowledgment of Christ as their savior:

> You are saying Jesus' death I recognize and honor . . . I accept it and I'm coming to express to the public that I love Jesus, that I've been changed, something happen to me, so it's a symbol. (Sermon, 30/12/90)

Baptisms are held approximately four times a year, at Christmas, Easter, and when there are enough new converts to warrant a service. They occur toward the end of evening services, following an altar call; they may be held on a Sunday or a Saturday evening, or in the context of a district convention (see Appendix I). The readings, prayers, sermons and testimonies of the service center on the candidates and the theme of baptism, thus integrating the baptism into the service and concentrating attention on it. Thus at a Sunday-night baptism, the sermon was preceded by a series of testimonies from previously baptized members of the congregation. The purpose of these testimonies was to encourage and give support to the new candidates. Three of the women testified that their daughter or grandchild was being baptized. Other testimonies recounted the experience of Pentecostal or nonconformist river baptism in Jamaica during members' late teens and early twenties.

Baptismal services are highly public and emotionally charged events; the church hall is crowded with saints as well as visitors, family, friends and well-wishers. The candidates are seated in the front pew, males to the pastor's right (congregation left) and females to his left (congregation right) (Figure 3.1). Female candidates are clothed in white dresses and head scarves (see Plate 3). Immediately preceding their baptism, female candidates are escorted to the back hall to put on white raincoats. This precaution

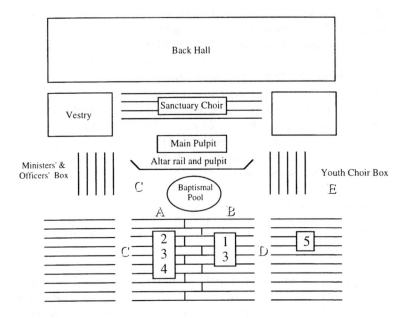

Figure 3.1 Plan of Church Hall and Seating Arrangements

Regular Seating:
1) Elderly women
2) Elderly men
3) Middle-aged men and women
4) Mothers with young children
5) Younger women

Seating During Commemorative Rites:
A) Male candidates for baptism
B) Female candidates for baptism
C) Men during 'Lord's Supper' and 'washing of the saints' feet'
D) Women during 'Lord's Supper' and 'washing of the saints' feet'
E) Sanctuary Choir during 'Lord's Supper' and 'washing of the saints' feet'

safeguards a woman's modesty by covering her wet and potentially revealing clothes. Male candidates wear white shirts and black trousers.

After the sermon, the pool which lies at the base of the pulpit, in front of the altar, is uncovered. Candidates are then asked to give their own testimonies in which they express their nervousness, their joy in salvation and their dedication and commitment to the new life they have chosen. They end their testimonies with a stylized request for prayer which underscores the conception that conversion is impermanent and requires steadfast commitment: 'Pray for me, as I mean to carry on.' At this point, members of the assembly press forward to sit or stand near the baptismal pool, while others climb into the gallery for a better view. Male candidates are baptized first; they are escorted individually by male officers of the church to the right (congregation's left) side of the pool. Women are similarly escorted by Mothers of the Church and enter the pool from the left (congregation's right). In the pool, candidates are received by a pastor and an exhorter dressed in long black robes. Male candidates stand facing towards the right (congregation's left), females towards the left (congregation's right). The pastor says a few words about the person and how they were saved. After acknowledging that he has heard the candidate's confession of faith, he immerses the candidate in the water in the name of the Father, the Son and the Holy Spirit.[12] Care is taken to ensure that the candidate's hands are arranged in prayer and that the whole body is submerged. Candidates are exhorted to 'bury the old man' – their old nature of sin and temptation – when they are immersed and to arise as righteous persons. As the candidate is raised from the water the entire congregation immediately begins singing a new chorus. The chorus continues as the candidate leaves the pool, and the next person prepares for baptism.

Calley interprets baptism as an 'induction rite' that separates full sect members from the world (1965: 89). In the NTCG and COG, however, 'Water baptism is not a door into the Church, but an act of obedience after one has been converted' (COG 1988: 22). Not all members of the congregation or church have been baptized by the denomination; some have previously been baptized by other denominations, and previous baptisms are acknowledged as sufficient provided they have taken the same form as that prescribed by the church. Further, baptism is not necessarily a one-off occasion: as an affirmation of his or her renewed resolve and

---

12. 'So by the confession of faith in Jesus Christ crucified for our sins and according to the commission given to me, I now baptize her in the name of the Father, the Son and the Holy Spirit.'

dedication, a person who has severely 'backslidden' may wish to be re-baptized, although this is unusual. This supports the argument that baptism does not in itself effect a transformation but is a public affirmation of change within the person and a reflection of their pure internal state.

Reception of Members

Although it cannot be interpreted as an induction rite, baptism – whether conducted by the denomination or an acknowledgment of a previous baptism – is the prerequisite for a service and formal ceremony known as 'reception of members' or 'the right hand of fellowship,' whereby the new convert is received into the congregation and denomination. The 'right hand of fellowship' affirms both the person's belief and membership in the local body of saints and the wider collective of saints. An account of one such ceremony follows.

Some of the newly baptized gave their testimonies and thanks for baptism. New members were asked to come forward and face the congregation so that everyone could see them and know who they were. The officers of the church were asked to flank the new members on their right and the Mothers of the Church to stand to the left. The sermon took the form of an address to the new candidates. It outlined church principles and the standards of life they were expected to uphold. The new members were urged to follow a life of Holiness and sanctification where they 'set themselves apart' by exhibiting a lifestyle and behavior that separated them from the rest of the world and from other Christian denominations. Their bodies were to be presented as a living sacrifice so that God could use them.

As a confirmation of membership in the collective of saints, new members were told that they had become part of the 'body of God' and that every person had been 'placed there for a special purpose.' Their membership in the local congregation was underscored by making it clear to them that they could rely on others; they were told they would not be alone and were encouraged to ask questions and seek help when they needed it, whether in doctrinal or temporal matters.

The Pastor summarized the teachings of the church, the new members were asked to pledge their loyalty to the doctrinal and practical commitments of the church and existing members were asked to renew their commitment. The Pastor then invited the congregation to receive the new members by walking past them and shaking their hands. The officers filed past first, then the Mothers of the Church; each spoke a few words of encouragement to the new members. The officers and Mothers were followed by the remainder of the congregation, accompanied by the singing of choruses. The new members then turned and knelt facing the Pastor, who was standing behind the altar rail; the Pastor shook hands with the new members and welcomed them into the congregation. The Pastor asked the officers and Mothers of the Church to come forward and pray for the new members, who remained kneeling at the altar. The Pastor then handed each new member a booklet that outlined the doctrinal and practical teachings of the church. Afterwards the entire congregation joined hands and began to sing, as the new members were escorted into the vestry to sign the church roll.

The 'Lord's Supper' and 'Washing of the Saints' Feet'

The 'Lord's Supper' is the communion service of the NTCG and COG. However, it is not a regular ritual, not sacramental and unnecessary for salvation (see also Calley 1965: 87). The 'Lord's Supper' may be followed by the 'washing of the saints' feet', or it may be held independently. These acts, whether held in conjunction or independently, should occur at least once a year (COG 1988: 22). King Street congregation celebrates the 'Lord's Supper' four times a year, once at Easter and Christmas and on two other occasions. Unlike conversion and baptism, the 'Lord's Supper' and 'washing of feet' do not form the subject of extensive exegesis. Like baptism, the 'Lord's Supper' may be incorporated into regular services, or a special service may be held.

The 'Lord's Supper' does not effect transubstantiation; instead, the service is described as a 'memorial,' a 'commemoration' and 'an opportunity to remember Jesus' sacrifice.' The bread and wine are described as 'representations,' 'emblems' and 'symbols' of Christ's body. Although 'commemorative' like baptism and conducted with the assistance of others at a public assembly, the significance of the 'Lord's Supper' relies less on the public expression and affirmation of one's internal state to others and more on the confirmation made to the self of one's own internal state that is a prerequisite for inclusion in the body of saints.

The 'Lord's Supper' is an act of humility: members are asked to examine themselves in light of the sacrifice which Jesus made for them and to consider whether they are worthy of receiving the supper. In self-examination, individuals assess their progress as 'Christians,' examine their relationships with God and others, and re-dedicate themselves to God. Members should communicate with God, confess their sins, shortcomings and failures as people and ask divine forgiveness. Like conversion and baptism, the 'Lord's Supper' re-establishes and reinforces communication where it has faltered; the blood that cleanses in the confession and repentance of sins at conversion also cleanses in the 'Lord's Supper.' Members need strength and fortitude to carry on as 'Christian'; hence, the blood that gives strength and nourishment at conversion is also a source of spiritual nourishment in the 'Lord's Supper.' The bread and the wine reinforce spiritual strength, as does adhering to the behavior and prescriptions set out by God and Christ: 'Jesus say eat my body. The bread is not body but a symbol. Eat my body. Eat through word, through fasting. The journey is long but my body will sustain you' (Sermon, 16/12/90). It is not enough simply to 'eat'; the symbol of Christ must already be understood and internalized as a measure and standard of living. The unworthy person who consumes the supper will suffer damnation; he or she will ail both physically and spiritually.

Unlike baptismal services and the reception of members, which are well attended and emotionally charged with happiness and joy, the 'Lord's Supper' and 'washing of the saints' feet' are sparsely attended and somber services, reflecting their contemplative purpose. Before they begin, the Mothers of the Church will prepare a table, located beneath the pulpit and behind the altar rail, for the supper. The table is spread with a clean white cloth which has been washed and ironed by a Mother and is laid with racks of individual wine glasses and bowls of communion wafers. The supper is covered with a another clean white cloth until needed.

As men and women arrive, they occupy seats on opposite sides of the church hall (men on the pastor's right and women on the left), sitting in alternate pews and leaving the pew in front empty for the distribution of the supper. Unlike regular services, there is no formal choir; choir members who are in attendance occupy seats in the youth choir box, perpendicular to the congregation (Figure 3.1).

When the 'Lord's Supper' and the 'washing of feet' were held together, there was a small to moderate turnout. These members were the older nuclear and core members of the congregation; approximately half were members of the Sanctuary Choir. There were few young or second generation members. A description follows below.

The service began, like other services, with singing and prayer. One Brother and one Sister led the congregation in simultaneous audible prayer. Afterwards the Pastor read out the purpose of the 'Lord's Supper' from a church service manual. He then called on a Mother of the Church to ask members to testify; she called on three young people, eight adult males and eight adult females. The testimonies marked the anniversaries of the member's salvation, gave thanks for the member's personal salvation, gave news of the salvation of other family members or friends, or gave thanks for the opportunity to be present for the Supper. The testimonies were followed by a short sermon on the importance and meaning of the 'Lord's Supper.' Following the sermon, the congregation rose to sing a hymn. When the hymn ended, a hush descended upon the hall as members knelt in prayer and self-examination.[13]

The period of prayer ended when one woman softly began singing the hymn 'When I See the Blood.' While the congregation sang, five male officers of the church approached the altar to distribute the communion wafers. As the Pastor dispensed the wafers to the officers, he said, 'This is my body which was broken for you.' The officers distributed them to each member while repeating the same words. Before consuming them, members again knelt and prayed silently. In the interval between the distribution of the wafers and the distribution of the wine, the congregation sang another chorus. The officers returned to the altar to collect the racks with the wine. The Pastor handed the wine racks to the officers with the words, 'This is the wine of the New Testament, as often he spoke, drink this in remembrance of me.' As they

13. It is rare for the congregation to kneel in unison in silent introspective prayer during a service.

distributed the wine, the officers repeated these words to each member. Some members drank the wine immediately; others prayed again before drinking. The congregation sang as the officers collected the glasses.

Like the 'Lord's Supper', the 'washing of the saints' feet' is an emulation of Christ's behavior and the carrying out of His example and command. Following the Supper the Pastor led straight into the 'washing of the saints' feet' by recounting the story of how Jesus had washed the feet of the disciples.[14] Unlike the sermon preceding the 'Lord's Supper,' there was little explanation of the importance of the act. The Pastor simply reiterated Jesus' words of command and humility:

> For I have given you an example, that ye should do as I have done to you. Verily, verily, I say unto you, The servant is not greater than his lord; neither he that is sent greater than he that sent him. (St. John 13: 15–16)

The Mothers of the Church, assisted by some of the officers, retreated to the back hall to fetch pitchers of hot water, basins, towels and aprons. The women in the congregation remained seated on their side of the hall and the men went forward to the space in front of the altar. The members of the congregation removed their shoes and began to wash each other's feet. Unlike the Supper, there are no special utterances involved in the act of washing feet. Women washed and dried their Sisters' feet, and men washed and dried their Brothers' feet.

Send-off

A 'send-off' is a highly emotional and anxiety-ridden occasion that marks the departure of individuals from the congregation. It is a secular-cum-religious means for marking physical departure and highlighting the potential danger of a spiritual departure from the 'body of saints.' A 'send-off' is secular in so far as it is not one of the practical commitments outlined by the COG; it does not approximate the attitudes and aspects of Christ, nor re-enact his behavior, nor mark a change in a person's status or internal state.

---

14. St. John 13: 4–17.

The religious nature of the 'send-off' is derived from an application of the principles of universal Christian brotherhood and fellowship to the exigencies of temporal life where people are continuing to relocate or emigrate. Although the saint may be physically separated from the community in which belief is nourished, he or she has not renounced membership in the wider body of saints but may simply be moving to another part of the body elsewhere, e.g., to London, Jamaica or North America (see Figure 1.4). The 'send-off' also acknowledges the danger that saints may depart from the faith and leave the body of saints if they cannot find fellowship with other saints in which their spiritual life can continue to be nurtured and grow.

A 'send-off' celebrates the degree to which a person has succeeded in maintaining the dispositions induced by religious belief and it encourages the saint to remain steadfast in their belief despite physical change. Young people are given extra encourage-ment to 'stick with God', and the wish that the person will take up membership in another congregation is stressed repeatedly; for example, if a Sister who was a choir member moves to Kingston her move will be described in terms of the addition she will make to the Kingston choir.

A 'send-off' is held in the church, within the context of an evening service. Like the service, it is composed of elements of worship behavior, i.e., prayer, music and testimonies. The depart-ing saint sits on an elegantly carved chair behind the altar rail, facing the congregation. Relatives and friends, who may or may not be members of the congregation, take turns to stand in front of the assembly and speak or sing his or her praises. At the conclusion of the 'send-off' the saint kneels before the altar, with the pastor, ministers, exhorters, officers and Mothers standing behind to lay on hands and pray for him or her. Some members prefer not to have a 'send-off'; however, remaining members usually manage to hold a mini 'send-off,' with food and gifts,[15] in the elderly club or the auxiliary in which the saint participated.

15. Gifts can include small amounts of cash called 'love-tokens.'

Christian Dedication and Funerals

The rites of 'Christian dedication' and funerals are not limited to members of the church but may be undertaken on behalf of 'non-Christians' as well. Therefore, they cannot be interpreted as a straightforward symbolic expression of the community of believers, but are better understood as a symbolic expression of the potential membership and potential growth of the body of saints.

Presenting a child for 'Christian dedication' or 'infant dedication' is not the equivalent of a christening or baptism in other churches. Dedication is not the means whereby the child is incorporated into the body: rather, dedication is a public demonstration that the parent(s) will raise the child according to Christian values and teach it about Jesus. Parent(s) and 'Godparents'[16] need not be members of the congregation. The parent(s), accompanied by 'Godparents,' approach the altar rail with the child. The pastor or a minister will say a few words, exhorting the parent(s) to provide a 'Godly environment' for the upbringing of children (for example, by encouraging private worship in the home, teaching the child to read the scripture and pray, participating in regular public worship at church, and so on) so that the child may come to accept Jesus as their savior at an early age. Following a series of formal questions concerning their intentions to be Christian parent(s), parents are given a certificate stating that the child has been dedicated in the church. The infant or child, dressed in a white gown reminiscent of a christening gown, is then passed to an exhorter who prays for the future of the child. The act of 'infant dedication' self-consciously commemorates the time when the mothers of Salem asked Jesus to bless their children;[17] the officiating pastor and exhorter portray the actions of Christ, and the parent(s) and 'Godparents' portray the actions of the mothers of Salem.

---

16. Godparents are chosen by the parents as a substitute in the event that they will be unable to carry out parental responsibilities. According to some informants, if the child is a girl she will have one Godmother and two Godfathers, if it is a boy he will have two Godmothers and one Godfather. Sometimes there will only be one Godparent of each sex, which is seen to be following 'English custom.'

17. Matthew 19: 13–15. The hymn accompanying dedication is invariably 'Mothers of Salem.'

Calley interpreted 'infant dedication' as a ritual response to anxiety concerning the liminal position of the unsaved child, through which the child becomes a junior member with an intermediate position between being unsaved and saved (1965: 91). If baptism cannot be understood as a rite of induction that denotes membership, then 'Christian dedication,' which does not require the conversion of either the parent(s) or the infant, cannot be interpreted as a sign of junior membership. The speeches accompanying dedication stress that the dedication is not akin to christening or baptism. 'Christian dedication' underscores the religious intentions of the parent(s), and can only note potential conversion and inclusion in the body of Christ for both the infant and its parent(s). Since not every parent is necessarily a 'Christian' or a member of the church, the 'non-Christian' parent must also come closer to the Lord if she is to honor her obligation to raise her child properly.

In death, members do not depart from the body of saints but simply leave the local community of the congregation to join the saints in heaven (see Figure 1.4). The funerals of non-members cannot mark an exit from the group because the deceased may not have been part of the body. Since being a 'Christian' is an internal state that can only be partly expressed through external actions, one cannot speculate or stand in judgment upon the nature of the deceased who was not a member of the congregation or denomination. Instead attention is focused on the assembly of mourners, many of whom may not be 'Christians'; funerals present an opportunity to preach to the living in the hope that they will convert. In this respect, funerals, like 'Christian dedication,' can seek out potential converts and members but do not necessarily lead to their incorporation in the congregation or the body of saints.

Born of the Spirit: The Baptism by the Holy Spirit

The paramount expression of the moral efficacy of religious rites to cleanse, re-establish and maintain communication between man and God is the concept of the baptism by the Holy Spirit. Members make a conceptual distinction between 'sanctification' and 'baptism by the Holy Spirit.' Sanctification is an ongoing process of cleansing through ethical rigor in which the believer achieves 'higher heights and deeper depths' of spiritual knowledge and belief. According to church doctrine, baptism by the Holy Spirit is subsequent to 'a clean heart.' The body is a vessel which must be cleansed and maintained before it can be filled with the Holy Spirit:

> You got to be clean. Your heart has got to be clean . . . your life in general have got to be clean to live a Holy life before the Lord, then you can be used as a vessel for him. (Lorraine)

and

> The Holy Spirit don't dwell in dirty place and if you're not really sincere and pure or whatever, they claim that you won't get the overflow. (Martha)

The metaphors used to describe baptism by the Holy Spirit are those which apply to a vessel: 'in-filling' and 'outpouring.' It is believed that baptism by the Spirit can grow quietly inside a person until one day they are suddenly 'filled' and start to 'overflow.' Overflowing or outpouring is manifested in the ability to 'give utterance' or 'speak in tongues' (glossolalia):

> When you get filled, it's a process of growing until it overflows . . . that's when you start give the utterance, because if you have a cup and you pour a little bit of water in there today and a little bit tomorrow, you know . . . and whenever it flows over it's going to empty out on something. (Martha)

As on the day of the Pentecost,[18] the gift of tongues is interpreted as the initial evidence that a person has been baptized by the Holy Spirit: 'Utterance to prove that you really have him' (Elma).

Although baptism by the Holy Spirit is a spiritual ideal, it is acknowledged that not all members possess the gift. Absence of the Holy Spirit does not deny the validity of a person's faith; some members acquire the gift relatively soon after salvation, while others will wait years, and some may never manifest baptism by the Holy Spirit:

> Nowadays Christian people get saved and all six, seven years, then nothing touch them in church. They don't even shake . . . but nothing shake them, can't feel anything because we haven't brought them to

18. Acts 2: 4–11.

the place where they can be nurtured in God and where something start. You know when you just get saved and something start in your shoes, and it boil up and come up here and it move up to your tummy and it come up into your chest and it stick in your throat . . . Glory to God! Glory to Jesus! And it come a little way and the tongue start to get loose and before you know it you go ba-ba, ba-ba, ba-ba, ba. Yessir, and then before you know it a new language start coming out. (Sermon, 27/5/90)

Waiting for the Spirit is known as 'tarrying for the Spirit.' Members who have the gift often joke about how long they had to wait and how hard they prayed to God for the gift. There are several ministers who relate their own tarrying experience in sermons and services, and it is such a focal point among members that it has even been written about by a member of the ministry (Brooks n.d.: 27–8).

Although baptism by the Holy Spirit is 'a gift' from God, because a person can only be filled if their internal state is pure and clean, the effect of religious steadfastness is that members believe that the more rigorous they are in their faith and practice the more likely they are to receive the gifts of the Holy Spirit. Rigor is demonstrated in fasting and praying:

Tarrying, you help the person to pray, pray true and the more you praise the Lord is the more the Holy Spirit take you out of yourself and take you into that realm until if you are to be filled at the same time you just sweetly fill and begin to speak in other tongues like at the day of Pentecost. (Lorraine)

Though now infrequent, the church used to hold 'tarrying services,' where people would seek the Spirit and be filled. The tarrying service has been replaced by an altar call, where members who are not filled are urged to approach the altar and pray for the gift with the assistance of the officers and Mothers of the Church.

The ability to speak in tongues is a two-way street: it is understood that God can speak in tongues through the person or the person may speak (pray) to God in tongues.[19] Not all members

---

19. Glossolalia, 'utterance' or 'speaking in tongues,' are vocalizations which sound like language but lack semantic meaning (Spanos 1986), for example, the following utterances (without linguistic diacritic marks):

who have the gift of tongues understand the meaning of their utterances; to understand utterances one must also have the gift of interpretation. If a person speaks in extended tongues, they may be uttering prophecy, sounding a warning, or delivering a message to the church. If the utterance has relevance for the church, it will be interpreted by the speaker or another person, but this is rare. The manifestation of tongues during public worship is limited to the preacher and a few members who will shout praises in tongues or in English. Prior to a sermon a prayer may be offered invoking the Holy Spirit and asking Him to fall upon the service, guide the preacher and open people's hearts to the message. During a sermon the preacher will work up towards a period of ecstatic behavior. The preacher will constantly 'seek the Spirit' and engage the congregation by asking 'Are you with me?' 'Is somebody coming?' 'Can I preach now?' or he will shout repeated praises like 'Praise the Lord!' 'Hallelujah!' or 'Amen!' Some members of the congregation will respond to the message by interjecting shouts of praise, moaning and swooning. When a service attains this level of ecstatic behavior, it is generally accepted that the Holy Spirit has fallen on the service and is doing His work. Though the use of tongues and other manifestations of the Holy Spirit are present in large public worship, they are more sustained and intense in smaller private worship meetings, i.e., at prayer or fasting meetings. In large services extended utterances are usually left un-interpreted; the occurrence of the utterance is sufficient. A saint is understood to be interpreting her own utterances if she follows it with an epithet like 'Amen' or 'Praise the Lord.'

---

polama hando,
pulama hando,
polama hando,
polama hando
(A man in St. Vincent's)

or

huntala hun,
ma tan diɛ
huntala hanandada di:
kontala hanandala
huntala handala handí
kuntala haníi: honto
(A woman in St. Vincent's) (Goodman 1972:105*f*)

To be filled with the Holy Spirit is to be anointed and empowered for service. Members speak of being taken out of themselves and being put into the spirit world.

> You can't do anything of your own self, me as I'm here talking to you now is just my real self, but to get into the spirit or the realms of God, the Holy Spirit would have to anoint me, take me out of my self, power, strength and when that fire come down, because we been baptized with the Holy Ghost and fire, so when you're anointed you have that power, you're not in yourself, you been taken out of yourself. . .. (Lorraine)

In the world of the spirit, members can 'see' things, or 'discern' things they would not ordinarily be able to see with their 'natural eye.' By 'seeing through the spirit,' members with the gift can detect physical and spiritual danger for themselves and others. There are occasions when the service or current activity is interrupted because someone has seen something, or the thought of someone has come to their mind. At these moments the assembled group will cease what they are doing and will pray or conduct an intercessory prayer for the person who may be in danger. The gift of spiritual sight can also affirm and reinforce personal belief because it is understood that the Holy Spirit guides and instructs a person in their faith. The Holy Spirit, like the blood of Jesus, is able to protect the believer from harm. It is believed that despite the violence with which a person shakes or jumps when they are filled they will not be harmed, because the Spirit would not harm them. A person may also be able to speak in tongues if he is possessed by the devil, but only a person who is filled with the Spirit will be able to 'discern' that the person is possessed by evil and not good.

Conclusion

For the NTCG, individual conversion is regarded as a radical change in a person's nature. Thus for saints, a 'Christian' is defined in terms of an internal state; a man or woman is a 'Christian' because of what he or she believes, not simply because of his or her actions. A person's new 'Christian' nature is deeply embedded in the substance of the body, in the blood, the stomach. (Sin is similarly located within the individual, where it is described as 'bad blood', an inherited 'sinful nature' and 'thinking poorly of others.') It is internal substances of the body, not easily identifiable external signs, that identify 'Christians,' i.e., 'a people with blood on their hearts.' While deeply seated, this new nature radiates outwards and can affect the visible appearance and behavior of the person, for example by changes in countenance and dress, bodily dissociation and worship. Although this internal nature can be manifested externally, for saints the possibility of inferring the internal state of a person's nature from external appearance and behavior is limited. In contrast to the system of wider social values, in which the most significant aspect of African-Caribbean identity is that inscribed on the skin, saints insist on a fundamental identity inscribed on the heart which is only partially and indirectly visible to others, especially to 'non-Christians'. Within the congregation, the 'Christian' nature of the person is announced to others through baptism, the reception of members and recurring testimonies.

The new nature which a person receives at conversion is that which approximates the 'moods and motivations' which members ascribe to Christ. The internalization of the symbol of Christ provides members with a model for ideal and proper conduct in the social world. However, the internalization of the symbol of Christ is never complete and never permanent; the new nature of the person is seen as fragile and vulnerable, threatened by forces in the very social reality which it seeks to negotiate. The new nature and the model for social relationships which it provides requires continuous religious work for it to be nurtured, sustained and safeguarded. This is accomplished through religious belief and ritual, where the 'Christian' 'dies everyday' and 'prays without ceasing.' Rituals like the reading of the Bible, prayer, responding to an altar call and the self-examination of the 'Lord's Supper' reinforce the nature the person received at conversion. Saints thus choose to emphasize an aspect of identity – that of being 'Christian' – which is not only seen as more important than the superficial identities of ethnicity or social status, but is also willed not fixed and individual not collective. This view of a human nature brought into being by human agency resolves the crisis of presence which occurs when the individual is not valued by others or integrated into society. It restores individual agency over passivity and contradicts the logic of a racism that is based upon visible and cultural differences and assumes a fixed internal essence. Similarly it is significant that the continuous cultural work of religious belief and ritual is aimed at maintaining the nature of the transcendent person, not the boundaries of an ethnically defined group. Hence, religious behavior in the NTCG also contrasts with the nature of social relations through which African-Caribbean people, in Britain at least, interact with others.

The saints of King Street congregation are like early Christians in that membership and community are not based on non-fictive kinship, race, ethnicity or nationality but on shared religious dispositions and an appeal to others who share the same world view. Only when the individual converts and becomes a 'Christian' does he or she become a member of this collective, and it is only then that community is engendered and achieves validity in the sphere of social interaction. Only by one's becoming and remaining a 'Christian' can the collective be prefigured and expressed to one through the symbolic acts of intercessory prayer and the 'Lord's Supper.' Further, the sense of collective based on shared religious belief means that the only significant social distinction to be made is that between 'Christians' and non-'Christians.' This obfuscates the drawing of immovable and permanent boundaries around the group, because the boundary can easily be redrawn to include others who have become 'Christians' through conversion. The potential to extend the boundaries and widen the ambit of those it encompasses is expressed in the acts of 'Christian dedication,' in preaching to the unsaved at funerals and in evangelism.

Mary Douglas (1982) suggests that the apparent spontaneity, lack of control and diffuse sense of the collective in West Indian Pentecostalism expresses the fluid and transient nature of social life experienced by West Indian migrants in Britain. However, within a system of religious practice which emphasizes fluidity, there is also a powerful emphasis upon personal discipline and control. A more complete interpretation of African-Caribbean Pentecostalism acknowledges that it is read and enacted by followers as a surrender to the will of God, expressed by a lack of control over the body, an in-filling by the Holy Spirit, and a commitment to a disciplined and ethical life. Pivotal to this conjuncture is the person as a 'Christian'. Conversion not only engenders the link between man and God and paves the way such that the collective can be realized and represented to the individual, it also requires that the person forego individual impulses and obey God. Control is exercised at the level of the person in the strict maintenance of a distinction between good and evil, which can be expressed, as Douglas suggests, as a distinction between the inside and outside of the physical body. In the NTCG there is an emphasis on purifying and cleansing the body, which is achieved by the blood of Jesus at conversion, the 'Lord's Supper,' obedience to God and striving to live a sanctified or 'holy life.' The 'reception of members' and the performance of recurring testimonies indicate to others the degree to which the person has been successful in exercising self-control. Sin as an internal state can also imply a sense of control, since it suggests that the person's internal state is not cleansed or purified because he or she has not obeyed God and His commandments. Ironically it is only through the strict control of the will and body that bodily dissociation – which can be seen to echo the diffuse sense of collective and which Douglas felt expressed the transience of social life – can be experienced, for example at conversion or in the manifestation of the gifts of the Holy Spirit.

Religious behavior provides members of the NTCG with the means to construct and maintain an alternative identity as 'Christian.' This identity, which begins and ends with the person – thus giving deeper meaning to the idea of identity based on self-ascription – mediates questions of suffering and status because it can be used to negotiate social experience and to structure personal relations with others in society. Members' belief resolves the question of suffering by deflecting it from its object: racism and discrimination cause suffering by addressing the individual who is defined on the basis of externals, but since belief remakes the person such that he or she is defined on the basis of his or her internal nature, the logic of racism is no longer valid. Once belief establishes the claim for a different identity as a 'Christian,' it can be elaborated further and used to mediate questions of status by steering a course through contested social experience.

Chapter 4

'I may be Black, but we're from the same hand, the hand of God': The Construction and Mediation of Identity

When students are asked to define culture, they almost always cite religion as one of its characteristics and for some religion is culture *in toto*. Two scholars speaking about the African-American church, C. Eric Lincoln and Lawrence Mamiya, underscore the indissolubility of religion and culture; religion governs cultural values, and in turn culture governs the forms religious expression takes (1990: 7). If religion is culture *in toto* and if ethnicity is understood as an expression of cultural identity, then it is not a great leap in logic to understand why religion can be interpreted as an expression of ethnic identity. The conflation of religious participation with ethnic identity occurs in everyday thought such that 'ethno-religious' is a valid conceptual category for the media[1] and non-academics. Academics also sometimes think in terms which confound ethnic expression and religious participation (*inter alia* Fitzpatrick 1987; Gans 1994; Greeley 1972; Poblete and O'Dea 1960; Won Moo Hurh and Kwang Chung Kim 1990).

The equation of religious participation with ethnic identity is particularly acute with regard to the diverse religious practices in the African Diaspora. Much of the research concerning Black religious practices interprets them as a form of explicit cultural expression in response to a given social, political and economic context, e.g., *Black Gods of the Metropolis* (Fauset 1944), *The Negro Church in America* (Frazier 1964) and more recently M. D. Williams' *Community in a Black Pentecostal Church* (1974).[2] The implicit

---

1. Note the inconsistent use of the term 'ethno-religious' when reporting armed conflict. The war in the former Yugoslavia is 'ethno-religious' conflict, while Islamic jihads are not conceived in the same terms.

2. See also Baer and Singer 1981; Barrett 1977; Daniel 1942; Hogg 1960; Simpson 1955, 1956.

Plate 4 'Testimony, National Youth Convention'. Source: Author

assumption that religious identity is manifestly 'Black identity' is a position which is reproduced in the English material (i.e., Calley 1962, 1965; Cashmore 1979; Hill 1963, 1971a, 1971b, 1971c; Pryce 1979). The Black Church in the US has been variously interpreted as a stumbling block to assimilation (Frazier 1964), a form of voluntary isolation (Orum 1966; Silberman 1964), an avenue for the power and prestige otherwise denied Blacks in society (Drake and Cayton 1962) and a means for creating a sense of ethnic community and ethnic identity (Nelsen and Nelsen 1975).[3] However, religious participation in America is more than an expression of ethnic identity, it is also a forum for the creation and acquisition of racial and political consciousness and identity (cf. A. L. Brown 1994; L. Reese and R. Brown 1995). In a different approach, Lincoln and Mamiya conceive of Black churches as institutions involved in the resolution of a series of dialectical tensions (priestly/prophetic functions; this world/otherworldly orientation; universal/particular message; communal/private nature; and a dialectical stance of resistance/accommodation) (1990: 10–15). Each institution negotiates these tensions in its own way, adding to its unique culture (1990: 18). While it may be valid to think of African-American religious practices as expressions of ethnic and racial identity, is African-Caribbean Christianity in Britain an expression of ethnic identity? Is the message of the NTCG one of racial and political consciousness? Lincoln and Mamiya's model is useful for rethinking African-Caribbean Christianity. They note that the structure of belief for Black and White Christians is the same, though the 'valences' of belief differ. In African-American Christianity greater emphasis is placed on the theological view of the Old Testament God as avenger, conqueror and liberator. The suffering humiliation and triumph of Jesus resonates with Black experiences, and ideas of human equality for all are underscored (1990: 3–4). If Black and White Christianity can be understood to differ, then within the sphere of African Diaspora religious practices the 'valences' of African-Caribbean Christianity may differ, as will African-Caribbean Pentecostalism's negotiation of dialectical pairs. In the different multicultural context of Britain, the emphasis of African-Caribbean

3. See Lincoln and Mamiya (1990: chapter 1) for a brief review of the different theoretical approaches to the Black Church.

Pentecostalism may not necessarily be weighted towards ethnic and racial expression.[4]

Any assumption that Pentecostalism is ethnic expression ignores the gains made from the analysis of conversion and Pentecostal participation: the transformation of the individual with received categorical identities to an individual with a self-ascribed and self-achieved identity as a Christian. Several episodes suggest that there is no simple congruence between ethnicity and faith for the members of King Street. On my first visit to the church, an usherette presented me with a card which requested information concerning my name, address and religious affiliation. Later during the same visit, an officer of the church seated himself beside me and asked, 'Are you new?' 'Yes,' I explained, adding that I had attended an African Methodist Episcopal Church in the US several years ago. This prompted the officer to ask, 'Are you a Christian?' Without understanding the meaning of his question, I replied 'Yes.' His response was one of greeting and acceptance: 'Well then this is the place for you! Welcome!' A week later, during my first visit to the church elderly club (almost all African-Caribbean attendees), the Mother in charge was concerned to point out that the group was organized for 'any nationality, any color' and that it catered for 'Christians and the whole community,' not simply church members. When I told her of my research plans she commented:

> My culture is different from yours, but that doesn't mean we can't learn about each others' culture. I may be Black, but we're from the same hand, the hand of God. We're born the same, we wee [sic] the same and die the same.

It is commonplace to hear statements concerning identity like the following:

> The psychologist say you are not who you say you are, neither are you who people say you are, but a combination of who you say you are and who people say you are. I don't think I agree with everything about that. If we want to get a good impression of who we are, just get that consciousness of almighty God. (Sermon, 26/5/90)

---

4. For a discussion of how Britain's multicultural context differs from either Jamaica or the US, see chapter 2; also Sutton and Makiesky-Barrow 1994.

It soon became clear that for members of the NTCG, faith and ethnic identity were neither indivisible nor interchangeable concepts. This is not the case for all sections of Britain's African-Caribbean population. For Rastafarians, for example, there is a close association between religious and ethnic identity.[5] The divergence in the identities expressed through religious practice is also evident in the Caribbean, where Austin-Broos argues that Pentecostalism and Rastafarianism present different solutions to the racialized situation of Black Jamaicans (1991–1992: 307):

> The solution from a Rastafarian view was separation, pan-Africanism and a return to their own particular place. [While] Pentecostalism . . . involved an attempt on the part of White American missionaries to subsume Jamaicans within their moral and spiritual world . . . [t]hrough proclaiming the possibility of spiritual protection for all . . . the [Pentecostal] movement acted to neutralize race and class and reconcile its followers to New World conditions. One religious movement revolted against the hierarchy of the region and sought to separate Jamaicans from it. The other moved to redefine the hierarchy and seek integration with it. (ibid.: 307–8)

The political element of self-representation inherent in Rastafarianism has formed the focus of much work (e.g., Cashmore 1979; Gilroy 1987; Pryce 1979) which in general sees it as a creative response among the second generation of Black-British, organizing political consciousness and providing a vehicle for its expression and mobilization. Rastafarianism and Pentecostalism can both be interpreted as messianic-millenarian movements of the oppressed, which provide their adherents with a means of making sense of the suffering they experience, given their placement within a racially divided society. However, as Austin-Broos noted for the Caribbean, they diverge in the means through which their respective ideologies offer a resolution of suffering. The ideology and symbolism of Rastafarianism is grounded in the very essence of what it is to be Black in a society charged with White bias and discrimination. The beliefs of Rastafarianism replace European values with values which celebrate Africanness and Blackness: belief is congruent with ethnic identity. Unlike Rastafarianism, the ideology and belief system of Pentecostalism is not overtly and

5. For discussions of Rastafarianism in Britain, see Cashmore 1979; Gilroy 1987; Pryce 1979 and *The Independent* May 3, 1991.

explicitly grounded in members' experience of racism and discrimination – it does not invert European values to replace them with ones which celebrate Africanness. There is no necessary categorical congruence between 'Black identity' and belief. Rather, there is an emphasis upon an inner non-ethnic essence produced and maintained through faith and religious work on the part of the individual. Hence, the resulting politicizations of identity in Rastafarianism and Pentecostalism differ enormously. This does not mean that identity among Pentecostal Blacks cannot be politically mobilized, but rather that its expression is more subtle and complicated. We are reminded of the plural meanings assigned to 'being Black' in Britain in the 1990s.

Conceptualizing Identity

Paul Gilroy provides an important clue for conceptualizing identity. He suggests we rid ourselves of reductionist tendencies and open up categories like 'race' or class so that they become tentative categories which can accommodate various meanings (1987: 19). The various meanings are socially and politically constructed and like all meanings can change; they are not only 'different over time but may vary within the same social formation or historical conjuncture' (ibid.: 38). In order to understand the diversity, dynamism and complexity of Black identity better, we should focus on how the category of identity is constructed and given meaning by actors.

Following critical advances in ethnic and identity theory made by Frederick Barth (1969) and Anthony Cohen (1985a), identity is understood as a cultural category filled in by actors with symbols of their own choosing. The following discussion examines the symbolic themes[6] which members of the NTCG manipulate to construct a sense of community and identity which can be deployed in interaction with other groups of people.[7] The main themes chosen for discussion are ideas about nationality, general status markers, language, work, education and food. Being

6. The concept of symbolic themes used here is informed by Victor Turner (1967: 19–47).

7. Barrett (1977) and Williams (1974) have also examined the use of symbolism in the construction of identity among Black religious groups.

symbolic in nature, these themes are multivalent. They can simultaneously bespeak the dichotomy between 'us' and all 'others' on several different levels: 'us' as 'Christians' and them as 'non-Christians'; 'us' as 'Pentecostal Christians' and them as 'non-Pentecostal Christians'; 'us' as minority ethnic group and 'them' as the dominant group in society; or 'us' as minority ethnic group and 'them' as other minority ethnic groups.

Members of the church define themselves in opposition to other categories of people. The general categories of 'others' as perceived by members are continually used as referents against which the 'we' is measured and given form. However, it is important to note that members never define themselves in direct opposition to being Black, Jamaican or West Indian. Selective aspects of experience and ethnic identity are evident in the construction of members' identity as Christians. Members' perception of their identity as Christians is not made independently of their perceptions of 'ethnic identity.' Since social life is continuous, we can expect feedback between members' perceptions of themselves as Christians and their perceptions of themselves as Jamaicans. Belief determines which symbols will be used to construct a sense of ethnic self which is compatible with a sense of religious self. Belief permits certain views of ethnic identity and obscures other views. To understand this is to understand the relationship between ethnic and religious identity and the sum total of members' identity.

The context for the data analyzed here is the realm of social and religious gatherings of King Street congregation and the National Youth Conventions of the NTCG. The context is not one of visible social interaction between groups: instead it is one where people are primarily telling themselves and others what they perceive to be their identity. In the case of the National Youth Conventions, members are publicly proclaiming their identity to British society (see Plates, cover, this chapter and chapter 5). The data are the symbolic themes, expressed verbally and through practice, which the clergy, officers and lay members manipulate in the construction of community and identity. There was little or no interaction between members and others in the religious sphere. Hence, the identity categories created by the actors appear in a void of interaction – saints are preaching their identity to the already converted, while others who are unsaved are missing or unreceptive. The actions and statements of members provide a clear example of what Anthony Cohen (1985a) means when he suggests that ethnicity can also be a statement made to the self by the self. Yet, there is also room in this approach for remaining sensitive to the wider social, economic and political context and its articulation with the community as imagined by members. Sandra Wallman (1978) has noted that ethnic boundaries have two sides, and the issue of power in determining the nature of inter-group relations and political representations of self for African-Caribbeans in contemporary Britain is a crucial one. Hence, the themes which members mobilize in the construction of community and identity are chosen precisely because they represent those issues which are contested by others as well as by members at the point of social interaction between two ethnic groups. Further, Abner Cohen (1980) has recognized that the symbols which mark the community can change with each new political formation. Thus, these symbolic themes are those which express members' identity and placement in Birmingham in the early 1990s. Hence the church provides an arena in which messages are exchanged and through which members can locate themselves in the wider 'common-sense' discourses about Black people in Britain.

The views of one generation do not necessarily represent, nor exclude, those of another generation. This is especially important for African-Caribbeans in Britain (Allen 1982; Gilroy 1987; James 1989, 1993; Lawrence 1982a, 1982b). However, as Cohen (1985a) has suggested, the boundaries of community are capable of incorporating difference and diversity among members. Since the primary focus of research was older female migrants, many of the symbolic expressions of identity presented here emanate from that quarter. Public expressions of identity manifested in the arena of religious services and activities – from the pulpit and church social events – also represent the views of the older generation. It should be borne in mind that members of this Pentecostal church, especially the elderly, represent only one view of what it is like to be African-Caribbean in England.

Ethnicity

Terms like 'Colored,' 'Black,' 'Jamaican,' 'Caribbean' and 'West Indian' are all used by saints to talk about themselves. Despite current politically correct usage – the replacement between the 1950s and the 1980s of the terms 'Colored' with 'Black' and 'West Indian' with 'African-Caribbean' or 'Caribbean' – the diversity in the terms used by people is striking. In general, people both in the church and outside tend not to speak of themselves as 'Jamaicans' or as 'West Indians' but instead of 'coming from Jamaica'. This sense of place, with a distinct nationality for those who live there, is maintained by the use of prepositions like 'in,' 'from,' 'there' and 'with': 'I'm from someplace in the world, I'm from Jamaica of course, and I'm this side of the world . . .' (Sermon, 26/5/90). One can be a White 'Jamaican,' a Black 'Jamaican,' an Indian 'Jamaican,' etc. As Sister Ashe put it:

> A girl, one time, who is a White, she born and grow in Jamaica, one time she was on the telly in a beauty contest and they ask her where she come from and she says, "I'm Jamaican my mom and dad born there and I born there, I'm a Jamaican."

In contrast, the term 'English' is synonymous with an ethnic identity and describes White people. Hence a woman may say, 'My son is married to an "English" girl.' However, like Jamaica or the Caribbean, Britain is a seen as a place of origin for diverse people. Younger people maintain that although their parents came from Jamaica and can thus be considered 'Jamaican,' they are 'British' because they were born or grew up here.

As a place, Jamaica is located in a region which people call the 'Caribbean' or the 'West Indies.' People from the Caribbean acknowledge that there are similarities between them:

> If I say I saw some lovely breadfruit out the shop, you know what I'm talking about 'coz we're from the same place. When you talk to an English person about breadfruit it's like talking a different language – don't understand, it's a different experience. (Lorraine)

However, saints are equally prone to underscore the differences of island origin, attitudes and linguistic differences, for example, the social and cultural differences of 'small island' or 'big island' people, or when a man confirmed that he was from Barbados by responding, 'You hear me speak.'

People also refer to themselves in ethnic terms. Many older people employ the term 'Colored' to identify and describe themselves and the group to which they belong. Thus 'Colored' people are 'my people,' 'we' or 'own people.' 'Colored' people are felt to understand the needs of their own people better and will go further than other people to meet these needs. The term 'Colored' refers to a specific ancestry and social status which may, in some contexts, be differentiated from being 'Black' on the basis of skin color, physical appearance, lifestyle and behavior (see chapter 2). For older people, the term 'Black' takes its meaning from experiences of racism and discrimination. The term is commonly used to describe actors and events which take shape in contexts where racial dichotomies are potentially significant. For example, a person will describe herself as 'Black' when speaking of her work experience ('I was the only "Black" woman in that section'), when describing a different religious affiliation or when describing an encounter with a prejudiced shopkeeper.

Although 'Black' can be self-referential, it is sometimes contrasted to being 'Colored' when it is used as an insult to describe someone who is disloyal to people of their 'own kind.' For example, when an African-Caribbean woman's grandson had been attacked, she described his attackers as 'Black'; when another woman was conned by a firm which specialized in shipping goods to the Caribbean, she described the African-Caribbean owners of the firm as 'Black.' Younger people reject their parents' use of the term 'Colored,' preferring to describe themselves as 'Black'; for them this is a term that encompasses not only an oppositional identity to White, but also a sense of shared culture and experience. It would be misleading to imply that older people never use the term 'Black' in the same ways as younger people; in fact older people often substitute the more general use of the term 'Black' for 'Colored.' However, among the people polled, both young and old, distinctions are maintained within the general use of the term 'Black' between people with different national and cultural origins and different experiences of racism and discrimination. While a person may describe herself as 'Black' at work, she will differentiate herself from Black African workmates. Contrary to the cultural politics of the 1970s and early 1980s, the term 'Black' is not extended to Asian people. Asians are perceived as maintaining a distinct identity.

Them . . .

Members perceive the world as a competitive place where people fight for their rights to belong to a group and seek to preserve an exclusive identity: 'There is widespread persecution, nation versus nation, race versus race . . . seek to maintain identity at whatever cost, at whatever price' (Sermon, 14/4/90). 'You have no rights, people are lost, because they are fighting for their rights' (Sermon, 8/7/90). Society is preoccupied with nationality, race, class, and the pursuit of material wealth. This has an adverse effect on those involved, which can be described vividly in terms of physical violence:

> . . . vision of unchurched people around you. When Jesus saw the multitude he was moved with compassion. He saw them helpless, scattered over barren mountains, battered, bruised, lonely, frustrated, flat out on the ground. (Sermon, 30/3/91)

Because it is preoccupied with these matters, the world and its inhabitants are suffering from a 'spiritual drought.' It is a 'morally lax' and 'promiscuous' place characterized by the pursuits of pleasure, an 'unholy place,' an 'un-Godly place.' The people are 'backslidden' and 'unchurched.' People of the world are perceived to be 'empty' and 'unfulfilled' because they are engaged in the struggles of the world and lack the experience of God.

The world is associated with death or inactivity. People of the world are occasionally described as animals; they are the 'fish which float' on the ocean after a storm. While saved members of the church are sheep, the unsaved are goats, crows and dogs which feed upon the rubbish or dead carcasses of the world. The world is an unclean place characterized by pestilence and slime. The current condition of the world and its inhabitants is summed up by the view that this is a 'terrible time' or, in the words saints borrow from Rastafarians, a 'dread time.' Overcrowding in prisons, the use of drugs, prostitution, child abuse, abortion, etc., are all indications which reaffirm the validity of members' belief.

Although members set themselves apart from the world, they do not escape its perils. The world threatens the spiritual life of members and misunderstands saints' identity in much the same way that it threatens members' secular identity. If members grasp for material things and live according to society and its values, they will be corrupt. If members succeed in leaving the world behind, it can still threaten and pass judgment on them. Society tells them they are 'too churchy' or that they think they are 'the only Christians.' "The world don't understand; that's why they think you so strange. Think we are religious maniacs living off in space . . . pie in the sky . . . not real" (Sermon, 24/2/91). 'Are you one of those people who are afraid that people brand you a religious maniac, because you muse on things of heaven?' (Sermon, 9/6/91).

It is acknowledged that God does not tie himself to any particular denomination and that other people worship God in their own way. However, a clear distinction is made between Christianity and other faiths (notably Hinduism and Islam) and between Pentecostal churches and other Christian denominations. While the Catholic church is perceived as one which 'burns incense' and where priests speak for people, 'incense burns within' members of the NTCG in the form of the Holy Spirit. Other churches which are not Pentecostal are referred to by members as 'nominal churches.' These churches are criticized for having lost touch with heaven, for being too secular and for not reading the Bible, and if they do read it, they are criticized for reading into it.

> The view that God wants you to be rich is all a part of worldly spirit of the time, want all you can get, get all you want, but hold onto the outward trappings of Christianity . . .. Look around, they are yielding more to the pressure of the age than to the Holy Spirit. When that happens we are worldly . . . when believers lose sight of heaven it is because worldliness has stepped in. They are more concerned with making it down here than up there. (Sermon, 14/4/90)

Like the world in general, other denominations and religions are associated with death; they are inactive and cold. The COG and Christianity differ from 'Eastern religions' whose 'saviors are dead'. In a world of religious diversity, members must be wary of 'false witnesses' and 'false cults':

> There are those people who are telling me they have found a new way. They have found Buddhism . . . they have found Shintoism . . . they have found the Mooneys . . . they have found the Jehovah's Witnesses . . . they have found all kinds of cults under the sun, and you know why these people have found these cults and are happy to be Muslims and what not? Because they have no responsibility . . . their God is dead and they are not accountable. (Sermon, 27/5/90)

... and Us

While people in the world are divided, frustrated and sorrowful, members' self-image is of a 'free' and 'happy' people, full of warmth, sharing and love. People in the world are lost, they are unclean, licentious and immoral; they can drink, smoke and have sexual relations outside marriage. Members, however, are 'saved,' 'redeemed' or 'chosen,' and as such they are cleansed because they maintain the standard of sanctification.

Members' general self-image as brethren *vis-à-vis* non-brethren parallels and highlights certain aspects of their general self-image as a community of 'Coloreds' or 'Blacks' *vis-à-vis* the dominant majority. Two general attributes which they apply to themselves are those of a 'sharing' and 'clean' people, whereas the dominant others are stereotyped as 'unsharing' and 'dirty.'

Sharing is not simply the redistribution of possessions, food or money, but also sharing oneself. Sharing is offering your time and abilities to others: running errands, helping each other in times of crisis, offering lifts, and advising each other in dealings with officials. One should share one's company with others at work, home and church. This is a trait which the English are not seen to possess, because they maintain limited interaction with members outside work contexts. Although there are individual exceptions, members are not invited into an English person's home. The most idealized expression of sharing is at times of bereavement. A sharp contrast is drawn between the way 'they' mourn and the way 'we' mourn. While the English only have a handful of mourners, when someone from the Caribbean dies his or her whole social network shares the bereavement. At this time, one shares not only by attending the funeral, but by helping to dress the deceased, staying with the bereaved during 'nine-night,'[8] contributing food, presenting gifts or giving money. In the field of religious participation, sharing in all its manifestations can be embodied in the saying 'to have fellowship.' It is believed that when a person leaves a nominal church after service on Sunday, there is no contact with other brethren or fellowship until the following Sunday. Members

---

8. The wake for the deceased, during which family and relatives visit the bereaved over the nine nights following the death. For an account of the significance of repatriated burial in the Caribbean see James 1993: 245–6.

criticize themselves when they find themselves behaving in a manner they perceive to be indicative of English behavior.

Issues of cleanliness and purity are often invoked to draw boundaries among groups, and in this respect members are no exception.[9] Members' image of spiritual cleanliness *vis-à-vis* the English echoes their images of cleanliness and hygiene *vis-à-vis* non-members. A common theme of discussion among women at the elderly club is the personal hygiene and food practices of other groups of people. One woman told a story about an English workmate whose overalls were so greasy they shone. Other stories focus on the repugnance they felt for English food practices such as wrapping fish and chips in old newspapers or leaving unwrapped bread on the doorstep. Here, as in sharing, perceived ethnic differences are both incorporated into the discourse of identity and transformed into moral and transcendental values.

Members clearly distinguish the denomination from other Christian denominations and faiths by self-consciously referring to the church as a 'Pentecostal church' and a 'Holiness church.' The appellations 'Pentecostal' and 'Holiness' serve as shorthand for doctrinal and practical principles which distinguish the denomination from other Christian faiths, although the most commonly drawn contrast is with the Roman Catholic church.

The portrayal of the church as a 'Black Church' or 'Afro-Caribbean' church is invoked less often. The label of 'Black Church' is derived from the way the world perceives the church as an ethnic enclave and defines its role as a source of ethnic self-help:

> There are some people who try to get us in a certain group and tell us what our role ought to be, and some of our churches sadly are becoming like a social service department, but nothing is wrong in going out in social service, but the main purpose of the church is to talk about Jesus Christ and Him crucified. (Sermon, 26/5/90)

Further, since the title of 'Black Church' focuses on issues of race and not doctrine it cannot be used clearly to distinguish the denomination from other Christian faiths:

---

9. Williams notes the manipulation of symbolic cleanliness among members of the Zion Holiness Church (1974: 125).

When you say Black-led church there could be a stipulation there, because it could be a Black-led church, but then they are not real born-again Christian, because you have the Baptist who is Black-led, you have the Presbyterian who is Black-led as well. You have other Pentecostal church who are Black-led as well. It depends how Christian they are . . . . (Mother Green)

In contrast to other faiths, members believe that the faith embodied in the church is one of spiritual vision and truth based on a literal reading of the Bible unspoiled by learned interpretation. Unlike other churches, which are cold and inactive, the church is described as a 'living church' which is 'hot,' 'born of fire.' It is a noisy and active place full of 'amens' and 'hallelujahs,' a place where people are free to worship by 'clapping hands' and 'stamping feet.' Since the church is founded on faith and righteousness, it does not need the outward physical trappings of stained-glass windows or pine pews which characterize other churches.

Nationality[10]

Ideas of nationality and 'origin' used to differentiate people in British society are also employed by NTCG members to distinguish themselves from others. However, more important are the often asserted ideas of common kinship with God. Members variously describe themselves as 'children of God,' 'people of God,' 'His people,' etc. This 'common heritage' is affirmed and extended by the use of the fictional kinship terms 'Brother,' 'Sister,' 'Mother.' Secular citizenship in the nation of Britain is replaced by spiritual citizenship in the imagined community of God's nation; members

10. There are two senses to the term 'nation' and hence ambiguity in the meaning of 'nationality.' In its first sense, a nation is a collectivity of people, akin to an ethnic group and characterized by solidarity and self-consciousness. Its people share a common history, language, religion and 'race.' When the sense of nation includes the idea of being grounded in a common territory, it invokes the idea of a state, a political entity which exercises sovereign rights over a territory. The maintenance of a state's sovereign rights over territory can involve the extension or exclusion of rights to the resources of the territory–citizenship. When belonging to a nation and a state are conflated in thought, as it is for some segments of Britain's population, citizenship may be premised on nationality. Nationality refers to the citizenship of a nation-state in this context. See Danforth 1995; Gellner 1983; Llobera 1994.

are 'citizens with God,' 'fellow citizens in the house of the Lord,' 'citizens with Jesus not England,' etc.[11] National citizenship is therefore seen as unimportant: ". . . if born in England if came from the Caribbean, God has seen your substance" (Sermon, 14/4/91); ". . . in Africa, the West Indies, Great Britain, God is able to keep you" (Sermon, 11/3/90). Like Britain, which possesses the military and diplomatic tools of statecraft, the imagined community of members is sometimes described as an 'army' and members as Christ's 'ambassadors.' The church and her people as an imagined community, like other imagined communities,[12] is perceived to possess its own culture: "The church army have language, dialogue, lifestyle, culture" (Sermon, 2/6/91). This formulation neatly side-steps debates about how, and on what terms, African-Caribbeans may be included in the British nation, for this inclusive spiritual nation is not premised upon racial differentiation: "White people coming to church, color doesn't matter . . ." (Sermon, 9/9/90); ". . . the people's Christ . . . the people, everyone Black or White . . ." (Sermon, 2/12/90).

If a person's citizenship is spiritual and not secular, the millenarian view of 'this world is not our home' becomes logically valid: "You don't belong to this world, your citizenship is in heaven" (Sermon, 3/2/91). Similarly, the sense of difference which members maintain between themselves and others, and the sense of difference which others maintain between themselves and church members, can also be understood in these terms. Citizens in the house of the Lord are 'strangers' and 'foreigners' in Britain, where members perceive themselves to be 'pilgrims.' "For the believers this is not home, heaven is home. We're just passing through. Church of God is at the airport, ready to go at any time, when you get on board, keep your seat, fasten your seat-belt" (Sermon, 13/1/91); "I am a stranger, pilgrim in this world . . . we are so strange in this world" (Sermon, 13/4/91). Thus members maintain a position which simultaneously negates the privileged

11. The source for spiritual citizenship is taken from Ephesians 2:19; 'Now therefore ye are no more strangers and foreigners, but fellowcitizens with the saints, and of the household of God . . . .'

12. For Benedict Anderson (1983), the nation is an imagined political community because its members can never know all the members of the community called the nation, but they do not doubt its existence. Like identity, nations are cultural constructs based on the mobilizations of symbols.

position of others who might claim ownership of Britain and deals with social exclusion and the subjective sense of being 'strangers and foreigners.'

Status and Material Wealth

Status markers and material wealth which are used to differentiate people in society have little value among members of the church:

> ... happiness is not bank account, number of houses, number of cars, numbers of friends, but that the life of Christ is living in you ... the little the righteous man has is better than the abundance of the wicked ... you may not have much, I may not have much, but we have Jesus, rather than houses and land. (Sermon, 24/8/90)

The denigration of prestige and status markers generates some of the richest religious oratory. This oratory can be interpreted in two not inconsistent ways. One reading suggests that it is about 'compensation' for members' relative status deprivation in mainstream society. Another reading suggests that it outlines a charter for membership and behavior within the group and involves an element of political and cultural critique.

If high socio-economic status is a necessary prerequisite for value and effectiveness in the wider society, it is of negligible, even negative worth for inclusion and membership in the society of Christians:

> You can get to heaven without health, without wealth, without fame, without riches, without jewelry, without high learning, without high earning, without culture, without beauty and without 10,000 other things, but you can't get there without Jesus. (Sermon, 19/5/91)

Although the socio-economic status of members may not be positively or highly esteemed, "You may be insignificant in Great Britain, you may not be worth much, but among God you are worth a lot" (Sermon, 11/3/90).

If status differentiation is unimportant to God and to Christ, it should also be unimportant to members. Status markers should not be used to differentiate members within the church. Members may have different offices or roles to perform within the church, but they are all members equally:

> Everybody is equal, no one is special . . . but when God looks down, what he sees in the church are not some people who are better than others, nobody up here [in the pulpit] is a better quality person than anybody down there [in the congregation]. (Sermon, 6/10/91)

and

> I don't care who you are. I don't care where you come from. I don't care what position you hold in your church. I don't care what post you are holding up tonight, commit your ways unto the Lord . . . remember God does not require a beautiful vessel, He requires a clean one . . . I don't care off which table you are eating. I don't care if your cutlery is gold-plated or gold. I don't care if it's silver-plated. I don't care if you drive a BMW. I don't care if you drive a Rolls Royce. I don't care if you live in Buckingham Palace. What I'm saying tonight, God does not desire a beautiful vessel, he desires a clean one. (Sermon, 27/5/90)

While the usual avenues for the attainment of status and material wealth may be denied to members in the wider society, members may still achieve these goals through the alternative route of spiritual provision. While the children of God may not have the visible benefits of status and material wealth in the here and now, they are millionaires by dint of sacred kinship and sacred citizenship; since their Father is rich in houses and land, they stand to inherit a fortune.

When wealth is achieved, it is closely related to God. God is sufficient, He provides what may not be attainable in the secular world. "God blesses us with homes, cars and fine things" (Sermon, 4/2/90). "Thank God for all we got in this country" (Sermon, 17/9/90). Material benefits are not in themselves sinful or corrupting, but it is what a person chooses to do, or not to do, with them that is potentially damning. Sin is greed and selfishness; those who are fortunate should share what they possess. One preacher spoke of how when he first arrived in England he was earning £5 a week, and out of this he put money aside to purchase a car. Once purchased, the car was put into the service of the Lord by offering brethren lifts to church. In a similar vein, the donation of food or money for the poor can also be regarded as an act of faith which is reminiscent of the attribute of sharing which members ascribe to themselves as Jamaicans. One young Sister recounted how, when visiting a congregation in London, she only had £5 in her purse when a collection was taken. Since she did not know how she would get home, she put it in the collection reluctantly. At the end of the service, a Sister presented her with some money she owed her; for the young Sister, this was proof that God provided for her needs. Occasionally members are asked to go through their larders and contribute any food which is not immediately necessary to a 'barrel'[13] for the needy. Similarly, ambition is not a bad quality in itself, but one should have the ambition to be like Jesus, not for power and things of the world. At 'send-offs,' a person's secular achievements are left unmentioned; rather, attention is focused on their spiritual achievements.

Even where such goals are attainable for members in the wider society, they may choose to reject them in order to reaffirm their status as Christians. A female preacher, visiting from Fort Lauderdale, recounted how she was offered a higher position in the state education system but turned it down because it conflicted with her responsibilities in the church and her status as a separated and sanctified 'Christian.' She said to her superior: 'I know you mean me well. You tellin' me I can make it in the world, you tellin' me that the world has got a place for me, but I'm sorry I got to tell you I've been separated unto Him' (Sermon, 6/10/90). Although the theme of work is examined below, it should be noted at this point that the value of work for the acquisition of status and material benefits is also questioned:

> You say you are tired after work. Your mothers worked and they did the same things . . . .. We can do all things through Christ. Don't take all the overtime you can get. What is the money doing for you? (Sermon, 9/9/90)

and

> Men with a burning desire, stuck to the factory wheel, look forward to the weekend when they get the pay packet. Divide it, send some home, pay the rent, etc. Decide, no I'm tired, let me tell the supervisor two more weeks and I'll pack it in. God will take care. (Sermon, 24/3/91)

---

13. A 'barrel' is a large cylindrical shipping container, often used to ship food and clothing to Jamaica.

Language

The themes of ethnicity, 'us,' 'them,' nationality, status and material wealth illustrate the explicit symbolizings of boundaries. Language, work, education and food are aspects of culture where differentiation is implicit. The symbolic theme of language is multifaceted and complicated. In addition to the potentiality of glossolalia, members are fluent in at least three dialects, each of which possesses multiple symbolic meaning in their own right. Members speak Patois, what they refer to as 'Queen's English' (Standard British English) and what they call 'Authorized Worship Language.' In the course of interaction with each other and with others, members are continually confronted with linguistic choices. The idiom used for expression is partly determined by the parameters of audience and subject matter. Although language choices are strongly associated with demarcated domains, the individual speaker's choice of dialect is not necessarily defined situationally but is also indicative of the speaker's social allegiances, which can transcend the exigencies of their particular circumstances (Benson 1981: 42). Given the parameters of audience, subject matter and allegiance, language can be a marker of the multiple and shifting boundaries in the construction of identity and can also be used as the basis of interaction between members and others.

Patois Jamaican Patois[14] is seen by the English as a diacritic of members' Jamaican ethnic identity and racial difference. The stigmatization associated with Patois is expressed in statements like "they think we can't speak English properly" and "they ask me where I learned English so well." However, members mobilize Patois as a symbol of group identity and can reinvest it with new meaning. Patois is used in communication and interaction with others with whom one is familiar and who are perceived to be the same, while excluding others who are not the same. For example, in the wider African-Caribbean community, one of the justifications given for the establishment of separate West Indian day-centers for the elderly was that the elderly were fed up with constantly

14. Patois is the form of English spoken by ordinary people in Jamaica, which differs from Standard British English in diction and grammatical construction. See Bailey 1966; Cassidy 1971; Cassidy and LePage 1967; Morris 1982.

being asked to repeat their requests to White workers who lacked comprehension of Patois.

Patois is used to convey the mundane and trivial aspects of secular life in conversational exchanges, e.g., when relating an incident one had with the water board, a shopkeeper or a relative. It is also the primary medium for cultural expression. It is used to express sentiment and to relate experiences of life 'back home' and the rich oral tradition of the Caribbean, i.e., riddles, song-games, stories, folksongs, poetry and literature.

'Queen's English'   'Queen's English' differs from Patois not only in grammar and diction, but also in pronunciation. Members describe it as a 'posh voice,' a 'proper voice,' and as one of the 'principles one has to adopt to get ahead.' It is spoken primarily with others who are not known and who are perceived to be different, e.g., at work, in shops, and in dealing with council officials or the anthropologist.

'Queen's English' is also spoken with Patois speakers when the context is a public one, at public events hosted by the church and church auxiliaries. During Sunday services the notices and addresses are given in 'Queen's English,' and people will speak it when chatting in the foyer. 'Queen's English' is used to explicate a Biblical passage. Patois, however, can be inserted to facilitate meaning, express an allegory or render a parable.

Does Patois operate as a 'secret code' for signaling ethnic identity (cf. Eidheim 1969)? Susan Benson notes that ethno-specific traits, such as the use of Patois, do more than simply indicate ethnic affiliation to outsiders; they may also operate as a means of focusing and maintaining solidarity between sharers of the same cultural orientation (1981: 42). The use-value of Patois as a means of maintaining solidarity may vary across generations. For older members, there is continual movement between Patois and 'Queen's English' which can be a source of conflict and anxiety to them; they say they have 'difficulty in putting together English' or 'can't deliver an account in English.' Members and others constantly have to make a choice between two different codes of grammar and diction, e.g., replacing the first-person pronoun 'me' with 'I' or the non-gendered third-person pronoun 'ihm' [*sic*] with 'he' or 'she'; or 'pear' with 'avocado,' 'Irish spud' with 'potato,' 'grip' with 'suitcase.' Members feel they have to 'dot their i's and cross their t's' in public interaction with others, or they may risk conflict in communication.

For some older members, language choices are clearly polarized. However, among younger members this may not be the case, and the value of Patois as a means of solidarity may be attenuated. For those younger people either born or raised in Britain, language choice is not simply restricted to Patois and Standard British English but also includes British regional dialects indicative of urban sub-cultures, e.g., the use of cockney among young Blacks in London (Benson 1981: 42 and Gilroy 1987: 194–6).

'Authorized Worship Language' (AWL)   While language differentiates people in the wider society within the church language is denuded of divisive powers. It is understood that God hears people, speaks to people and speaks through people. The experience of being saved is a 'call' or described as 'when God speaks to me' (see comments by Lorraine in chapter 1): When this happens, the particular form language takes is unimportant:

> . . . suddenly . . . you hear a voice speaking – you look around, nobody around – if I were in the West Indies, a lot of people they would run away, and you know what they would say? They would say it is evil spirit. Praise Him! But when the Spirit of the Lord ready, He will call so that you understand. Praise Him! If you speak in English, He will talk in English. If you speak Spanish, He will talk Spanish. If you speak in Greek, He will speak Greek. If you speak Hebrew, He will speak in Hebrew. You will understand that God is speaking . . ..
> (Sermon, 25/5/91)

Similarly, when people communicate with God language and eloquence are unimportant, as He hears any language, whether it is Patois, 'Queen's English' or 'Authorized Worship Language.'

While everyday activities are transacted in Patois and 'Queen's English,' the religious sphere is differentiated by the use of 'Authorized Worship Language':

> . . . many of us are spiritual schizophrenics, we are one thing in church and another thing outside. The whole cycle switches into a different gear. We talk different. We behave different. We dress different. And it's as though the world we have in church has no relationship with what goes on outside. When you come to the church, know you just

sloops,[15] switch and you pray and go on different, and you think in authorized worship language and talk authorized worship and we thee and thou. When we go back in the other world where they hardly say thee and thou, it's as though we become a different person, and it's as though God is not portable. I want a God who is not only in church. I want a portable God! (Sermon, 5/10/91)

'Authorized Worship Language' denotes a change of lexicon characterized by the use of forms not ordinarily present in everyday speech, i.e., 'thee,' 'thou,' 'lendeth,' 'behooves' (see Appendix III). Unlike glossolalia, the use of AWL is not spontaneous; rather, its occurrence is restrained by context and its extent is limited to the use of quotations and stylized forms of address. This should not be misconstrued as suggesting that AWL is in any way impoverished; the use of such forms and the ability to pray, testify and preach using AWL fluently requires skill and a thorough grounding in scripture and hymns. An inspiring sermon is one constructed from scriptural references, song lyrics, Patois, and allegories and parables based upon common cultural experiences.

Although the significance of language in the wider society is thus minimized and transformed, language retains the potential to be mobilized as a mark of differentiation between brethren and non-members. When a person becomes a 'Christian,' his or her manner of speaking and subject matter, like dress and other forms of behavior, are said to change:

And even by my talking, I didn't know that people was noticing me and listening to me that much. Last week, Thursday . . . I was walking along with this White lady and I said, "Come on love, the road is clear, we can cross now" and she says, "Which church do you go to?" I said "I go to [King Street] I'm a Pentecostal." She said, "Oh, say no more, because from the moment I hear you talk something in me click; something in me click with you because I can tell that you are a Christian." And from there we hold such a wonderful conversation and when the bus came I go and sat with her and we been talking about the goodness of the Lord. (Lorraine)

---

15. Possibly a variant of the Patois word 'swips,' pass swiftly and easily; take up swiftly and easily, by analogy with 'sloop,' the single-masted sailing vessel (cf. Morris 1982: 171).

At a service for the reception of members, the Pastor reminded the new converts that they should lead a life of holiness in lifestyle and in speech. A 'Christian' is instantly recognizable by the manner of their expression "when you walk into a group, eyes turn on you, your laugh is noticed, your voice is noticed" (Sermon, 21/4/91).

Like AWL, glossolalia can be seen as a diacritic of identity, where it is deployed as a boundary between members as 'born again Christians' and nominal Christians. In one sense, because it lacks any secular social referent, glossolalia is the most absolute of the non-distinguishing languages which members speak. When members of the COG first began to speak in tongues in the late nineteenth century, it was believed they were speaking foreign languages like Spanish, Hebrew or 'African' and were therefore empowered to evangelize in foreign countries using the native language (Conn 1955: 24–5). 'Speaking in tongues' is viewed as a reflection of the Holy Spirit, not, as in other linguistic forms, as a choice made by the individual. In theory, all saints have access to glossolalia; therefore it is a democratic medium which transcends and dissolves differences of race, gender, class, etc. In practice, however, glossolalia can divide saints because not all members are baptized with the Holy Spirit. Among members who possess the gift of tongues, a distinction can be made between men and women. For men, extended glossolalic episodes occur in the context of regular public services like Sunday worship and Monday evening prayer meetings when they are preaching. For women, their occurrence appears to be less clearly defined; they may occur while preaching or as an intervention from the floor when others are preaching (see chapter 5).

Although language and the content of speech is used to reify the difference between 'us' and 'them,' language simultaneously forms the basis of interaction between members and non-members. While members should strive to lead a lifestyle which is set apart from the things of the world, members also have a responsibility to spread the Gospel of Christ and message of salvation to the world. This responsibility is effected through the medium of language in evangelizing, witnessing and testifying. Members should praise the Lord with every breath they take; they should cry out, shout out, sing out and tell as many people as possible.

We are Christ's ambassador. An ambassador visits England, ambassador visit Jamaica, Barbados. Call a meeting, that person coming so far has something to say. You are Christ's representative in this world. (Sermon, 16/9/90)

. . . every person in the body of Christ is called to be a witness, we are all called to the harvest field and we are responsible to God for this . . .. There was a Sister who was a member of this church . . . I remember one night in her testimony she said, "If I go to the Bull Ring [market] and get a good bargain, then I'm going to come back and tell my friend and take her to the Bull Ring so that she can partake of the good bargain that I have found," and Christianity is like that. (Sermon, 27/5/90)

Despite differences in personal styles, sermons represent a very rich area for analysis. The standard themes presented in sermons tend to be few: evangelism, prayer, how to serve the Lord, addressing the unsaved and encouraging the saved to be steadfast. Unlike the themes of sermons which are restricted, the actual language used to convey themes is far from impoverished or circumscribed. Religious language presents the speaker with a wider range of choices than he or she would have in everyday speech. In church, sermons, like the rest of the service, will be delivered in 'Queen's English' peppered with AWL and biblical quotations (King James' English) and Patois or Jamaican expressions and colloquialisms. Sermons are constructed from a combination of statements of theme, biblical quotations, allegories or parables, glossolalia, invocation of congregational response and songs, either in the form of recited or sung lyrics.[16] These elements are present in all sermons to varying degrees, and are manipulated by both men and women.

Many preachers begin their sermons with a short scripture reading. This passage becomes the reference point of the sermon, and the repeated statement of the theme serves to punctuate and structure the delivery. Within the sermon, the preacher will quote biblical maxims and epithets or simply list several scriptural references. These quotations engage the congregation in active participation as the congregation joins the preacher in reciting the quotation. The use of quotations, parables and Patois are constit-

16. See Martin (1990: 113–34) for a discussion of language and evangelical religion in the Caribbean.

uents in a shared system of beliefs, ideals and values. Only a 'Christian' will be fluent in scriptural quotations, and only African-Caribbean brethren will understand the experiences incorporated in parables and understand the use of Patois.

Work

As with race, nationality and language, occupational different-iation and stratification is also minimized and transformed within the ideology of the church. Membership is not contingent on whether one is a lawyer, nurse, factory employee, unemployed or a pensioner. Within the church, secular work is replaced by spiritual work. The imagery employed in a member's respon-sibility and commitment to spread the message of salvation is one of work; members are 'doing God's work,' 'working for the harvest,' 'working for the crown.'

Understanding members' responsibility to spread the gospel requires taking a closer look at their conscious perceptions of how their relations with others should be structured. The conflicting demands of sanctification and the responsibility to spread the message of salvation to the world governs the nature of these relations. While saints should not conform to the ways of the world and should not strive for the things of the world, they should conduct their lives in such a manner that others will want to emulate their behavior. This is a difficult ideal to achieve in practice:

> The lord of the harvest calls us to sanctification . . .. You see we have been conditioned from childhood to be part of a group. Individualism is discouraged in our society and so separation as a spiritual concept is very difficult for us to accept . . .. A sanctified life makes us more easily identifiable as disciples of Christ. I bet you the Hindus and these people I see around here, the Sikhs, they wear all of their uniform. You know exactly what they are when you see them, what's our problem? They be in the freezing cold wearing them little slippers, and them thin little silk things. They don't have a problem with it. We got a problem because we don't want to be separate. (Sermon, 6/10/90)

If saints strive for acceptance, they forfeit the very basis of their Christianity. The 'tendency to be accepted' – to adopt the values of the world – causes saints and the church to 'lose the cutting edge.' Their distinctiveness is lost and they become like other churches and nominal Christians of the world. Members can only be purposeful on earth if they are heavenly minded, for this will provide the necessary motivation and strength; they should strive to maintain the "standard of holiness . . . at home, work and in [their] daily lives" (Sermon, 28/5/91). They are continually reminded not to place their family before the Lord in their order of preferences. On one occasion a preacher visiting from the US admonished members for being 'unequally yoked' with unsaved friends:

> . . . be ye not unequally yoked . . . with unbelievers for what fellowship? . . . For the Bible said what fellowship, for those of you who have got good friends on the job, for those of you who go shopping with your unsaved ones, for those of you who claim that your best friend is not saved, that they understand you better than the saints, this is for you. Come out, come out from among them and be ye separate, sayeth the Lord. (Sermon, 6/10/90)

Or as another put it " . . . house, wife, children, car, are they your gods? Don't put material things before God. Let God be first in your life." (Sermon, 10/2/91).

While secular friendships and the domestic sphere are problematic, it is secular work which presents the greatest challenge to the maintenance of a 'Christian' lifestyle and identity. As was noted above, saints should not allow secular work commitments to overshadow their commitment to God and the church. On a return visit from Florida, a member of the church testified that he found it difficult to attend church because he was working all the time. When he had finished his testimony, the pastor warned him to 'Watch that job!' In another service, an unusual example where the church was compared to other faiths and found wanting, members were reminded that Jehovah's Witnesses ensure that they do not take a job or do anything secular 'which cuts across their commitment to their harvest' (Sermon, 5/10/91).

This responsibility can become onerous:

Me and my assistant manager, we have a good relationship but sometimes because I am a Christian, because I am a child of God, he sometimes try to abuse me in certain ways. He try to swears [sic] in front of me and say all manner of things. He's not an atheist but because I'm around he acts like he's an atheist. You see my point. And certain times, I have to say to myself, "God, you got to prove yourself." Come on now wherever you are, our workplace could be the harvest field. It is the harvest field, that where souls want to deliver, and it's one of the hardest place for us to fulfill Christian life at work . . .. It's alright when we're jumping in church . . .. Oh glory be to God! It's alright when the spirit of God is moving, but when you're out there and people smoking in your face and swearing at you, it's not so easy. (Sermon, 27/5/90)

What God has done for us . . . is not something we can lock up and shut it up in a can and not tell anyone. There are people who will tell me that they will work at a place for years and nobody knows you're a Christian . . .. Two weeks ago, I was at work and I was walking down the corridor and someone shouted to me from one of the offices and I went in and I thought it was something to do with work and this lady said to me, "Tell me what it's like to be born again." And it was like a question out of the blue and I stood at that door and for a second or two, I was a bit dumbfounded, because I didn't expect her to ask me that question . . . and brethren and friend, Sisters, young people, I told her what it's like to be born again . . .. (Sermon, 27/5/90)

Education

Secular Education   Most older church members received a partial primary school education, supplemented with religious instruction. In some cases, formal education was followed by apprenticeship in a trade such as carpentry or sewing. While the formal education received in Jamaica may not have been to degree level, it was felt to be sufficient for employment in Jamaica. Upon arrival it was noted that education and skills were not easily translated into sufficient preparation for employment in England. The education and training received at home were devalued by others. Early studies are replete with accounts of occupational downgrading (Foner 1979: 106; Glass 1960: 71; Patterson 1965: 68–9; Richmond 1973: 83).

Among members, education is associated with high status, good occupation, desired lifestyle and good speech in both England and Jamaica. However, absence of education can equally be used to symbolize lower status, inferior occupation, undesirable lifestyle and poor speech. Thus, education is one of the symbols co-opted by others to stigmatize migrants as inferior and different (see Carby 1982b). The educational attainment of migrants was mobilized by others not only as a justification for inferior employment, but as a diacritic of ethnicity and migrant status. This explains the reluctance of migrants to use education as a criterion of English class position and differences within the migrant population.

However, unlike the value assigned to Patois as a means of cultural expression and a strategy of linguistic inclusion and exclusion, members are less willing to accept the use of inferior educational provision as a fixed diacritic of ethnic identity and difference. They concede that education differentiates individuals and that some people may lack 'proper education,' but they will not concede that education has any value as a diacritic of essential ethnicity. We have seen that the congregation incorporates both educated professionals and non-professionals. Although the educational attainments of older members may be devalued and the educational opportunities of some younger members frustrated, education in itself did not loose its cultural value as a symbol of occupational mobility and prestige:[17]

> Some of us have problems putting together English. We say me instead of I, we don't dot our i's and cross our t's . . .. We came here and worked hard . . . raised family here. I raised family there . . . worked hard, one day say, 'get your passport together.' We made a sacrifice for young people's education. We took the jobs you wouldn't even do today. They wouldn't even train us in skilled jobs . . .. We worked hard and God blessed us . . . we put money into our children to educate for jobs. (Sermon, 4/2/90)

The minister then pointed to the suit he was wearing and said it was a gift from his daughter, who had a good job.

Members assert their intelligence and challenge state provision of basic formal education. At the church's Women's Festival, Sister

---

17. For a different interpretation of the significance of education for Jamaican migrants in Britain, see Foner 1979.

Louis, a politically aware and active woman in her early eighties, challenged the state's curriculum for language education and said that she would not stop pressuring the government until Patois was taught in the classroom. Mother Adler endorsed Sister Louis's position by adding, 'Who feel good about that? We are still intelligent people.' The church has taken practical steps towards meeting the need for better basic educational provision and the need for an education which reflects the cultural identity of Black-British children in a multicultural society. It has established a 'supplementary school' (for children aged five to eighteen), hosts career fairs and in the past held business- and computer-training classes.

For over ten years the main objectives of the Saturday 'supplementary school'[18] have been 'to supplement Black children's statutory education in the subjects of English, Mathematics and Cultural Studies. Each child is stimulated and encouraged to realize his/her fullest potential, enlarging on their personal confidence, self-esteem, concentration and cultural identity.'[19] The school is funded by an Inner City Partnership Program' and is staffed by local volunteers from the church and the community who 'reflect the children's black identity.'[20] It should not, however, be assumed that the school is specifically designed to supplement Black cultural studies. During school holidays, the 'supplementary school' runs a holiday program and each program has a different theme related to the multicultural urban environment in which the children live.

Education in the Church   As with nationality, race, general status markers, language and work, the value of secular education as a means of differentiation is minimized and transformed. God

18. I volunteered to teach four to six year olds basic English and Mathematics for six weeks. Some of the class groups were named after famous black figures in history. My group was named after Mary Seacole. Although the children I worked with were too young to benefit from the direct teaching of Black history and culture, the books we used to practice reading were specially designed to reflect their cultural identity and Caribbean background. On one occasion, we drew the Jamaican flag and discussed its colors and what they represent. On another occasion, we discussed the different animals found in England and Jamaica and the sounds they make.

19. Supplementary Education Project, Evening Finale Program (August, 1992) and *Welcome*, quarterly magazine of the NTCG, n.d.

20. Ibid.

chooses people regardless of intellect or educational attainments: "I don't care who have more education or who can hardly deliver themselves an account in 'Queen's English.' We need God" (Sermon, 6/1/91). "You may have a BA, an MA or a PhD, but without Jesus you can do nothing" (Sermon, 10/2/91). However, this does not mean that education is unimportant. As with the symbolic theme of status and material wealth, it is what one chooses to do with one's education that is important. Education and religious instruction are necessary if members are to uphold their commitment as Christians to evangelize and spread the message of the Gospel to others:

> I dare say God has spoken to some of you. God has even challenged many of you in your educational preparation to be able to learn languages . . . to be able to acquaint yourselves with other groups of people that you might go and minister. (Sermon, 7/10/90, delivered by a minister who is a school teacher)

The denomination and the local congregation provide members with the opportunity for religious instruction so that they may effectively minister to others. Every Sunday, before morning service, members of all ages attend Sunday school. The denomination's headquarters offers various courses leading to certificates and diplomas in theology at the national level which are intended for members 'engaged in or about to embark upon the practice of Christian ministry' and ranging from pastors to lay persons.[21] In 1963 the denomination founded a Bible Institute at King Street congregation. The Bible Institute differs from Bible school in that it offers certificates in theology and prepares members for ministry.

The graduation ceremony of the Bible Institute demonstrates the symbolic manipulation of the theme of education. One graduation I attended was held on a Sunday afternoon in the church and followed the general order of a Sunday service, with choruses and hymns, a scripture reading and collection, though the sermon was replaced by an address. The president wore an academic gown and mortar board, as did the graduates, while first-year students wore a uniform of maroon berets, blazers and jumpers.[22] The address of the guest speaker focused on education

21. Course flyer.
22. Sweater.

and ambition. He noted that 'learning makes a person ambitious for power and the things of the world,' but he beseeched the students to 'have the ambition to be like Jesus.' The value of their religious instruction was not so they could graduate and maybe one day become a bishop, minister or national overseer, but so they could be equal members of the body of Christ. The speaker mentioned his own educational frustrations. He was not disappointed he had not become a medical doctor. He would not trade his experience, because it is a 'tremendous thing to be engaged in God,' and 'secular employment only answers the secular needs of this world.' This theme was interspersed by the theme of self-sacrifice and the need to disentangle oneself from the things of the world if students were to be successful in their ministry. Although formal education to meet the secular needs of the world was being played down, he constructed his message through academic references to C. S. Lewis, Alexander Solzhenitzyn and others. Like the insertion of Patois colloquialisms and the construction of allegories and parables based on the common experiences of life back home, the use of literary quotes is a common device in the construction of religious oratory.

Food

Food as Practice   Caribbean foodstuffs and identity as a West Indian are inextricable (cf. earlier comments by Lorraine regarding breadfruit). The perception of Jamaicans, by members and others in England, as a lively, warm and sociable people is exemplified by the commensality associated with food. There are several contexts in which food is prepared and distributed among members of King Street congregation and others; these range from the twice-weekly luncheon of the elderly club to religious conventions and Sunday evening services.

Food is integral to the activities of the women's elderly club and has a strong Caribbean flavor. Such foods are simply palatable and familiar. When the women arrive for a session of the club they are offered a cup of mint tea, which is served only after the devotion has been offered. Later in the session, women may purchase a subsidized meal which is prepared in the church's large kitchen and served by some of the Sisters and Mothers of the congregation. The menu usually varies between 'rice and peas', oxtail stew, fried chicken, escoveitched fish,[23] vegetables and occasionally dessert. The Mother in charge once tried to organize daily menus, because she found catering to everyone's individual preferences frustrating and expensive. The Mother asked the women what they would like to have on the menus; she suggested macaroni and cheese or meatballs as alternatives. In response one woman half-jokingly replied that she wanted ackee and saltfish. Ackee and saltfish is not only more expensive and difficult to prepare but is also the 'national dish' of Jamaica. The Mother laughed at the teasing and let the issue rest.[24] Before eating lunch, each woman quietly says grace.

In addition to the main lunch, the distribution of food at the club includes selling, buying and sharing. Members with allotments or gardens may bring callaloo, pumpkin, rosemary, onions, tomatoes or other produce to sell. Sisters of the church often produce home-made foods like coconut drops or ginger beer which they sell among members and friends to raise funds for the church. If a woman is going to the nearby shop to buy harddough bread or meat for dinner, she may pick up a few groceries for a friend at the club. If a member has baked something at home, like beulah or totto cake,[25] she may bring some to share. If there is a celebration in someone's honor, like a mini 'send-off,' the Mother in charge will go to the shop and purchase some Schlöer[26] and cakes. Before these are consumed, members are invited to say a few words, the person may be presented with a small gift, and a prayer, but not grace, will be said.

The church hosted two special events at which food was on sale, a Christmas fête and a Caribbean night. The Christmas fête was an informal event to raise funds by selling Christmas cards, calendars, jumble,[27] shoes and food. The food on sale was West Indian but not particularly special or unusual except for the sale

23. A way of preparing fish steaks by marinating them in vinegar, onions, black pepper, green pepper and occasionally hot chilies.
24. The West Indian menu at the club is not unique to the NTCG. Apart from Patois, another issue cited as justification for the establishment of clubs which cater to the West Indian elderly was food. Other such clubs in the neighborhood, sponsored and run by secular organizations, also specialize in serving exclusively West Indian food.
25. Cakes made with ginger, molasses and brown sugar.
26. The brand name of a popular non-alcoholic substitute for wine.
27. British English for used clothes, goods and bric-a-brac.

of home-made sorrel drink, home-made ginger beer, syrup, peanut cakes, patties,[28] escoveitched fish and fried chicken. The Caribbean night was a conscious display of ethnicity aimed not at others, but at themselves. The original intention may have been to reach a wider audience, but nonetheless the gathering was composed primarily of church members, family and friends. The festival was not simply about being Jamaican but about being West Indian. There was a formal program where historical and descriptive vignettes of each island were read from tourist pamphlets and guide books. When each island's turn came, people from that island were asked to identify themselves by raising their hands. In the event, only one man from another island raised his hand, the remainder either being Jamaican or choosing not to participate. The evening proceeded with riddles, poetry, games, folksongs and a limbo competition. 'Special food' which takes considerable time and effort and is specifically Caribbean, such as ackee and saltfish, dumplings, fish fritters,[29] sweet potato pone,[30] grater cake[31] and gizzada[32] was on sale throughout the entire evening. The sale of foods at church-sponsored public events is not unique to the NTCG. At a 'Ladies' Day' held by the Seventh Day Adventist congregation, the food on sale included hot-dogs, 'run-down,'[33] 'tie-a-leaf,'[34] and totto cake. However, when the Sisters of the NTCG held a Women's Festival as part of the city-wide celebration of women's day, food was not on sale. The only apparent inter-section between religious beliefs concerning the consumption of food and drink and the consumption of comfortable ethnic foods is a negative one – the proscription governing the use of alcohol. Unlike in other African-Caribbean social get-togethers, alcohol plays no part in social events hosted by members; instead, guests are served a fruit punch or a non-alcoholic substitute for wine.

28. A Jamaican form of Cornish pasty usually made with curried minced beef.
29. Shredded salted cod coated in batter and deep fried in oil.
30. A savory-sweet pudding made with Caribbean sweet potatoes, coconut, coconut milk, sweet spices and raisins.
31. A sweet made with grated coconut, usually in pink and white layers.
32. A tart made with toasted grated coconut as the filling.
33. Mackerel cooked in reduced coconut water, seasoned with onions, tomatoes and salt, and served with baked sweet potatoes or plantains.
34. Parcels of cornmeal, carrot, desiccated coconut and sultana batter tied up in banana leaves or foil and dropped into boiling water.

Unlike the above occasions, where the distribution and consumption of food forms an integral part of the event, within the context of religious services, conventions and auxiliary meetings there is a clear delineation between the distribution and consumption of food and the spiritual aspect of the event. Nowhere is this more evident than at fasting services, held once a month, and at Ladies' fasting meetings. Here it is the marked absence of food that helps to emphasize the spiritual purpose of the service; it is usually traditional Jamaican foods which end the fast. On a regular Sunday, the congregation will disperse for Sunday lunch and return for the evening service. Members who have no one with whom to share lunch may be invited to share a traditional Jamaican Sunday lunch with a family and return with them for service in the evening. On a fasting Sunday, the service is not interrupted for lunch. A Sister may stand in the foyer and sell hot patties or gizzada after evening services. During district, regional and national conventions, the program is punctuated with long breaks for meals. When the Young Adult Ladies Ministry holds a monthly meeting at a members' home, the hostess will usually offer a light snack once the meeting of the auxiliary has ended and prayers have been offered. The snacks range from biscuits and crisps[35] to 'cheese and bun.'[36] When the Young Adult Ladies Ministry wanted to celebrate its Christmas dinner, we were all bussed to a Caribbean restaurant in nearby Dudley.

Food as Verbal Symbol   There are few examples of food imagery in religious oratory. When it does occur, it is often based directly on a biblical image:

> The true position of the church according to the teachings of Christ is to be the salt of the earth and the light of the world . . . to be the salt of the earth and the light of the world. What does salt do? It flavors and flavors and gives good taste . . . .. The bible says the Christian is the salt of the earth, therefore the world must be able to taste of us. See what God has done? We are the salt of the flavorings [sic] of the world. (Sermon, 27/5/90)

35. British English for potato chips.
36. A Jamaican version of a cheese sandwich where malted fruit loaf is substituted for bread.

Alternatively, the imagery of food as sharing can transform ethnic difference into transcendental moral values, as in the parable of 'water soup.' A Sister testifying about the goodness of God and his ability to see her through spoke about how in Jamaica, if a person was hungry, all they had to do was put a pot of water on to boil. People passing by the yard would look into the pot and add to it. Eventually, through sharing, the water would become food. The 'Lord's Supper' is the only religious context in which sustenance is integral to the service, and this is not specific to the NTCG or African-Caribbean Pentecostalism. Here the imagery of food is used to point out the symbolism of Christ embodied in the host, wine and Bible and the need to partake of the 'Lord's Supper' and read the Bible for spiritual nourishment.

In the extremely few examples where the imagery of specifically Caribbean food appeared in religious oratory, the comfortable taken-for-grantedness of ethnic food, 'yard food,' was contrasted with the constant self-scrutiny and alertness necessary for the 'Christian.' In the first example, a minister delivering a sermon argued that 'rice and peas' (a standard Jamaican dish) was too familiar. If you eat the dish too often and take it for granted, you soon become bored with it; consequently, if members were not careful, their spiritual life could become like that. Another minister, encouraging people to attend a seminar on evangelism, warned those who wanted to attend that they had to pack their own lunch, as it was not going to be 'a rice-and-peas seminar.' The purpose of the seminar was evangelism and how to win souls for Jesus, not socializing. These examples contrast a comfortable and unthinkingly inhabited ethnic identity with a 'Christian' identity which requires conscious commitment and effort – a very different position from the previous use of ethnic food as a basis for practical sociability.

Members' Models of Identity

One of the starting points for this discussion was that the relationship between an ethnic identity, variously constructed, and an alternative identity constructed out of religious belief was not necessarily congruent. Given different constellations of identity affiliation, how do individuals perceive the relationship between religious identity and ethnic identity? More specifically, how do they perceive this relationship when one identity is premised on exclusive ethnic identity and difference and the other on the common unifying experience of shared religious belief, where religious symbolism transcends ethnic, racial and cultural difference? Do saints see ethnicity and belief as two mutually exclusive identities? Are ethnicity and belief shifting constellations of identity, or do they form part of a unified field of identity?

The following views concerning the relationship between ethnicity and religious identity are taken from an opportunistic sample of women in the church. There is a sense for all these women that Christianity is more than ethnicity, though their models indicate variation in the meanings they attach to their participation in the community. For some respondents, the church was part of a specifically Jamaican history and style of religious worship. For Sister Louis, for example, the church is "a part of culture kept from Jamaica, brought it with you, part of identity, it relates to custom, culture, tradition." For Sister Smith, the daughter of a family in the church and a single middle-age professional woman, "ethnicity is important, it is about feeling comfortable in worship." Similarly, Mother Harvey felt that the church in England was not very different from the church in Jamaica: the church is 'a bit of Jamaica' in England, 'a bit of culture' she couldn't do without.

Other respondents, like Mother Adler, chose to stress how adopting Christianity meant dealing with racism by abandoning a confrontational attitude:

> religion and 'culture' are separate, you can't go to 'culture' to have religion (or *vice versa*). Christianity covers the entire culture in some ways. My 'culture' never want to mix with person and as soon as I become a Christian it have to be changed; there should be no partiality . . . 'culture' is there but you have to adjust yourself in terms of your Christianity . . . Background of 'culture' helps people to come to church, meet people that worship in the same way.

or

> Christianity helps you to deal with racism, develop your Christianity. There were people I didn't like, that I was prejudiced against . . . I had a prejudice in my heart, but broke it down. (Mother Harvey)

While these are all the views of older women, the same opinion can be found among members of the second generation; however, younger people are much clearer about the ways in which the character of the church and the problems of suffering which the church addresses can be linked to the experience of racial exclusion. Sister Debbie Adler, a young single woman raised in the church by her parents and a university student, offered the following explanation:

> Pentecostal worship originated not as a result of West Indian culture but as a result of the command Jesus gave the disciples . . .. Whether West Indian or European, the Pentecostal worship is the same. What is, however, different is the way it is expressed. As Black people, we are much more vibrant and more expressive in our actions than other cultures; therefore the way we express our worship is going to be just that different, i.e., jumping, clapping, music, speaking in tongues and running . . . because I am a Christian, I am not exempt from the pressures of racism and discrimination. However, through prayer and constant dedication, God helps us to deal with the varying distressing situations. When one becomes a Christian s/he is changed, therefore our actions and speech should not be as before; so if someone strikes us, or hits us, we are told to turn the other cheek . . . but we can get angry and sin not.

All these respondents, however, shared the view that the relationship between 'ethnicity' and 'religious identity' was one of overlapping constellations of identity (see Figure 4.1).

For others, however, especially those whose major point of reference was Britain rather than the Caribbean, the connection

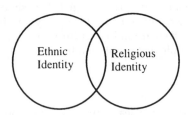

Figure 4.1 Ethnic and Religious Identity as Overlapping
Constellations

between the church, its history and ethnic identity was more complex. For example, Sister Mary Adler – a former social worker, single, in early middle age, a daughter of a church family and religiously very active – held different views. She felt the church was not about ethnicity but that it should be – and she made a contrast between a church passively based on Jamaican 'roots' and one actively committed to confronting racial issues in Britain:

> Black churches come that way by history, other churches weren't welcoming. Maybe it doesn't meet cultural needs enough. It's entrenched in the old Jamaican style, not looking for change, not challenging social issues or awareness. Christianity pushes aside ethnic identity and because I'm Christian I can't ignore that side of me. I treasure and value Blackness, but I don't exist in Blackness. People want a middle-class White ideology.

However, she added that she sat up and took notice when an element of 'what life was like back home' or the experiences of the older generation are inserted into a sermon. Like the women above, this Sister felt her Jamaican roots and 'Christian' identity overlapped; however, together they did not overlap or address issues which she faces as a Black person in Britain. The model of the relationship between her 'Jamaican,' 'Christian' and 'Black-British' identities can be represented as in Figure 4.2.

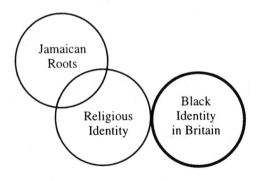

Figure 4.2 Ethnic and Religious Identity as Overlapping Constellations but Distinct from Black British Identity

The views of others suggest that 'Christian' identity transcends ethnic identity while offering a new inclusive identity which may be used in the sphere of inter-group relations. For example, Sister Young, a middle-aged woman who was raised in a Pentecostal church in Jamaica, felt that if she moved to another town and could not find a NTCG, she would join a White Pentecostal church. Sister Dwire was converted to Pentecostalism in Jamaica. She and her sister are the only family members in the church. She is middle aged and works as a secretary. She said, "You identify with something you already know. Culture is attached to religion, but I'm not in the church because of culture but because it's where I want to be." The views of these women can be expressed diagrammatically as in Figure 4.3.

How do religious leaders interpret the relationship between ethnic identity and religious identity and how do they interpret the significance of the position of the church? For the Pastor of King Street:

> Black churches, we came in from the West Indies – of course we are Black, won't be White because we live in England. So your people that came along who are Black as well, there's affinity to them – you know their needs, you can dialogue with them. And when we came in this country as from other areas of the world . . .. It [religious participation] means the same thing you do that side [where you came

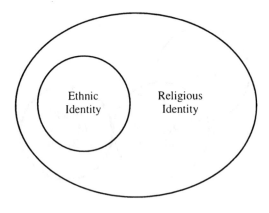

Figure 4.3 Religious Identity Transcends Ethnic Identity

from] where church is concerned. The English counterpart of church, here you could see is a little different, isn't it? So if there was no Black church everybody would be like the English, or none at all . . .. "A little of Jamaica"? In a sense, yes, but a lot of Christianity, Christianity. The people in Jamaica and some part of the other West Indies, say, for instance, feel that they ought to go to church. They got to spend their time worshipping the Lord. It means a lot to them. They come along, as they do, to England, feel "Oh you don't have to go to church, people go to the pub and drink and other places of amusement." They will either have to do that or continue to do what they used to do in Jamaica. Keeping your culture and your Christian conviction alive as well, Christian conviction. In other words, you broaden your horizon living in England, but you don't violate your conviction.

Joel Edwards, a younger NTCG minister who is also the co-ordinator of a nationwide African-Caribbean Evangelical endeavor, has said:

We are really experiencing a kind of identity crisis and it's very healthy: it's very painful, but it's very healthy. We are beginning to look at the label 'Black Church' much more seriously. We are now asking ourselves what the label means, what are the implications and ramifications of being called a 'Black Church.' Our schizophrenia is expressed by the fact that when we want a grant from the local authority, we are definitely a Black Church, but if somebody accuses us of not being sensitive to cross-cultural issues, we say, "We're the Black Church, but we're open to everyone and we have a few white members." . . . People are looking at the label, not because we are denying our essential blackness. It is not really true that we are a Black Church in an international context, but the label will ghettoize the Church if we are not careful. It tends to be exclusive rather than inclusive, in spite of our message and our responsibility of evangelism in a multi-cultural society . . .. To call a church a Black Church does not locate it in terms of its doctrinal stance; it says nothing about what we believe, and it leads to an assumption that all Black Churches are Pentecostal or Holiness . . . we have to look at ourselves as to how we are identified and labeled.

. . . I think it's necessary that if we are going to be true to the Gospel, true to the task of evangelism, that we don't promote the worship of culture above the worship of God. Heaven help us to find a proper balance, that we do not become assimilated and lose our selfhood, but neither do we become fossilized in a state where we don't see what the Lord is doing himself. (1991: 4)

It is clear from the comments of both men that while a sense of self as a 'Christian' can be part of a comfortably inhabited ethnic identity, 'Christian' identity is not coterminous with an essential ethnic identity. Christianity transcends the particulars of time and space, but it can be used to address experience in any socio-political historical juncture. In the context of Britain, where one receives a Black identity from others, one must strive to reconstruct and maintain not only a dignified sense of being Black but also one's identity as a 'Christian.' Being a 'Christian' can aid in the maintenance of a 'Black,' 'West Indian' or 'Jamaican' identity by playing a part in coming to terms with the sometimes painful experience of being Black in a society which denigrates blackness and also by providing a community in which the person can inhabit a reconstructed 'Black' identity which is both dignified and comfortable. However, this can only be accomplished if one continuously reaffirms belief and identity as a 'Christian.'

Summary and Conclusion

Returning to the debate referred to at the outset, how should members' participation in African-Caribbean Pentecostalism be interpreted? And how does this relate to the view that active forms of resistance, like those of Black male youths, are necessary in challenging racism? In her work among Tshidi Zionists, Jean Comaroff (1985) argued that we should reject a naive view of resistance. Tshidi Zionists were not engaged in active resistance, but this did not mean that they were not contesting and redefining their situation. This view can guide us in understanding the significance of members' participation in the NTCG and other African-Caribbean Pentecostal denominations. While African-Caribbean Pentecostalism as embodied in this denomination may not be waving the yellow, green and black[37] flag of resistance, this does not mean that members are not engaged in controlling and redefining their situation. Paradoxically the right of self-determination in the politics of representation is achieved through relative passivity. African-Caribbean Pentecostalism enables members to deal with the non-negotiable facts of racism by

37. The colors of the Jamaican flag.

providing them with the means necessary to control their own thoughts regarding themselves.

This means is the process of symbolic transformation: members transform the symbolic code of the wider secular society in which they are disadvantaged and replace it with a new spiritual code in which they are advantaged. Through symbolic transformation, the themes of nationality, status and material wealth, language, work, education and food are retained such that they appear to echo wider societal values, but they are given new inflected meanings. Members possess access to this code and can grasp the new meanings by virtue of their identity as Christians and their membership in the community of King Street and the denomination. As well as communicating new messages, these symbols also provide the practical means whereby individuals can experience their membership in the community of saints. In the spiritual code, the transformed symbols of nationality, status and material wealth, language, work, education and food neither celebrate selective aspects of essential ethnic identity in a revivalistic[38] sense, nor operate entirely independently of essential ethnic identity. They both incorporate and transcend ethnic particularity. What is distinctive about the symbolic transformation in which members engage is that it is premised on unification and inclusion as well as inversion.

The theme of nationality which divides people in the world is substituted with an inclusive form of spiritual citizenship and nationality. Members apprehend the symbol of spiritual nation-ality and experience the community marked by this symbol through the process of conversion and the resulting tie of sacred kinship with Mothers, Brothers and Sisters in the congregation. The attributes of status and material wealth which are also deployed in the secular world to differentiate people are of no importance for members. Members' symbolic code offers an alternative means of spiritual provision and ties this to egalit-arianism as a charter for behavior within the group. Occupational status and employment are substituted by the inclusive spiritual work of ministry and evangelism. Spiritual work denotes the individual's relation to the community, as every Christian has a responsibility to do God's work, and the individual's relation to the world since evangelism stipulates the nature of interaction

---

38. See Linton 1943; Wallace 1956.

between members and others. It is in the themes of nationality, status and material wealth and work that the conceptual distance between a Black identity and religious identity are the greatest. By subverting the symbolic code in which the lack of status, wealth or power is stigmatized and replacing it with an alternative code, members subvert some of the very criteria around which a Black identity derived from Black experience in Britain might be constructed and is indeed constructed in other African-Caribbean political movements.

The manipulation of the symbolic themes of language, education and food highlight the problems of a straightforward reading of religious participation as ethnic expression. Since divisive language is replaced with an inclusive language, on one level language can be interpreted as a transformed symbol akin to nationality, status, material wealth and work. Authorized Worship Language provides the means through which members can experience their community, make sense of the world and interact with others; it is the medium through which members learn their system of belief and in turn evangelize others, while the change in subject matter and manner of speech signals the individual's Christian identity to others. However, AWL is not the only cultural form contained within the symbol of language: it occurs in conjunction with Patois and Queen's English. It could be argued that through its inclusion in religious oratory Patois is honored and de-stigmatized and that therefore the mobilization of Patois in the religious realm is a celebration of ethnic identity, but there is also the inclusion of AWL and Queen's English which requires explanation. Patois, colloquialisms and allegories based on the experiences of actors as members of an ethnic group are inserted only when words fail, when the symbolic code of religious identity expressed through the mediums of AWL and 'Queen's English' is insufficient to express the meaning of an essential ethnic identity.[39] Unlike other symbols, the meaning of education is not completely inverted and transformed. Instead, education is a bifurcated symbol, manipulated by members in the construction of a religious identity, but also retained as a political representation

39. Confronted with a similar problem, Leslie Gill interpreted the use of Aymara language in Bolivian Pentecostalism not as an expression of ethnic identity, but as a confirmation of belief. Given the emphasis on 'speaking in tongues,' Aymara is considered as valid as Spanish for communicating with God (1990: 718).

of ethnic identity. As a symbol of religious identity, formal education differentiates members in society and is therefore substituted by religious instruction such that members are literally taught the basis of their belief and symbols of their community as well as being qualified to minister, evangelize and recruit new members for inclusion in it. Some of the value of secular education is retained, i.e., the use of learned knowledge in religious oratory and the application of professional skills to the activities and administration of the church. The provision of supplementary education is a space where members and non-members together can make political representations about Black identity. Food appears to be predominantly about ethnic identity. The preparation and sharing of food and meals provides the means whereby members experience a symbol of their ethnic identity while constructing a field of communication and interaction denoted by that symbol. However, the relationship between food as ethnic identity and fasting as an aspect of religious identity is clearly punctuated. The symbols of language, education and food represent not the revival of an ethnic identity, but serve to anchor ethnicity ambiguously to religious participation in such a way that religious identity is not independent of ethnicity.

As Anthony Cohen (1985a) reminds us, the community encompassed by a symbolic boundary encompasses heterogeneity and is thereby strengthened. Within the community of brethren there is variation not only in the age, gender and socio-economic circumstances of members, but also in the range of meanings which saints attribute to their identity. The community incorporates members who believe that their participation signifies religious identity, those who believe it can signify ethnic identity, and those who believe it should be mobilized as a political resource.

Although members appear to be engaged primarily in the process of expressing identity of the self to the self, they are simultaneously challenging the relations of power which determine the placement of the boundary. By explicitly drawing the boundaries of identity around that which is religious rather than that which is ethnic, members assert their right to self-representation. This does not mean that the painful and unavoidable facts of racism and disadvantage in Britain are denied within the church: as we have seen from member's comments, they are often explicitly acknowledged. The church offers a way of transcending the suffering engendered by such forces, and to label it 'compensatory' is to strip it of its power. To begin with the assumption of 'compensation' is to take for granted the ways in which the religious practices of the church work to offer a resolution of the problems – not least of which is a meaningful identity – confronting its members, and to assume members to be incapable of criticizing the injustices and evils of the society which surrounds them.

Being a 'Christian' offers members an alternative basis for the construction of identity and difference. It is their identity as 'Christians' which serves as the basis for their interaction with others in British society. Rather than define themselves as 'Black' in White society, church members identify themselves as model 'Christians' in an imperfect Christian society. This has important implications both for relations with unsaved Blacks and with the wider society: when members say they have to "ax culture and make friends"[40] they are simultaneously addressing Black culture and the dominant culture. It is significant that, just as contrasts are drawn between the corrupt world of the unsaved and that of the saints, distinctions are also drawn between personhood in the world and that of the 'Christian.' One of the issues at play in conversion was the rejection of an identity inscribed on the skin for one inscribed on the heart. For saints, in the unsaved world people are content to live with received identities; but to be a 'Christian' involves an act of will; to continue to be a 'Christian' requires constant effort, vigilance and self-scrutiny. Inasmuch as 'Christian' identity is constructed, the 'Christian' person is also constructed – one makes oneself, and God is the only arbiter of that project.

It is, however, equally significant that although the church advocates the inclusion of different groups through evangelism and conversion, membership in this congregation remains exclusively Black. The general absence of fellow White brethren is elided; rather than confront this, members resolve to step up their ecumenical and evangelistic efforts. This ambiguity renders the church an attractive alternative for members. If community identity were simply about being Black, it would devolve into another diacritic which others could use to exclude them. Hence the reluctance to label the church a 'Black Church,' 'Afro-Caribbean Church' or 'West Indian Church.' The symbolic markers

40. Quoted from an address by a young Sister at the annual National Youth Convention (14/4/90).

of the community of brethren are 'an ambiguous unity' (Abner Cohen 1980) of cultural and religious significance, and to reduce them to either would threaten the role of the church and the ability of members to negotiate the terms of their existence in contemporary Britain.

Chapter 5

Wives, Mothers and Female Saints: Women in the Church

The previous chapter illustrated that for members of King Street congregation, Christianity provides the lens through which identity is focused. However, it must also be added that gender conditions the way we perceive and experience our identities as persons. African-Caribbean gender has been the focus of dominant representations and as such could have been examined as a contested theme in the preceding chapter. Inasmuch as religion is a primary ideological site for the construction of the person, it is also a site for the construction of gender. Constructed through religious belief while simultaneously mediating experience as a person, the gender processes of the NTCG merit a separate discussion.

This study of gender is based on the premise that gender is culturally constructed sexual difference. Three basic questions underlie the argument: First, what are the ideas which surround gender? Secondly, if the conceptualization of gender entails agency and differential ideas of agency, what is the nature of agency for men and women in the church? The material presented takes the form of reflexive commentary: the symbols of gender manipulated in imagery and metaphors, social practice, and the structuring of agency; and the roles and activities in which males and females may be effective. Thirdly, why do women and men subscribe to the resulting model of gender?

Gender and Religion

The development of a gender focus within the field of Religious Studies echoes the development of gender studies within Anthro-

Plate 5 'Testimony in Song, National Youth Convention'. Source: Author

pology.[1] Informed by a Western feminist perspective, early work argued that the religious sphere was a patriarchal site which contributed to the subjugation and oppression of women (e.g., Holden 1983). Comparative material on women in other religious traditions inside and outside the Judeo-Christian framework suggested that matters were not so clear cut. We could not argue for the universal oppression of women in all forms of religious ideology and practice (King 1995: 6). Thus the status of women in religion was framed in terms either of a negative and oppressive model or a positive and liberating model (e.g., Sered 1994a, 1994b). To the idea that religion could be read as empowering was added the further distinction between women's religious participation which on the one hand, served practical and individual interests resulting in the temporary alleviation of individual women's circumstances by working within the parameters of the existing gender order (e.g., Berger 1976; Constantinides 1979; Steady 1976); and on the other, those forms of participation where strategic collective action challenged the pre-existing gender order, resulting in a permanent increase in the power and status of women (e.g., Baer 1993; Brusco 1995: 137; Falk and Gross 1989; Forman 1984; Saghal and Yuval-Davis 1992; Sered 1994a, 1994b).

In 'Women and the Inverted Pyramid of the Black Churches in Britain' (1992), Elaine Foster notes that although there has been a quantitative and qualitative rise in the participation of women in the churches, there has not been a corresponding increase in their access to positions of power, understood as legitimate authority vested in the churches' hierarchic offices. By occupying offices and positions of power within the churches, Black Churches give Black men a sense of self-worth that White British society has denied them. However, as she correctly acknowledges, Black men only hold power within the church on the approval of the women who constitute the majority of the membership. Foster describes the arrangement where men hold visible authority while women wield background influence as one of 'silent collusion' which can be understood as part of the dynamics of the relationship between Caribbean men and women (ibid.: 47–9). Since women are the mainstay of the churches, Foster asks, is there anything that is 'womanist' about the 'Black churches'? She argues that although

1. For a review of this material, see Bynum, Harrel and Richman 1986; Falk and Gross 1989; Holden 1983; King 1987, 1995; Madsen 1994.

the churches have given women strength and the means of fulfillment in the face of racism, the churches are guilty of sexism (ibid.: 55).

The themes of sexism and oppression did not raise themselves among the women of the NTCG, although the differences between men and women often did. In her collection of poetry, *The Real Me*, Esme Lancaster not only describes her experiences as a Black woman, political activist and Christian but also illustrates one way in which the relationship between religion and multicultural politics can be harnessed by women.[2] As a minister in the New Testament Assembly, Io Smith is aware of the sexism of the church, but she is also aware of the opportunities for old and young and male and female which are often denied in other religious traditions (Smith and Green 1989). It is misleading to read women's religious participation in terms of externally defined dichotomies which make use of narrow definitions of power, oppression and advantage. To understand the dynamics of gender in Black Churches, we need to put aside the preoccupation with visible office as power and a preconceived idea of who is a 'liberated Black woman' and focus instead on everyday relations between men and women and the construction of gender in the churches.

There has been a recognition that religion defies generalization and that there is a need to study the complex and ambiguous processes which contribute to the construction of both male and female gender in religion (e.g., Brusco 1995; Gilkes 1986; Hacket 1984; Holden 1983; King 1995). In addition to a dual gender focus, the challenge of difference which the Black feminist critique brought to women's studies and anthropology is also a critical starting point for the development of gender studies in religion. Early-wave Black feminism proposed a 'unified Black identity' which posited 'the experience of racism as defining the difference with White women' (Anthias and Yuval-Davis 1992: 102). However, there is growing recognition that the conceptualization of a 'unified Black identity' and 'unified Black sisterhood' resulting from racism is as problematic as the previous idea of universal sisterhood. The lives of Lorraine, Elma, Martha and other women inside and outside of the church and fictional characters like Tanty, Adella and Selina poignantly illustrate that differences obtain among Black women as well as between Black and White women.

2. See also Brown et al. 1990.

Gendered identity, whether Black or White, cannot be understood without reference to the specific historical, cultural and social circumstances and experiences which provide the contexts for construction. Because religious participation is critical for configuring gender, we need to recognize that there is also variation at this site.

Gender and African-Caribbean Religious Practice

It is highly improbable that the constructions of gender within the diverse forms of African-Caribbean religious practice would be the same. An example is provided by a comparison between Rastafarianism and Pentecostalism. Writing with reference to Jamaica, Austin-Broos establishes Rastafarianism and Pentecostalism as 'complementary,' 'gender specific' ways of negotiating the moral worth of working class men and women (1987: 1; 1991–1992). In the contexts of both Jamaica and Britain, Rastafarianism is reified in the literature as a Black male religion which constructs a Black male identity in the face of emasculating oppression and racism (Barrett 1977; Cashmore 1979; Gilroy 1987; Kitzinger 1969; Pryce 1979). In addition to inverting the dominant values of society, Rastafarianism also inverts the patterns of Jamaican working-class gender relations and domestic organization. Rejecting the power of women as head of the household, with the capacity to nurture, feed and socialize children, Rastafarianism posits the agency of mature men who, as fathers, have the responsibility to procreate widely (Austin-Broos 1991–1992: 308) and look after their sons (Kitzinger 1969: 254, 259). Austin-Broos notes that by rejecting the idea of monogamous Christian marriage and substituting it with the potentially polygynous "joining of hands," Rastafarianism combines the idea of the nuclear family with its own idea of African masculinity and thus paradoxically duplicates 'the status and freedoms of the middle-class patriarch' (1987: 17–18 and 1991–1992: 308, after Barrett 1977).

The placement of Rastafarian men at the center of remade domestic organization rests on their placement at the center of religion. Unlike other forms of African-Caribbean religious practice, where men have formal leadership roles but women form the majority of the membership and are recognized for their greater spirituality, in Rastafarianism, men outnumber women where they are morally superior and women must seek access to spirituality through men, (Rowe 1980: 15, in Austin-Broos 1987: 18–19). As 'virgins' and 'Queens,' women have no control over their sexuality or social and physical reproductive capacities; they are left little authority in the domestic sphere and none in ritual practice (Kitzinger 1969: 253–4; also Barrett 1977: 2, 184–5, 142, 209). The religious ideology of Rastafarianism replaces the figure of a God endowed with the feminine attributes of nurturing, love, warmth and patience with a virile and powerful God who seeks just retribution and who, 'in contrast to the accepted modes of fatherhood in Jamaican peasant society,' is a responsible and generous provider (Kitzinger 1969: 261).

If Rastafarianism appeals to males and legitimizes male dominance, then what is it about Pentecostalism, a seemingly male-dominated, sexually orthodox tradition, which appeals to women? In Jamaica, social adulthood is contingent upon having offspring, but single motherhood, visiting unions and female-centered households are considered of dubious moral worth relative to middle-class norms. Austin-Broos suggests that in this context Pentecostalism accommodates the circumstances of women and helps them to resolve some of the ironies inherent in Jamaican conceptions of sexuality, gender and social status (1987; 1991–1992: 308–9). If being a single mother is an inescapable fact of life, a woman can be redeemed of the associated social stigma. While her status as a single mother and her relations with men create problems in other Christian denominations, these circumstances may very well be imperative factors in conversion and acceptance into the Pentecostal fold. The sin and social stigma of single motherhood is washed away by the blood of Jesus at conversion, and striving for sanctification and baptism by the Holy Spirit is sufficient justification for a woman to break or regularize a visiting union (Austin-Broos 1987: 23–4). Working-class Pentecostalism also acknowledges and supports the spirituality of women which can be expressed in institutionalized ritual roles and positions of formal leadership and authority, i.e., as deacons, bishops and pastors (ibid.: 11). Interestingly, Austin-Broos notes that the emphasis of lower-middle-class Pentecostalism differs from lower-class Pentecostalism; here less attention is focused on fornication and single-motherhood, and women are more subordinate, possessing fewer ritual and leadership roles (ibid.: 13).

While these accounts provide a glimpse of women in Rasta-farianism and Pentecostalism in Jamaica, there is little attempt to account for the construction of female gender and the practices of women in Rastafarianism in Britain; limited evidence suggests it is somewhat similar to Jamaica (Cashmore 1979: 78–9). By contrast, men and women both participate in the NTCG. Women are not marginal but remain at the center of domestic and religious organization. How should this be interpreted in the context of Britain when both Black men and women are affected by racism and discrimination? It could be suggested that differential religious participation reflects the specific circumstances of different segments of Britain's African-Caribbean population and provides them with different identities premised on the inversion of the dominant values of society and the rejection of 'common-sense' assumptions concerning Black people. It is tempting to suggest that Rastafarianism is a religious movement of the economically disinherited Black man while Pentecostalism is a religion of the relatively economically inherited Black woman. But this would be a crude model which ignored the participation of women in Rastafarianism and the large numbers of men in Pentecostalism while also underplaying the complexities of gender images within the NTCG.

Approaching Gender

A useful approach for understanding gender processes in religion is to focus on the cultural construction of the 'person' and on how people experience themselves as 'persons' (Strathern 1980, 1981, 1987a, 1987b, 1988; see also Moore 1988: 38–41). The cornerstone of this approach is the realization that if the dichotomies of culture/ nature and domestic/public are cultural constructions, then the concepts of individual and person (see chapter 3), inequality and power are also culturally constructed. If 'persons' are culturally constructed categories, how are they assigned value? Value may be assigned by reference to ideas about inequality understood as difference. If we suppose that persons are differentiated on the basis of inequality, we must understand what is meant by inequality. Inequality may be the attribution of different interests, motivations, choices and actions to persons. If power is a corollary of a person's interests, then we must understand the scope within which that person may express and/or exercise his or her interests–agency. Marilyn Strathern argues that our focus must shift 'from the nature of inequality between the sexes, to the construction of inequality through sexual difference' (1987a: 6). Instead of seeking absolute power as the difference between men and women, we seek to understand how the actors construct relations and assign power to one category of people and assign another an unequal position.

With reference to conceptions of personhood, Strathern explodes the idea of social agents. She notes that actors are not simply the 'doers of things done' but may also work on behalf of someone else. Therefore, the interests and motivations in terms of which they act cannot simply be read-off their actions – interests may be ambiguous. Hence, the source of one's effectiveness may be equally ambiguous. This raises the question of what constitutes effective action. Strathern introduces the concept of agency as a 'shorthand' for questions about how 'people allocate causality or responsibility' to persons which entails ideas about the 'sources of influence and the directions of power.' For Strathern, the concept of agency requires a focus on 'the contexts in which will is relevant to action' and thus how will is defined in society. She argues that the idea that persons may be accountable for their actions may typify particular social categories under particular circumstances (Strathern 1987a: 22–3). The concept of agency helps us to understand how certain acceptable forms of efficacy are tied to certain social categories. Since efficacy is seen as part of person-hood, it remains to be seen how capabilities and responsibility come to be associated with gender.

In addition to understanding how males and females are constructed as persons, a concept of dynamism and variability within the categories of women and men is crucial for under-standing gender processes in the NTCG. Connell (1987) presents a model for the study of gender that examines how men and women are assigned value with reference to cultural value systems and the activities of men and women and the domains in which they conduct their activities. For Connell, what is needed is a theory of practice in which the 'gender order' of each society is the result of a series of interlocking and potentially contested and conflicting 'gender regimes' – in churches, schools, workplaces, homes, etc. The value of his approach lies primarily in his view that gender is a process, the outcome of a set of social practices which connect nature and culture in a non-reductionist manner. Social practice continuously produces new meanings and forms which in turn can be negated and transformed to produce newer meanings and forms (ibid.: 78–9). This perspective prevents us from reifying the structure of gender and assigning pre-eminence to a single key determinant. Thus it is possible to account for inconsistencies and contradictions in any society's gender order, and to see how women as individuals, both structured by and participating in the structuring of the gender practices of the patriarchal society which they inhabit, may come to have different and perhaps inconsistent 'gender identities.' From his work we can begin to see why 'woman' as mother, sister, daughter and wife may possesses different value attributions all within the sphere of the family. The categories of 'man' and 'woman' are multifaceted; the value of woman as 'mother' is composed of a constellation of labor, power and cathexis which differs from the constellation that values woman as 'sister.' By the same token, we can also come to terms with the broad range of women's status in society overall.

The second virtue of Connell's approach is that it provides the necessary conceptual space to recognize that in heterogeneous societies, any one gender regime like the family is subject to multiplication, variation and diversification. Thus we can accept that Jamaican or African-Caribbean gender regimes can differ in several respects from White British ones. However, it is not enough to recognize differences of ethnically specific gender regimes: we need to assess the nature of difference. To what extent are African-Caribbean gender regimes in Britain affected by dominant ideologies of race and gender and the forces of the state and the labor market? Can the differences of African-Caribbean gender regimes simply be attributed to being separate and autonomous from other gender regimes because they are replications of Caribbean ones? We cannot rely on a static, dated, partial and suspect view of Caribbean culture to posit a separate and auto-nomous African-Caribbean gender regime in Britain (Phoenix 1988). The construction of ethnically specific gender regimes in Britain results from the effects of wider forces on autonomous conceptions of gender – the construction of gender in dominant White British gender regimes and the dominant White British gender order (Anthias and Yuval-Davis 1992: 108; see also Ware 1992).

Of further utility is Connell's concept of gender identity as the outcome of social practice within interlocking and potentially contested gender regimes. Within the diversified gender regimes of heterogeneous society, it is thus possible to see not only that Jamaican concepts of gendered identities, e.g., mother, differ from White British concepts, but more significantly that there may be inconsistencies and contradictions in gendered identities between different Jamaican gender regimes. In other words, the Jamaican concept of mother held in the regime of the family may differ from that held in the regime of the church. Further, through social practice, actors possess the capacity continuously to make and remake gender identities. It is therefore possible that through social practice, actors can use the concept of identity in one regime to contest and remake identity in another.

Gender and Pentecostalism

Pentecostalism varies widely in the extent of formal authority and leadership allocated to women. This variation results from each denomination's mediation of a theological position of absolute male dominance and a substratum of negotiated gender roles. It is the mediation of gender roles inherent to the process of Pentecostal gender construction that makes it difficult to concede that women are oppressed or reap only temporary benefits from religious participation. As with ideas of the person, Pentecostalism develops new meanings of gender and new social relationships within socially prescribed boundaries (Cucchiari 1990; Gill 1990: 708, 712 and 1994: 131). Although Pentecostalism may not topple the existing order, it has the capacity to transform gender.

Studies on Pentecostalism in the United States (Lawless 1983, 1987, 1988, 1991), Latin America (Brusco 1995; Gill 1990, 1994) and Italy (Cucchiari 1990) provide significant evidence for the transformation of gender. In these contexts, the wider gender order is characterized by male dominance. In Italy and Latin America, ideas of patriarchy, machismo and a complex of honor and shame circumscribe the lives of women as wives, mothers, daughter and sisters. Participation in Pentecostalism enhances the circumstances and status of women, not by directly questioning traditionally subordinate female roles, but by challenging ideas regarding traditional male roles. Ideas about gender in the churches are not made in isolation; instead, they address critical issues arising in the hegemonic gender order. In these accounts Pentecostal women 'benefit' from relations with men who are less typically 'male' as defined by the hegemonic gender order (Gill 1990: 717; 1994: 135). Pentecostal men become less typically male through a reformation of machismo (Brusco 1995) or a transformation of patriarchy (Cucchiari 1990).

Brusco records that in Colombia, the traditional male role is one of machismo (a complex of behaviors such as aggressiveness, womanizing, drinking and gambling) which results in a high degree of sexual segregation, the divergence of male and female interests, goals and motivations, individualist consumption patterns, and attenuation of the male roles of father and husband, which jeopardize the safety of women and the security of the domestic unit (1995: 78). However, an acceptance of the ethos and lifestyle of Christianity is incompatible with the maintenance of machismo (ibid.: 137). Women benefit from male conversion; as men fulfill the Pentecostal male role of husband and father, the focus of their interests converge with those of women–the domestic sphere (ibid.: 145). Similarly, Gill notes that for rural/urban Aymara migrants in Bolivia, the significance of Pentecostal participation is the modification of male forms of behavior (drinking and gambling) which are potentially harmful to women (1990: 708, 717; 1994: 133).

If the ideal Pentecostal male is the seemingly patriarchal and authoritarian husband and father, how is he less traditionally male? The answer to this puzzle requires a shift in analysis from practical observations to the examination of how gender is symbolically constructed and given meaning within the church (Cucchiari 1990: 696). Complex and ambiguous ideas of gender at this level are informed by the interplay of different models of personhood, agency, kinship and domestic organization. Although God and Jesus are models for man and legitimize male dominance in the church, it is significant that the Pentecostal God and Jesus are imbued with feminine as well as masculine qualities (Brusco 1995: 117; Cucchiari 1990: 689–90; Gill 1990: 717, 1994: 134). The traditional Sicilian father is 'aloof,' 'judgmental' and 'punishing,' but the God worshipped in the Pentecostal community is feminized. God is maternal, empathetic, loving and emotionally vulnerable but not completely devoid of masculine qualities, is also a craftsman who has the power to shape the will of others

(Cucchiari ibid.). The melding of genders in the symbolic image of God and the blurring of male and female spheres provides a model for the possible redefinition of gender (Cucchiari ibid.: 693; also Brusco 1995: 117; Gill 1990: 717; 1994: 134).

If the hegemonic gender order of a society values authoritarian patriarchy or machismo, why would a man subscribe to the model of gender provided by the church? Brusco (1995) appeals to the idea that although machismo is the ideal, there are a range of male roles in Colombian society. The social and financial costs, as well as the high male mortality rate associated with machismo, make it unlikely that all males will conform to this role; thus the male role as constructed by Pentecostalism is an alternative for Colombian men (ibid.: 114–15, 120). Cucchiari, however, suggests that the Pentecostal gender regime is a revitalization movement for a hegemonic gender order in crisis and that men and women perceive the benefits of Pentecostalism differently (1990: 699–700). In a milieu of honor and shame, the availability of education, contraception, abortion and divorce and the increasing independence of women are perceived as threats to male sexuality, identity and prestige (ibid.: 698). Cucchiari argues that men participate in Pentecostalism because it reconstructs the 'lost golden age of patriarchy' and creates a domain where they can regain the leadership, authority and honor which is under threat in the hegemonic gender order. Although women have gained greater independence by changes in the dominant gender order, they lack the prestige formerly associated with their roles of wife and mother. Hence participation in Pentecostalism is a means whereby women can transcend the gender subordination of the new patriarchal order and shift power and prestige in their direction while acting in a way that does not contradict traditional values (ibid.: 700–1). The recognition that there is variation in societal gender roles, that the construction of gender within Pentecostalism is not made independently of wider ideas concerning appropriate gendered behavior, and that men and women may share the culture of Pentecostalism differently but in ways that are not mutually exclusive are relevant to understanding the process of gender in the NTCG and why both men and women subscribe to models of personhood and gender in the church.

While there is clearly a transformation of ideas of masculinity and appropriate male behavior in these diverse forms of Pentecostalism, is there a corresponding transformation in the meaning of femininity and appropriate female behavior? In the rural Pentecostal churches of Indiana and Missouri where folklorist Elaine Lawless (1983, 1987, 1988, 1991) worked, women theoretically could not have authority over men in the church, yet she met women who were not only itinerant preachers but pastors of their own congregations. Lawless' data suggest that there are two ways in which women reduce the threatening aspects of being a preacher and a pastor. First, women can maintain the idea of female subservience to man and God by basing their legitimacy to preach on external spiritual agency–'a call from God' (1991). In this argument, God confirms the subservience of women by employing them as 'handmaidens,' and the autonomous agency of women is attenuated. Secondly, women also appeal to a model of women as mothers (1987, 1988). The pastoral work of nurturing, counseling, empathizing and praying for others agrees with ideal maternal attributes. Hence, pastoring is an extension of the already condoned female role, and women consolidate the basis of their pastorate by manipulating maternal and reproductive imagery in their sermons and interviews (1987).

Although there are no formal positions of authority or leadership for women in the Pentecostal community studied by Cucchiari (1990), the close association of women with the spiritual can be manipulated to give women a public voice. There is, however, an ideological distinction between the spiritual gifts of women (understood as illegitimate) and the ministries of men (understood as legitimate), which undermines the potential for formal leadership among women (ibid.: 689–92). Cucchiari argues that the ambivalent attitude towards women's spirituality and leadership results from the contradictions between two intersecting models of family in the church. These are the model of the egalitarian family of God's children, where men and women are reduced to 'abstract "souls" shorn of all hierarchical social identities, including gender,' and a model of 'brothers and sisters in Christ,' which in a culture infused with ideas of honor and shame represents a hierarchical model of familial relationships (ibid.: 696). Within the highly conservative manifestations of White American and Sicilian Pentecostalism, evidence suggests that the redefinition of female gender and agency is accomplished by appealing to ambiguous interstices of meaning which result when different models of agency, personhood, kinship and domestic organization are played off against one another.

The gender processes within the NTCG are broadly comparable with the dynamics outlined for other Pentecostal traditions. In the NTCG there is a mediation of gender, the creation of new meanings and the transformation of gender accomplished on practical and symbolic levels. The outcome, however, is not the transformation of male dominance, but the tempering of a perceived tradition of female dominance which is at odds with and pathologized by the hegemonic gender order.

Imagery: The Head and the Neck

'For the husband is the head of the wife, even as Christ is the head of the church'[3]
'Man is the head, but woman is the neck'[4]

Church members do not differentiate between a 'Christian' man and a 'Christian' woman. Members are quick to point out that 'God is no respector of persons,' whether rich or poor, Black or White, male or female. Both male and female 'saints' must go through the same process of salvation, repentance, conversion and baptism. Whether male or female, all saints must lead a 'sanctified life,' a life that is 'Christlike' or that emulates Christ. However, a high proportion of congregations are composed primarily of women and there are currently more female converts than male. The circumstances which may lead one to seek conversion or the manner in which a person is saved may be gendered, e.g., sending a child to Sunday school, the evangelism of women by women, or a mother waiting up for her son. Yet, 'Christian' identity is not explicitly constructed around specific male or female issues, but out of issues which confront both male and female members equally.

While at one level of abstraction being a 'Christian' or a saint is not a gendered identity, at the level of social practice gender is important. It would be difficult, if not impossible, to be a saint without adhering to the norms and expectations that apply to men and women respectively and which differentiate them. The

3. Ephesians 5: 23.
4. Jamaican proverb used by women informants.

pervasive idiom of conjugality and kinship within the church that encompasses the ideal of the 'Christian family' and draws upon assumptions concerning actual kinship and family organization serves to order the meaning of male and female, the relations between men and women, and the status accorded to men and women, as well as the roles and activities which are available to them.

Within the church, men are regarded as patriarchs, the authority of the household, the providers and protectors. Men are strong: they are the leaders and ultimate decision-makers. As providers, they are authorized to make financial decisions concerning the household and the church. As husbands and fathers, they are entitled to admonish and discipline. The relationship between Christ and the church is taken as a metaphor for the relationship between husbands and wives. 'Husbands love your wives, even as Christ also loved the church. . ..'[5] The metaphor of Christ and the church also legitimizes the authority of the husband. 'For the husband is the head of the wife, even as Christ is the head of the church . . ..'[6] As in Italian and Latin American Pentecostalism, there is a suggestion that God and Jesus can at times be endowed with feminine qualities. On one vivid occasion a male preacher grabbed his breast while likening the breast of God to the nourishing and comforting breast of a mother (see also the first testimony in Appendix III). Here too the sufficiency of the traditional male role is challenged: husbands have responsibilities as well as power. A 'good man' is clean, sober and monogamous. It is not enough for men to be providers and disciplinarians; women challenge men to surpass the 'ideal male role,' to be instrumental and take on attributes which are traditionally accorded to women. Women want men to be responsible and caring, to have stamina and to be the backbone of the family and church:

> We don't want our men chicken [sic] in Church of God . . . men to be like that. We want caring men . . . We want caring men. We don't want any minimal men, too many min [sic] people about . . . too many min men about. They sit down . . . is always the woman lifting her hands. (Sermon, 10/3/91)

5. Ephesians 5: 25.
6. Ephesians 5: 23.

Here the ideal model for the family and gender roles provided by the church is a 'model for,' not necessarily a 'model of,' the social world of church members. It contradicts the variety of Jamaican family practices, and for some members it contradicts their own lived experiences in both Jamaica and Britain. At the same time, these exhortations point to the reality that although men can be responsible providers, it may still be necessary for women to contribute towards the economic provision of the domestic unit while bearing most of the responsibility for social and domestic reproduction.

Women, by contrast, stand in relation to their husbands as the church stands in relation to Christ. 'Therefore as the church is subject unto Christ, so let the wives be to their own husbands in everything.'[7] 'Wives, submit your selves unto your own husbands as unto the Lord.'[8] Women are seen as 'the weaker vessel'; as wives, they should be subservient and passive but also be helpful, serving and supportive. As a wife, a woman should respect the authority of her husband and defer to him. A good woman is wise, sober, modest and discreet. When women in the church cite the proverb quoted at the beginning of this section, in one sense they are supporting this view. On another level, however, it can be read very differently. After all, the neck is not simply subservient to the head but supports it and controls its movements; and Jamaican women are well aware, as their life histories indicate, that they are often the ones bearing the most domestic responsibility.

Biblical women serve as role models, both positive and negative, and there is great variation in the female role models chosen: the wanton woman at the well who spread the gospel to the Samaritans; the wise and prepared virgins; the sisters Martha and Mary and Dorcas and Lydia, who sewed clothes for their brethren. Women are rarely likened unto the Virgin Mary. When asked about the significance of the Virgin Mary, women suggested that she was important because she was the mother of Christ, but they did not single her out as a model of 'woman.' The range of female biblical role models mediates between the ideal role and actual roles of women. It acknowledges the different domestic circumstances of women, while also acknowledging the different interests and agency of women that are vested in these different roles. Biblical

7. Ephesians 5: 24.
8. Ephesians 5: 22.

stories of female role models can also be ambiguously deployed, e.g., the use in the following sermon of the story of Abigail and Nabal:[9]

Thank God for his wife, Abigail . . . thank God for the wife Abigail! This was a woman of vision . . . this was a woman. Maybe you know . . . maybe the Bible says, "Man is the head of the home . . . man is the head of the home," but when this woman hear of what was going to take place . . . the woman, Abigail, said to her servant, "Saddle an ox, put some food, get ready . . . put there plenty food" . . . When you hear death is at the door, you want to do something about it. You want to prevent it . . . She heard what was going to take place in her household . . . Abigail, the wife, she get going to stop bloodshed from coming into her house and when she meet David she get down off her horse, she bowed[. . .] Praise the Lord! . . . that woman of vision, she can stop that gap . . . she didn't consult with her husband. The writer says there's a time, there's a place for everything. If maybe she did say to her husband, "You know I'm going to send off food to David, although you didn't send it." Maybe he would get miserable and upset and want to do something about it, so the wife didn't tell him anything at that time . . . You see when it's wife and husband everything belongs to you, what belongs to the husband, it belongs to the wife. So since the husband didn't want to help, the wife helped. It was in her position that she could help, so she take action . . . and praise God, her household because of the action that she had took her household was spared . . . In a time of crisis, everybody running for their life . . . so she run out and when she came back, she find her husband drinking. He was drinking until he was drunk. He was making merry with his friends . . . imagine brethren . . . It is a time of crisis. . . ..

. . . this is about woman facing crisis . . . in time of crisis . . . but sometime men make women run into crisis also [murmur of agreement from congregation]. Sometimes women get into crisis because of husbands not facing up to their responsibility, because this was a man who not facing up to his responsibility. He was only a provider. . . .. (Sermon, 10/31/91)

The most pervasive definition of women in the church, however, is as mothers. Yet not all cultures define 'woman,' 'wife' or 'mother' in the same way, nor do they necessarily establish the same

9. I Samuel 25.

connection between woman, wife and mother. The status of mother in African-Caribbean cultures is more important than that of wife in defining the social status of females as women (MacCormack and Draper 1987; Smith 1988: 137; Sutton and Makiesky-Barrow 1980: 493). Parenthood is symbolic of maturity for women and virility for men (MacCormack and Draper ibid.: 146; Smith ibid.). A woman may become a wife later in life, after her reproductive career is ended, or not at all, while she is more likely to become a mother earlier on. Hence, Caribbean scholars have argued that parenthood is an attribute of each parent separately and is not (as in mainstream British ideals) an expression of the conjugal or co-residential union between them (MacCormack and Draper ibid.: 154; Smith ibid.). The uncoupling of parenthood from marriage in this way is commensurate with a gender system in which women can achieve social status and prestige independently of their relations with men (McCormack and Draper ibid.: 146; Sutton and Makiesky-Barrow ibid.: 478). Because motherhood is central to the idea of social adulthood, authors comment that the absence of a child is perceived as unnatural and unhealthy: barren and childless women are to be pitied (cf. McCormack and Draper ibid.: 147, 155; Sutton and Makiesky-Barrow ibid.: 493). However, when economic activity (e.g., economic migration) is incompatible with social reproduction, mothers often rely on 'kin' networks and foster out children. This practice provides the opportunity for social motherhood to women who may not have had children. Thus it may be useful to distinguish between biological and social mothers who provide for and enable others on the one hand, and women who are neither biological or social mothers and do not provide for or enable others the other.

Ideas of women as mothers in the church reflect distinctive Jamaican patterns. For church members, motherhood is symbolic of a female maturity which is not necessarily premised on a conjugal relationship associated with a biological act of parturition. The simplest reading of motherhood is as an emotional attribute specific to mature women. The capacity to mother is seen as an aspect of all women's nature, not simply those who have given birth; it is the act of mothering which is underscored rather than the status of biological maturity:

It is good to be here this morning, Mothering Sunday,[10] and although there might be people here who have not biologically brought forth young ones, but I know you too are nurturing and helping to bring up young ones. There are those of us who does [sic] as mothers . . . they are important because they are going to be able to fall in where the biological mother has perhaps failed or not able to keep up certain things. . .. (Sermon, 10/3/91)

Since the kinship role of mother is seen as an expression of the lived relationship where one does things for others, it has the capacity to cut through the formal Christian ideology of the church, where the role of mother is an expression of the act of giving birth to a child conceived in a sanctioned conjugal relationship between a husband and a wife.

Unlike women as wives, women as mothers in the church need not be passive and submissive. As mothers women posses the authority to teach, admonish and discipline any member who could be understood to stand in the relation of child to the woman; significantly this can include men.

Social Practice: 'Strength and honour are her clothing'[11]

The practical transformation of the body is not simply difference accomplished on the level of symbolic imagery. Connell argues that the effects of social practice – housework, childbearing, etc. – like the relations between genders, can be physically inscribed or manifested on the natural body (1987: 86–7). Although not as dramatic, the effects of social practice on the natural body are also visible among members of the NTCG.

There are clear codes of dress and adornment for members. Men should wear their hair clean and short. Young boys who are not officially members of the church but whose parent(s) are members occasionally wear 'tram line' haircuts.[12] Men generally

10. The American equivalent is Mother's Day.
11. Proverbs 31: 25.
12. A short back and sides haircut which may be long on top and has geometric or linear designs resembling tram lines which are shaved into the hair above the ear and the nape. An alternative is to wear the hair in a style following the boxer Lloyd Hunnigan, where the hair is cut short with a double parting shaved in just above the forehead.

wear suits or blazers to church; occasionally they will wear a smart sweater and a collared shirt. If elderly men are wearing hats on the street, they will remove them before entering the church hall or a religious service. Men should wear little or no jewelry except for a wedding band, watch or tie-clip.

There are, however, many more rules for women's dress and appearance. Women wear dresses or skirts to church. Clothing such as sleeveless dresses, short skirts or low necklines, which reveal too much of a woman's body and emphasize her sexuality, can be considered a potential threat not only to the wearer's sanctity but to the sanctity of the male observer.

> We can dress modest ... not showing your shoulders, armpit ... reason why that is said 'We are creating too much attraction for men' ... Women should not be dressed like men. These days you hardly know women from men and little things, too much bottom ... You're inviting them [men] and when them come what do you tell them? ... And there's a resistance, because we are human being ... Somebody talking to you, your very body is talking to you itself ... and sometimes you become yielded. After that passion is over sometime you regret it ... so what it is saying here now is how well you can avoid it. (Mother Harvey)

Outside of religious services, younger women may occasionally wear trousers to informal services such as evening prayer meetings, although when they do so, they keep their coats on. A woman should not wear make-up or jewelry. The proscription on make-up is fairly well observed, although some members may use cosmetics to even out skin tone, apply petroleum jelly to give the skin a healthy appearance, and may use sheer lipstick and powder sparingly. The ban on jewelry as a bodily adornment is also well observed. Jewelry on the body is restricted to a wedding or engagement ring and a fancy watch for Sunday or special occasions. However, younger women will wear jewelry on clothing if it can also be seen as serving a useful purpose, e.g., a hat pin or a pin to mask a dubious neckline or secure an errant scarf. Women should wear clothes which are modest, but this does not prevent clothing from being a legitimate and expressive means of adornment. Clothes are flattering, and the fabrics and trimmings are decorative.

Women should wear their hair long and natural because hair is considered a woman's crowning glory and veil; in fact, women's hairstyles range from long hair caught up in a snood[13] to being permed and cut fashionably. Women are supposed to cover their heads in prayer, and this is one reason given for wearing hats to church; the other is that it is 'traditional from back home' and as such a distinguishing mark of African-Caribbean ethnicity and religion. Most women will wear a hat to church, but some younger women will experiment with alternate forms of head covering, e.g., wide elastic head-bands, long strips of cloth wound around the head in a West African or Jamaican manner, or no head covering at all. Women do not feel that it is absolutely necessary to cover their heads before praying. Omission of prayer is considered more serious than not covering one's head. Most older women will wear hats inside and outside church. If they have removed their street hats they will cover their heads with a scarf kept in their purse to say a prayer.[14]

The style of dress and adornment in the NTCG can be compared with the gendering of dress in Rastafarianism. Both religious traditions manipulate nature and culture to transform the body. As with the NTCG, the manner of gendering dress within Rastafarianism reflects an ideal of the holy woman as pure and natural. Rastafarian women, like some women in the church, wear their hair natural, unrelaxed, in a snood or covered by a headscarf, though the effect of appearance is different. The ideal appearance of the holy woman manipulates a homonym of naturalness between female dress and the naturalness of the female body. Although there are echoes between dress and gender for women in Rastafarianism and the NTCG, there are no parallels between the appearance of Rastafarian men and Pentecostal men. Where the Pentecostal man appears as a creature of culture, clean shaven, dressed in a suit or blazer and perhaps a hat, the appearance of the holy Rastafarian is diametrically natural. The dreadlocks of the Rastafarian are a symbol of defiance to society and other cultural norms (Barrett 1977: 138). Barrett suggests that the care of Rastafarian dreadlocks is grounded in naturalism; hair is washed in water with herbs, and some men will not use a comb (1977: 139).[15]

13. A hairnet.

14. See Cucchiari (1990: 696) for a discussion of the head shawl worn by Pentecostal women.

15. However, Barrett also points out that there are Rastafarians who use a comb who are called 'combsome,' while Rastafarians who are just beginning to cultivate their locks are called 'cleanface' and 'nubbies' (1977: 140).

The onus of managing appearance falls on the women of the NTCG. This control of bodily appearance is part of the continuous religious work which female members must engage in to remain a 'Christian' and to enable others to remain 'Christian.' The strict control of women's appearance deflects sexual temptation to which both male and female members may succumb and thus 'backslide.' However, as previously noted, it is this formality and control which makes it possible for members to achieve the contrasting lack of bodily control associated with in-filling by the Holy Spirit. The wearing of raincoats during female baptism, the moment of public expression of commitment to belief, foreshadows the required control of female appearance. While the everyday body of the woman is strictly disciplined, when a saint is filled with the Holy Spirit she loses control over her appearance, 'ladies kicking off their shoes' (Sermon, 9/9/90).

Seating arrangements in the congregation present another form of social practice which not only reflects but constitutes gender divisions, presenting a symbolic grid which manifests divisions of gender, age and the intensity of religious commitment. Theoretically, a person may sit where he or she wishes; however, one chooses a place to sit according to the manifest order of gender, participation in the service and other divisions (see Figure 3.1). On the whole, women tend to sit on the pastor's left and men on the pastor's right. While younger married couples will sit together, most older husbands and wives sit separately. (A woman should not sit next to a man who is not her relative.) This practice is a source of amusement to members; the Pastor has asked the congregation to sit with their spouses on several occasions and no one complies. It is not unusual for members not to know who each other's spouses are, as Sister Ashe put it:

> . . . we can, but we don't. Certain time Pastor, when we have visitor, he call us to sit by our husband, that plenty of people who even in the church don't know who another husband them, don't know another them de wife. So he call us we should sit together. The couple must sit together that each and everybody can know, the visitor them and who even in the church can know who is a husband and who is a wife. . ..

Some people say this is 'traditional' from back home, like wearing hats, while others say it originates in the Old Testament. This division is stricter during the 'washing of the saints' feet,' when women will wash each other's feet and the men likewise. Segregation is also strictly observed during baptism, at which female candidates are seated on the pastor's left and male candidates on the pastor's right (see Plate 3, chapter 3). Female candidates enter and leave the baptismal pool from the pastor's left and face the women as they are baptized, while male candidates enter and leave from the right and face the men.

It is believed the closer a saint sits to the front of the church hall, the more committed he or she is to their faith. The first two rows of pews are rarely occupied unless there is a special service and every available pew is occupied, or a family has a child that is to be dedicated during the service. Elderly women tend to sit towards the front of the left-hand side and elderly men take up a corresponding position on the right. Middle-aged members and youth, who are not in the choirs or band, occupy the pews behind the elderly. Mothers with young children sit near the back, where they can make a hasty exit if necessary. Some young women will sit with their mothers, others will sit together. Infrequent attendees tend to occupy the pews under the gallery maintaining this left–right distinction. There is a group of early middle-aged women with children who sit in the back pews on the men's side, some of them are the up and coming generation of church women, part of the nucleus of membership.[16] The officers of the church sit in the officer's box to the pastor's right. Certain women can sit in this box on special occasions, i.e., the Pastor's female kin sit here during 'Pastor's Appreciation Day'; or if there is a visiting female minister, she will sit here with other distinguished visitors. The Sanctuary Choir sits in a raised box behind the pulpit, and the Youth Choir sits in the box opposite the officers. In the evening, the choir seating arrangement is altered as the focus of the service shifts from the pulpit to the podium behind the altar rail: female members of the Sanctuary Choir sit in the youth choir box, while male choristers sit in adjacent perpendicular pews.

16. Two of these women are the Pastor's daughters and one is the president of the Young Adult Ladies' Ministry. One of the Pastor's daughters said she liked to sit on that side to make a point, but she added that she moves over to the left for 'Lord's Supper' and the 'washing of the saints' feet.' When the future daughter-in-law of the Pastor visited, she also sat here.

Agency

> When God made Adam, he made Eve to 'company Adam; so the
> women in the church have role to play, so men alone can't man over
> the church, there must be some woman. (Sister Ashe)

Women and Language: Expressions of Interest

In many Pentecostal traditions women are prevented from
preaching. This ruling is based upon the scriptural edict: 'But I
suffer not a woman to teach, nor usurp authority over the man,
but to be in silence.'[17] This does not mean that women are silent or
are denied avenues to express their interests. One common theme
in Pentecostal ethnography is that women are never prevented
from testifying, speaking in tongues or prophesying, because this
would deny the spirituality of women and the agency of God. It
is, however, also clear that women can use these forms of expression to subvert male speech acts by monopolizing the service with
an extended testimony or interrupting a sermon by speaking in
tongues or prophesying. Different Pentecostal traditions draw
varying distinctions between formal and informal modes of
expression which accommodate women's speech, yet sustain the
theological position of male dominance. For example, while only
male Sicilian Pentecostalists possess the formal 'ministry' to pastor,
preach, teach, evangelize, heal and prophesy, women possess the
practically equivalent 'gifts' of evangelism, healing and prophesy,
and they 'testify' instead of 'preach' (Cucchiari 1990: 693–5; see
also Lawless 1991: 56). Similarly, Williams found that women in
an African-American Pentecostal church could deliver sermons,
but a distinction was made between the 'teachings' of female
missionaries (delivered from below the pulpit) and the 'preaching'
of male ministers (delivered from the pulpit) (1974: 31).

By contrast, in the NTCG female saints have full status as public
speakers. They may preach and moderate a service from the pulpit,
pray, testify, speak in tongues and recite the closing benediction,
as well as raising choruses and hymns. Sermons delivered by
women tend to occur in special services devoted to women, e.g.,
'Ladies' Day,' ' District Ladies' Ministry' Weekend' or the 'Ladies'

17. I Timothy 2: 12.

Regional Seminar.' Other opportunities for women to preach or deliver lessons occur in smaller meetings like evening services or auxiliary meetings. The majority of Sunday sermons, however, are delivered by the pastor or by male associate ministers and exhorters.

Formal Religious Speech: Sermons by Women   What does the use of formalized speech reveal about the nature of power and authority of speakers in the church?[18] Maurice Bloch (1975) argues that in a society where power and authority is based on ascription rather than achievement, the use of formalized language cannot be used to attain power and authority; political oratory is only an indication of power and cannot be used as a tool of coercion available to all. A challenge presented by a straightforward application of Bloch's theory to the setting of the church is the distinction between achieved and ascribed power. Membership within the church is an achieved status based upon conversion. Through sanctification and possessing a 'clean heart' members may be baptized with the Holy Spirit, which can endow them with gifts like the ability to speak in tongues, prophesy, interpret tongues, heal and the gift of spiritual vision. All members, whether male or female, potentially possess these powers and may thus serve as legitimate speakers. The potential for power cannot be questioned: if a saint claims to have received the Holy Spirit, others have no right to question the claim.

Anointment by the Holy Spirit endows the person with 'power for service.' The speaker should be able to hear from the Lord so that they can deliver His message. Prior to a sermon a short prayer may be said invoking the Holy Spirit to fall upon the speaker. Within sermons and services, glossalalic utterances punctuate and underscore emotional peaks in the delivery of the sermon and the service. The ability to hear from the Lord is sometimes explicitly stated by female speakers at the start of their sermons, reminding the congregation of the legitimacy of the speaker (also Lawless 1991). In this context, where status is achieved, baptism by the Holy Spirit and its attendant gifts not only indicate power but can also be used to attain more power and reinforce the speaker's authority.

18. Following Terrence Booth (1984), who has applied Bloch's (1975) theory of formalized language and political oratory in traditional society to an analysis of power dynamics and the competition for power in an Aladura church.

I'm hoping tonight the Lord will help me to go steady, because sometimes when I'm preaching I get a bit excited and miss what I'm going to say on paper. Sometimes the Holy Spirit lead us and directs us away. (female preacher, Sermon, 27/5/90)

Of all the things the Holy Spirit gave me to preach on. . ... (female preacher, Sermon, 5/10/90)

Another difficulty in applying Bloch's analysis of political oratory to sermons in the church is the restriction of language. Bloch (1975) argues that formalized language is characterized by a severely restricted and impoverished choice of words, syntax and style; by defining and regulating the manner in which things are said, the content is indirectly restricted and controlled, and with it the range of listeners' responses. He argues that the content of formalized language is restricted to a specified body of suitable illustrations, proverbs or scriptures. Bloch implies that the greater the restrictions on political oratory, the more it becomes like religious oratory. The ability of language to convey and communicate particular events and messages disappears. The individuality and historical aspect of events disappears, and specific events are merged into a timeless, eternally fixed order of things which is impervious to questioning and disagreement (Bloch ibid.: 6, 15). The use of language in the church is not a restricted code: as we have seen, members choose from and combine Patois, Queen's English and AWL to construct sermons, and the ability to convey particular events and messages does not disappear. Both men and women preachers draw upon these combinations.[19] At the same time, the parables and allegories employed by male or female preachers clearly draw on gendered activities and experiences.

19. While it does not appear surprising that women should employ 'Queen's English' in formal religious speech, it is also not surprising that they combine it with Patois. Until recently there was a common assumption in sociolinguistics that women tend to deviate less from the prestige standard and that they tend to employ less stigmatized forms of speech than men (for a critique of this, see Coates and Cameron 1988). With reference to African-Caribbean female speakers in Dudley, England, Edwards' work challenges the stereotype of the competent Patois speaker as the 'angry male underachiever.' Her findings suggest that there are no statistically significant differences between male and female Patois speakers and also demonstrate that Black women who are not 'angry underachievers' are frequent and proficient Patois speakers (1988: 49). What is significant with reference to the NTCG, then, is that AWL is not restricted to male speakers but is also employed by female speakers.

In the NTCG, formal oratory does not exclude women from positions of power; rather, formal oratory enabled by baptism by the Holy Spirit is one source of power which women can draw upon and use to express their interests. When speaking of the spiritual harvest, a male preacher will speak in terms of farming as it is practiced in Jamaica, while female speakers will speak of their commitments and duties as mothers, wives and daughters. In one sermon, the male speaker related the parable of the sons in the vineyard, and this was followed by a parable of a farming project at the church headquarters:

> We decided to plant some vegetables and to involve young people. Youngsters from the city have never seen a field; they don't understand our background. We planted [in Jamaica] our own peas, yam, corn. ... We understand about planting as reapers. They don't understand what growth is all about. We planted forty bags of potatoes. When it came time to reap it, twenty-two letters were sent to twenty-two Youth directors . . . only ten people came. Out of these forty bags, we got 400 bags. ... The harvest is plenteous [sic], but the laborers are few. (Sermon, 9/9/90)

A female preacher trying to illustrate the edict that no one should love their family more than the Lord related the following experience:

> Here I was, not only the eldest daughter, but the only daughter. I was the one near home. The responsibility of the care of my mother fell upon me, but I had a revival scheduled. They said, "Well we will let you go for this, but don't stay another week" . . . You know how it is . . . time to do duty for the family. It was a great revival . . . the Pastor asked me if I would go another week . . . you talk about instant confusion . . . All I heard was my mother saying, "Now don't you stay another week" . . . I was in a deep sleep, but the Holy Spirit woke me up with these words: "Any man that love mother [pause] more than me. ... you're not worthy to be my disciple." (Sermon, 7/10/90)

Another woman preaching about the role of women waiting at the tomb for the resurrection related it to a worried mother at home waiting for her child to come home:

> I don't know where the men were. It seems as though they had gone into hiding . . . but these women were there. They wanted to be there,

like mothers all over. There are some times when our children . . . I know when they are getting into trouble and the husbands would stay at home because they say that, 'Oh they not gonna bother go out.' They don't seem to have that in them, but there's this difference in women. There is this thing between a mother and a child . . . there's a difference between a mother's love or a woman's love and that of the man, so they said they couldn't stay where they were. They had to go see what had happened to the Lord. (Sermon, 10/3/91)

At a ladies' seminar, where there should have been a female preacher, the male preacher used parables that were based on women's experiences:

Hard to find time to pray . . . "I'm gonna push out the husband, push out the children, dismiss the cat, just me and Jesus" . . . that day they really gave it to you at work on the ward, everything came for you to do, you feel as though you want to head-butt the matron . . . you can talk to God in intercession from the ironing board. (Sermon, 5/10/91)

Most women felt that the gender of the speaker was unimportant. The crucial issue was that the word of God was speaking through the person anointed with the Holy Spirit. They did not prefer male speakers over female speakers or vice a versa, nor did they enjoy one type of sermon over the other as long as it was a 'good' sermon. Several subtle distinctions were, however, pointed out: The first was that the male speaker on a regular Sunday is addressing the entire congregation, whereas female speakers on special 'Ladies' Days' are addressing the women as mothers and wives and reiterating the principles they should uphold. However, this does not prevent the speaker from addressing the men in the congregation and telling them what principles they should uphold as well. Another factor was the specific qualities of women's voices:

. . . it's only with the voice, that's where the difference comes in, say a woman will be here now . . . it tends to be in a soft tone, but it penetrates through and it goes to your core. You listen and it goes straight through and the tears flow . . . you know it brings more emotion. (Martha)

Informal Religious Speech by Women   While the anointing of the Holy Spirit empowers speakers to deliver formal oratory, it is also a source of agency for exceptional and occasionally dramatic informal religious oratory ('speaking in tongues,' prophesy or discerning danger) which a person can use to draw attention to themselves. While glossolalia, prophecy and discernment tend to go unnoticed or unacknowledged, when they *are* acknowledged, the actor has the power to interrupt the service and/or alter the course of events (see descriptions of the church's 'Ladies' Day' and the 'Ladies' District Weekend' below). Although the in-filling of the Holy Spirit is not formally limited to either gender, male lay members rarely harness the agency of the Holy Spirit in this way. As was noted in chapter 4, its occurrence primarily among female lay members and Mothers of the Church seems to suggest that agency from the Holy Spirit has slightly different implications for female members.

By contrast, devotion and scriptural explication are another form of religious oratory practiced by women which do not require the anointing of the Holy Spirit. During elderly club meetings, devotion begins with a scriptural passage; the text chosen can be suggested by anyone present and varies accordingly. The choice may be based on dreams, vision, inspirations or communications from God; difficulty with the meaning of the passage or simple familiarity with it can also be the basis for selecting a scriptural passage. Any woman is entitled to read the passage aloud, and the women take daily turns. Following the reading, the reader or another woman, either of whom may not possess baptism by the Holy Spirit, will interpret the meaning of the passage by employing personal experiences, allegories or parables; other women are often invited to add their comments. The discussion is followed by individual simultaneous audible prayer. The emphasis in prayer is on praising or thanking God. He is rarely asked to take a specific course of action, but He is asked to watch over people who could be in danger or to take an expedient course of action according to the circumstances. Prayer ends when the last woman has finished; almost in unison, the women will then recite the 23rd Psalm or the 'Lord's Prayer.'

Within the church, the imagery of the head and the neck draws upon and constitutes gender divisions. This imagery works with the sexual differences between men and women and marks the different 'sources of influence and directions of power' which are allocated to people with different bodies. Roughly, men as Christian husbands possess agency where they are the 'authors of their own actions' and have been assigned that role by God. Women, however, are not the authors of their actions. The efficacy of women's actions is derived from their relationship with others. In its weakest form, women as wives possess only the necessary agency to support and ensure the continued agency of their husbands. In its strongest form, the enabling agency of mothers is embodied in the Jamaican concept of mother, where a woman's actions are directed at others to help them develop into actors.

However, analysis of formal and informal religious oratory reveals that people possess a third source of agency – the Holy Spirit. This source of influence and direction of power originates outside the human order and is thus not allocated to persons on the basis of human sexual difference. Instead agency, whether manifested in the gifts of the Holy Spirit or not, is allocated to all saints, and its deployment by actors blurs gender differences. Though a speaker will tend to draw upon the experience of being a 'man' or a 'woman,' the body of suitable illustrations and proverbs which a speaker draws upon is not constrained by gender. When saints preach, they may speak as saints in terms distinct from gender and express the interests of 'persons'; they may speak directly from gendered experiences expressing their interests as 'men' or 'women'; or they may speak across gender experiences and thus express the interests of the other gender.

In the church women as 'women' and women as 'saints' are assigned different social values. There are different expectations of 'women' and saints, and different standards of appropriate and inappropriate behavior apply to 'women' and saints, i.e., the contrast between the bodily control of 'women' and the lack of bodily control when saints are filled with the Holy Spirit. The different social values of women are registered in different types of agency. To return to Connell (1987), there appear to be two different sets of social practice which make and remake women as 'women' and women as saints, with the result that women can simultaneously inhabit two different and inconsistent gender identities. The different types of male and female agency vested in the different church roles available to men and women, and the way in which women can play off the model of persons whose bodies are different and the model of persons who are androgynous against each other, are examined below.

Roles Available to Male and Female Saints

There are a plethora of positions open to men and women in the church. Each auxiliary or department in the church and each congregation engenders its own organization and corresponding executive. Both Calley and Wedenoja have interpreted this multiplicity as a means whereby the individual acquires a sense of achievement and self-worth (Calley 1965: 32; Wedenoja 1980: 41). Whatever talent a person has is noted and fostered by other members. Ability is strongly emphasized; it is not simply academic but encompasses maturity, practical experience and, importantly, spirituality. The emphasis on ability as spirituality applies equally to male and female saints, but ability can be seen to be different-iated on the basis of practical experience as 'women' or 'men.'

Ministry   The category of ministers has several ranked positions: exhorter, licensed minister and ordained minister.[20] An exhorter is an apprentice, the first step in ministerial training; some denominations use the term 'lay preacher.' An exhorter can be either male or female, neither of whom has any ministerial authority other than to preach, but they may be called upon to pray, preach and assist a pastor with infant dedication, baptism, marriages and funerals. There was only one female exhorter in the King Street district; however, women are eager to point out that many women are now coming forward to train as exhorters. When an exhorter has gained more experience, he or she can become a licensed minister.

A licensed minister can pastor a congregation; male licensed ministers are able to perform infant dedication, baptism and funerals and deliver the 'Lord's Supper,' though without per-mission from the national overseer they cannot perform a marriage ceremony. A female licensed minister can pastor a congregation and perhaps perform infant dedication, but she cannot perform baptism, marriage or funerals:

> If is a lady she is a licensed person in the ministry, she serves just the same helping in the church. Now there are some things she wouldn't do . . . the male would do. That's go and baptize the convert, according to the old ruling of the church she wouldn't do that . . . [but she would] find a male member. She could go and pastor a church. (The Pastor)

20. The office of pastor is tangential to this ranking, as a pastor is a minister who has the responsibility of supervising a congregation.

There is a female pastor in the district who is unable to perform baptism. Her husband, who is a minister, baptizes the new converts. If he is absent, the district overseer baptizes them.

The next progression, for men alone, is to ordained minister, with all the rights and privileges of infant dedication, baptism, marriage and funerals. At weddings, the actual marriage ceremony is conducted by male pastors of the congregations. If the pastor is a woman, she would have to ask the district overseer or another minister to perform the ceremony. The participation of women in marriage services is limited to singing and reading the scripture. Unlike marriage and baptism, there is no specific liturgy for the dead. The funeral service is composed of a series of prayers, speeches, sermons, addresses, eulogies and songs, all of which women can perform. Yet, the sermon is always delivered by a man, not necessarily the pastor. Women participate by singing, delivering addresses and praying for the offering. Among my informants, no one had ever heard of or attended a funeral service conducted by a woman.

It was difficult to decipher why members felt women could not be ordained or perform the central rites which mark changes in the internal nature of the individual and potential or actual changes in membership. Members offered varied and confusing responses based on church ruling, female physical characteristics or biblical decree. With respect to infant dedication, the Pastor's wife, who also holds the position of Mother of the Church, a retired female pastor who is currently a Mother of the Church and two male officers replied that they had never seen a woman dedicate an infant. However, they thought that theoretically a woman could dedicate an infant because she is entitled to say a dedicatory prayer. The female exhorter was firm in her belief that a woman could dedicate an infant. Others simply 'didn't know.' During a 'Regional Ladies' Seminar,' the wife of the national overseer, a woman who is a licensed minister as well as president of the 'National Ladies' Ministry' auxiliary and Mother of her congregation, performed an infant dedication.[21] During the sermon which followed, the male speaker commented on the exceptional act that

21. However, the manner in which she performed it differed from observations at the district level. She asked ministers, who were all male, to stand behind the infant's family. When she finished the prayer, she passed the infant to the 'anointed ministers.'

had just occurred: 'I never understand how a woman could give natural childbirth and can't bless the baby' (Sermon, 6/10/91). This was greeted with loud clapping and agreement from the assembled congregation, which was mostly composed of women.

With regard to the issue of baptism, responses were grounded in women's physical characteristics and biblical scripture. Mother Green appealed to the belief that women are the 'weaker vessel.' She felt that a woman would not have the strength necessary to lift the candidate out of the water and she felt that if the woman was menstruating, it would not be right. The retired female pastor similarly emphasized women's sexual nature; she felt it would be too exposing for women to be in the pool. She added that it was not biblical and she had never read anywhere that a woman had performed marriage or baptism. One of the arguments, then, emphasized immutable differences (sexual nature, what is in the Bible) between men and women. Other arguments, however, tended to emphasize church rules or history, which could be changed. Thus, when asked whether the no-baptism rule existed because she was a woman or because she was not ordained, the retired female pastor explained that it was because a woman is not ordained. Indeed the emphasis upon the individual agency and the ungendered nature of spiritual life can be pressed into service here:

> They put all those [roles] in the bracket of the men because that's how it started, and as soon as you advance in the ministry and people eyes open and the women start to say we can do this and that can be done, *spiritually we can do it too* [emphasis added]. So it's something in operation coming up . . . if you are serving the Lord and you are out in the ministry field and you want to be in the ministry, why stop some people from doing that . . . women should be ordained, should baptize, that women should do marriage ceremony. . .. Why can't she if women exhorters go out in the mission field, why? Say for instance, if a missionary goes to Africa or anywhere and we are over there and people are saved, there's no man, they can't send to England here to get a man to baptize them . . . they would have to do something, you see? (Mother Adler)

Officers   While there is thus some ambiguity surrounding the idea of fitness for ministerial roles, the offices of officers and Mothers of the Church are unambiguously gendered. Here saints are differentiated on the basis of independent and complementary activities which are informed by the social categories of 'men' and 'women' as constructed by the ideal of the patriarch and the mother. The 'Church and Pastor's Council' in NTCG congregations is a board of seven male 'officers,' a male secretary and the pastor. Officers are nominated by the pastor and elected by members of the congregation during members' meetings; ministerial training is not a prerequisite. These men are responsible for the financial matters of the congregation, assisting members with spiritual, financial and temporal crises, and making decisions which affect the congregation. Two officers described their activities as follows:

> To assist pastor and make decisions, see to all the welfare, running of the church. We all sit down and discuss plans first before we come to members meeting, ... there's anything not right in the church and we know of before the pastor knows sometimes we contact the member and if we can come to a decision we leave it off there, but if it's a case that we have to, we can't come to any conclusion, then we take it to pastor. If you're walking contrary, then it's my duty to see you first and have a talk with you before I've got to go and carry it to the pastor ... carry it to the rest of men.

The emphasis is on leadership, decision-making, admonishment and discipline.

At present, King Street has only male officers. The question of whether a woman can, or should, be an officer is considered to be a '$64,000 question' by the Pastor. There is confusion in the congregation concerning the appointment of women as officers. This discrepancy can be explained by the multi-denominational background of members, what is considered to be a woman's role and frankly whether one asks a man or a woman. The role of officer is sometimes associated with the role of deacon. Deacons are found within Methodist and Baptist traditions with which most members have had experience and within which women can serve as deaconesses. Some women felt that in specific cases women could serve as officers. The Pastor was, however, reluctant to elide the role of officer with that of deacon. Women might assist and help in the church; however, counseling a pastor was a different matter – these men are 'special, selected men.' When it came to selecting women as officers, he said the church hadn't broached that topic yet. The Pastor justified the church's stance on appointing only men as officers by referring to a biblical quotation:

> Wherefore, brethren look ye out among you seven men of honest report full of the Holy Ghost and wisdom, whom we may appoint over this business,[22]

and he later commented:

> In some sense, we use the ladies in another office where they are called 'Mothers.' The Mothers in the church, another group, as the men are selected to become 'Church and Pastor's Council' and to serve the church and help the pastor, so the Mothers of the Church are selected . . . as Mothers to look about the affairs of the church, especially young women and all the different thing that would be in the home. They are serving with the pastor in that capacity, so in a sense they're officers . . . they're not official church officers but the function of them is in an office helping capacity.

Mother of the Church   Within Black churches in general, women as women are always accorded a recognized role ranging from the honorific to the consecrated. Women are responsible for carrying out domestic tasks, social reproduction, nurturing, comforting and socialization. In some Black-led traditions, these tasks are differentiated and vested in different offices held by women. In the American African Methodist Episcopal tradition, women serve as deaconesses or stewardesses. Stewardesses are responsible for providing the communion host, dressing and preparing the altar and preparing for baptism.

> The stewardess board should also dress the pulpit and altar rail with suitable clean white coverings. It is recommended that the stewardess board prepare the bread itself as a service of love and devotion rather than purchase it. Always white and perfectly clean, the linen used for the table may be embellished with white embroidered or crocheted symbols and made very beautiful. The utensils should be polished and shining. (AME Book of Discipline 1980)

While stewardesses are engaged in 'domestic tasks' or women's church work-cum-housework, deaconesses are engaged in the business of succor, comfort and nurturing. Deaconesses are consecrated single or widowed women who are responsible for

22. Acts 6: 3.

the general interests of the church and the pastoral care of the fallen, hungry or homeless; it is their duty to rescue the perishing, help the weak or unfortunate and minister to the sick. In the Church of the Cheribum and Seraphim, women are accorded several ranked grades (Booth 1984: 130–3). Three are relevant here: 'Lady Leaders,' 'Mothers in Israel' and 'Holy Mothers.' The role of the 'Lady Leader' is to care for female members and ensure that they are following the doctrine of the church; they care for strangers and arrange communion. A 'Mother in Israel' is senior to a 'Lady Leader' and acts as mother to the order, where it is her duty to organize the 'womenfold,' advising them and praying for them. The most senior female elder is the 'Holy or Spiritual Mother,' who ensures that peace is kept in the order, advises women and represents their interests to the equivalent of the pastor and the executive.

Though NTCG women cannot conduct all the rites and sacraments of male ministers or serve as officers on the 'Church and Pastor's Council,' they are given a quasi-official status as the Pastor describes, as 'Mothers of the Church.' In their survey of African-American churches, Lincoln and Mamiya describe Mothers of the Church as an honorific title reserved for the wife of the founder or the most respected senior females (1990: 275). In the Pentecostal church studied by Williams, a 'Church Mother' is appointed from among female missionaries (1974: 31). In his church, a Church Mother is a woman who has demonstrated her ability to keep female members in line and who possesses longevity, biblical knowledge and a commitment to the faith. The same qualities are necessary for a woman to become a 'Mother of the Church' in the Afro-Baptist tradition studied by A. L. Brown (1994). A woman need not have been a deaconess, been married to a man in the church or have had children. Traditionally, she was formally elected at a church conference, but now a woman can become a Mother by appointment or by being the oldest living female in the congregation. Ritually, Afro-Baptist Church Mothers are responsible for helping with the 'birthin' of new church members and preparing the 'Lord's Supper' (ibid.: 179–81).

In the NTCG, a pastor's wife should always be a Mother of the Church if she possesses the ability. The appointment of other Mothers in a congregation is at the discretion of its pastor. The number of Mothers in a congregation varies with the size of the congregation; King Street has six, including the Pastor's wife. A

Mother must be a good and respected Christian: 'I must be able to live a sober life as somebody can pattern me, I should not be wanton, should only have one husband and I must learn to behave myself properly' (Mother Harvey). Although members will offer the information that it is theoretically not necessary for a Mother of the Church to be married, all the Mothers in King Street congregation are married.

In the NTCG, as in the Afro-Baptist church (Brown ibid.), domestic tasks, social reproduction and socialization are vested in the one role of Mother of the Church. Her function is to look after male and female brethren and ensure that doctrine is upheld:

> If she looks around and sees a young or mature person acting contrary
> . . . it is her duty to admonish, advise, talk with them, not talk down,
> in a friendly motherly way . . . like a mother would talk to her son or
> her daughter . . . give direction. (Mother Harvey)

If two members have a disagreement, a Mother will try to settle it; if she feels she cannot handle it she will present it to the officers. If the officers are also unable to reconcile the parties, it is taken to the pastor and a Mother and an officer will act as witnesses. When a member has a minor financial crisis, a Mother may help out with money from her own pocket. Mothers are also responsible for the care of visiting members and ministers, ensuring that they have a place to stay and are well fed. They also make sure that the church hall is kept neat and clean.

There are no regular meetings of the Mothers; they meet as the need arises and discuss courses of action among themselves, usually over the phone. Mothers are not officially represented on the 'Church and Pastor's Council,' though there are times when the Pastor calls a joint meeting of the officers and Mothers. The Mothers were keenly aware that they could not legislate changes, but they could make suggestions and voice their disagreement or call the younger women together. In a congregation where women form the majority, as is the case in King Street and most Black Churches, Mothers have considerable power, as others have suggested (Lincoln and Mamiya 1990: 275). The Mothers in the NTCG have a judicious sense of the limits of their capabilities in problem solving; anything they feel they should not or cannot handle, they present to the officers and the Pastor. This does not imply that women are submissive. As the following example from fieldwork illustrates, women can and do defend their own interests. The officers had decided to encourage more people to attend a mid-week afternoon prayer meeting for everyone over sixty. This resulted in a scheduling conflict with another regular church activity whose attendees would provide the natural constituency for the prayer meeting. The Mother in charge of the other activity subtly 'thrashed' one of the officers for not clearing it with her first.

Mothers of the Church are responsible for preparing the 'Lord's Supper.' Although there is no set rule that states only men can serve the Supper, in King Street the Supper is administered by the officers (see chapter 3). Who serves the Supper depends on the size of the congregation and the preference of its pastor. The Pastor felt that 'A woman could do it, it's never likely so anyhow the men always do it, but suppose there were no men in the church something like that.' Mother Adler commented:

> . . . it doesn't matter if there wasn't a man then a woman will have to do, but as long as you have officers in the church is [*sic*] their responsibility or the minister . . . because women are usually the weaker frame, the weaker vessel and you take the Lord's sleeve and a lot of things they said, but if they doesn't have a man they'll have to use a woman.

After the 'Lord's Supper,' Mothers are responsible for preparing hot water and towels for the 'washing of the saint's feet.' The officers assist the Mothers by carrying in the basins of hot water. Afterwards, the Mothers collect the used towels and basins and prepare them for the next service. Before a baptism, the Mothers meet with the candidates to give encouragement and support and to vet the candidate one last time, as well as leading female candidates to and from the baptismal pool.

The ambiguities in the proverb of the head and the neck provide the basis for understanding the role of Mother of the Church. This role is informed by a Jamaican concept of motherhood, understood not as simply an act of parturition but as the acceptance of responsibility and doing things for others. By doing things for others, these women stand in relation to other members of the church as mothers to children. It is, however, significant that in contrast to the American African Methodist Episcopal tradition, where women who are given acknowledged positions of respect as deaconesses must be outside the structures of secular sexuality (single, widowed), in the NTCG Mothers should be married. As in so many other aspects of this church's organization, there is both an acknowledgment and a denial of the realities of members' lives: the role of Jamaican women in caring for children, the ideal of the Christian family. In addition to possessing agency as mothers, Mothers of the church possess agency as saints, for they should not only be mothers and wives, they must also be experienced 'Christians.' As both mothers and saints, Mothers of the Church possess the unquestionable agency to empower all others in the church, not only juniors or women. The nature of what Mothers of the Church do for others is as significant as the source of their agency. Unlike some other Black Churches in the US and Britain, which vest the responsibilities of domestic reproduction and spiritual guidance in separate roles for women, in the NTCG these responsibilities are combined in the Mother of the Church. Hence the Mother of the Church can be understood as enabling members of the family of God to develop as 'Christians,' i.e., by helping female converts publicly to express their changed nature to others at baptism, by assisting in the 'Lords' Supper' and the 'washing of saints' feet,' where saints examine themselves as 'Christians,' and by providing guidance, support and admonishment so that others may remain 'Christians.'

Auxiliaries

The auxiliaries of the church are organized around differences of gender, age or both, and the organized activities of male and female members can be understood with reference to complementary, independent and joint role patterns (Bott 1957). Hence, they provide an important context for understanding how lay men and women in the church experience, participate, and contribute to the gender processes of the church. The 'Ladies' Ministry' is only one of the many activities and associations recognized by the denomination's local and international administrative structure.

Ladies' Ministry

The 'Ladies' Ministry' is represented at the national, district and congregational levels; its executive organization is also replicated at each of these levels. The complement to the 'Ladies' Ministry' is the 'Men's Fellowship.' The president of the 'Ladies' Ministry' at the national level is the wife of the national overseer. This appointment is not a coincidence but is deliberately based on the conjugal relationship in Christian marriage, and is the basis of the recruitment of the 'Ladies' Ministry' president at each administrative level of the church. The president of the 'District Ladies' Ministry' will be the wife of the district overseer and similarly the president of the 'Ladies' Ministry' of a congregation will be the wife of its pastor. In the case of King Street, where the congregation is the Mother church for the district, the Pastor's wife is the president of the 'District Ladies' Ministry'; the office of president for the King Street 'Ladies' Ministry' is held by another Mother of the Church.

The 'Ladies' Ministry' is divided into three age grades. Young women join the 'Young Ladies' Ministry' (YLM) between the ages of thirteen to eighteen; from the age of eighteen to thirty-five a woman will be involved in the 'Young Adult Ladies' Ministry' (YALM); and from the age of thirty-five upwards a woman will join the 'Ladies' Ministry' (LM). A woman will not necessarily move from one group to the next simply because of her age, but she will follow her peer group. Similarly the 'Men's Fellowship' is divided into the 'Men's Fellowship' (MF) and 'Young Men's Fellowship' (YMF); young men will move into the MF around age thirty-five. Each segment of the 'Ladies' Ministry' and 'Men's Fellowship' possesses its own president and secretary/treasurer.

According to the Pastor's wife, the idea behind the separate ladies' auxiliaries is to involve everyone in activities which suit their age and peer group:

> . . . give each one something to do in their own age bracket. They can offer something to their peer group. . . .. They can go out into the community instead of getting lost, because there is so much work to do in the vineyard.

The official purpose of the 'Ladies' Ministry' is: 'To encourage spiritual growth, personal development, and leadership among women; and to contribute to the general welfare of the home, church, community, and the world.'[23] This translates into evangelism, temporal work such as fund-raising activities, providing baskets of food to the poor or bereaved, visiting the sick and spiritual endeavors such as prayer and Bible study.

Although the 'Ladies' Ministry' department is the umbrella under which each of these groups is organized, the YLM and the YALM are not seen as 'being under the shadow' of the LM. The LM, YALM and YLM are understood as working together and helping each other. Each section of the ministry will meet and organize its activities for the year independently of the others and independently of the 'Men's Fellowship.' Different sections of the 'Ladies' Ministry' and 'Men's Fellowship' may occasionally hold joint meetings and activities.

The members of the YALM see evangelism and support as the purpose of their group. The monthly meetings of the YALM usually occur in a member's home. The actual content of the meeting can vary and meetings are never identical. Some common elements are devotion or a reading from the scripture, prayer, music, a Bible study; a 'problem-solving exercise,' which may be an opportunity for the women to express in a stylized manner the problems they are facing at home, work, in church or with their faith, or sharing talents like plant-care, cookery, keeping fit, fashion and crafts with each other. At one meeting, we began with prayer and a lecture-sermon by one of the women on 'Equipping Yourself with the Armor of God' and the power of prayer. This was followed by a discussion of the lecture-sermon. Then we were asked if any of us had any problems. A prayer circle was formed by the women; each woman, whether or not she had voiced a specific concern, was given a turn to kneel in the circle, while the other women stood around her and prayed over her, some laying hands on her. At the end of the meeting we were asked to choose a prayer partner from a bowl containing slips of paper with each person's name and to remember our partner in our prayers.

Periodically the church holds a 'Ladies' Day' and a 'Ladies' Ministry Weekend' which celebrate the independent and complementary activities of the 'Ladies' Ministry' auxiliaries while they are engaged in creative fund-raising. One Sunday evening service

23. COG, Minutes of the 62nd General Assembly (1988: 65–6).

was dedicated to the women. The majority of speakers were the women of the church. A Sister from the YALM began the service. She arrived early and waited behind the lower podium, the usual focus of evening services. When the congregation had assembled, she led us in a few choruses, a prayer and a hymn. When she announced the lesson for the evening, she asked the men and women to read aloud separately, alternating the verses and reading the last verse in unison. The members of the Men's Fellowship were asked to pray while the women hummed softly. Then she called upon the men and women in the congregation to give their testimonies. During this part of the service, a drunken White man had wandered in from the street. Mother Adler had gone to the front of the hall to lead the rest of the service and as she was about to begin she noticed the visitor who had stretched out on a pew holding a can of beer. Mother Adler acknowledged the presence of the visitor and said 'he comes around and he is sick, sometimes I give him a hard time.' She appointed three women in the congregation to pray over him. Sister Duke and Sister Adams stood by him and prayed, challenging the devil to flee the body of the man, then Sister Duke began to speak in tongues and to tremble. When this crisis had passed, we returned to the service at hand. Mother Adler asked the MF to come to the front and sing for us. When they had finished singing, she asked the women to come up and 'buy their husbands down.' Before the men could return to their seats their wives had to make an offering to the evening's collection. If a man didn't have a wife, Mother Adler suggested that some women could get together and buy a man down. Sister Monroe then came forward to sing only a few stanzas of a song, but she decided to sing the whole song instead. Because she had gone over her allotted time, Mother Adler told her to stay where she was and people were encouraged to pay to 'get her out of trouble.' Then the young men were asked to come forward and sing, and they too had to be bought down. Finally it was the turn of the little boys to come forward and sing and be bought down. Following a short sermon by a visiting Reverend, Mother Adler took the opportunity to speak about the purpose of the 'Ladies' Ministry.'

Once a year a 'District LM, YALM, YLM Weekend' is held at the King Street church. This event brings together the members of the LM, YALM and YLMs from the different congregations across the King Street district. The weekend is designed to celebrate and bring attention to the work and activities of the Ladies' Ministry in the district. The Sunday Divine and Evening services are incorporated into the general program and are conducted by the Ladies' Ministry. The Saturday program was held in the back hall of the church. Women from all the different congregations were represented, but there were only two men. The theme for the weekend was 'Women on the Move in the '90s.' The program included songs, a 'keep fit' session and discussions and lectures. One lecture entitled 'Ministering in the Community' focused on the conflicting responsibilities that women as saints share. Women should be involved in 'winning the lost at any cost' not only in the community, but at home, in the work-place and in the church. It was noted, however, that women sometimes feel that they cannot ignore their responsibilities to their family to attend to their responsibility to God. When men in the church call upon women to do things, women should not say they cannot do it because this would be calling God a liar. Women need to learn to share their load with other women instead of trying to do everything by themselves.

The Sunday program, which coincided with Mothering Sunday, was held in the church. Mother Green, the president of the 'District Ladies' Ministry,' moderated the service and representatives of the different ladies auxiliaries also made contributions to it. Mother Green made an address and altar call where she asked the officers and ministers of the church to pray over the brethren. The children in the congregation showed their appreciation to their mothers by singing and reading poems about mothers. Then the Mothers of the Church were honored; they were asked to come to the front of the congregation, where members of the Youth Choir presented them with flowers. The remaining women in the congregation who were also mothers were asked to rise, and the Youth Choir went through the congregation pinning carnations on their lapels. Mother Green then introduced Sister Bunson, who gave a sermon on the theme of 'Women on the Move in the '90s'; Sister Bunson, spoke of biological and non-biological mothers. She likened the role of women in evangelism to that of a mother's work, and to the victories women had claimed in the last century, e.g., the right to vote, the women's movement and the freedom of Mary White-house[24] to speak out against what she believed was wrong. At the

---

24. A campaigner for conservative values in Britain.

end of the service, Brother Harvey climbed into the pulpit to give the notices; this was the only time during the entire service that a man climbed into the pulpit.

The evening service was moderated by Sister Kirkpatrick. We began with choruses and she asked six of the brethren to make one-sentence prayers. All the brethren who prayed were women. Following a chorus, Sister Kirkpatrick asked the Pastor of Palace View to pray for the sick. Following another chorus and a reading from the Bible by Sister Kirkpatrick, the female Pastor from Eastleigh was asked to pray. Sister Kirkpatrick then spoke about the fact that it was also the weekend of Birmingham's annual women's festival, 'where people on the other side of things were also talking about the same themes.' She said it was disheartening that this should only be once a year. She then turned to the subject of women's employment, arguing that although women may not have a BA 'they have more than a BA when it comes right down to it: women are good managers and they can be innovative because they have raised a family.' Mother Adler then came and moderated and asked Exhorter Harvey to pray. After this, the women of the different auxiliaries raised funds by singing in turn to the congregation. When the Sanctuary Choirs of all the different congregations stood to sing, Mother Adler pointed out that there was not one man among them (though usually there are). Mother Adler asked the Pastor of Palace View to take up a collection for the men to join the choir. Eventually two men joined the choir. When the choir had finished singing we were asked to buy the women down. Afterwards, the women of the other congregations continued singing to the congregation in turn. The celebration was interrupted when one of the women in the choir had a vision of a member of the church in trouble. We ceased what we were doing and prayed for the unknown man. Then two men held the collection plates for the general offering. Following this, Mother Green asked the district overseer to make presentations to the presidents of the different 'Ladies' Ministries' in the district, who were awarded first, second, third and fourth prizes for their activities.

The annual 'Regional Ladies Seminar' is held at the Mother church of the adjoining district. The focus of the meeting is a celebration of the 'Ladies' Ministries' throughout the north of England. This seminar is the largest national meeting specifically devoted to the women in the church. There is less play between the categories 'men' and 'women' and more emphasis on the independent and complementary activities of women and the joint activities of female saints. At one such meeting the individual achievements of women in the different 'Ladies' Ministries' in the region were celebrated; a report was made of the history of the 'Ladies' Ministry' in England and the current efforts of the women to establish a national home for the elderly. This seminar is a public statement of the efficacy of women and it is here that changes in the agency of women are registered; it was in this context that the national overseer's wife dedicated the baby.

Although the auxiliaries of the 'Ladies' Ministry' and the 'Men's Fellowship' conduct their meetings and activities independently, both are engaged in the evangelism of the wider community, a complementary spiritual endeavor which is incomplete without the efforts of the other. While the MF ostensibly provides a support group to men and evangelizes to men, women support each other and evangelize to women. The segregated meetings, such as the independent monthly YALM meetings or the combined district and regional meetings of the LM provide the contexts wherein women tell themselves what it is like to be a woman, and it is significant that being a woman is conceived primarily as being a mother. Women make few references to themselves as wives. When they do, it is to remind themselves that a woman should serve her husband and her family; no matter how good a husband is, if a wife is a hindrance she can bring him down, but a good wife can also save her husband in times of crisis, like Abigail, or she can save him through evangelism (cf. Brusco 1995). In the LM meetings, women confront the issues of motherhood and work and the contradictions that can arise from being a woman as wife and mother and being a female saint. Although these are separate issues arising from the complementary and independent activities of women, they are addressed through instrumental means which are shared with male saints: the ability to preach, pray, sing, testify and engage in Bible study. Women possess agency as a result of motherhood which can be compared to the nurturing qualities of God and Christ, but they also possess agency as female saints who are empowered by God.

There is a continuous fluctuation in the identity frameworks within which persons are described when the women and men of the church come together in joint meetings. On these occasions the relationships between men and women as separate social categories are played off against each other, e.g., 'buying a man down,' 'buying a woman down,' the alternate reading of verses, the YMF versus the YALM, the occasional contribution of the MF to the Ladies Day. The deconstruction and reconstruction of persons is not only accomplished at the level of gender but through generations as well: men are divided into husbands, young men and men; women are divided into the different auxiliaries which together form the 'Ladies' Ministry' as a whole. In joint services, the statements and actions of women make it clear that their agency as women is derived from their role as nurturing, comforting and caring biological and non-biological mothers and that they also possess agency as saints. When agency as a mother and agency as a saint are combined, as in the Sunday services of the 'Ladies' Weekend' and the dedication of an infant, the effect is powerful and the agency of women is not contested, but supported. While men may control the pulpit on most occasions, it should not be forgotten that women can also harness the agency of God and in so doing can also remind men that women are the financial, spiritual and demographic basis of the church.

Conclusion

There are three social categories of the person in the NTCG: 'men,' 'women' and 'saints.' The construction of each of these categories employs different levels of discourse and different forms of social practice, which have different implications for expected behavior, agency and relations of equality and inequality. The construction of these three categories of person can be understood with reference to two different models of gender identity in the church. One model employs the discourse and practices of Jamaican and African-Caribbean kinship and domestic organization. This model can be understood with reference to the imagery of the head and the neck which marks both the ideal of the patriarchal Christian family, where women as wives are subservient to the power and authority of men as husbands, and the experience of women as mothers of female-centered households who possess power and authority or as migrant women who (as their life histories indicate) have had to shoulder a heavy burden of responsibility. Thus within this single model of gender identity, there exist men as 'husbands,' women as 'wives' and women as 'mothers' from whom different things are expected and who possess different types of agency.

The second model constructs persons as undifferentiated saints with reference to a 'Christian' identity. Unlike the first model, in this model persons have in common the same expectations with regard to their behavior and they share the same type of agency. Although there are two different models for the construction of persons, the categories 'men,' 'women' and 'saint' cannot be understood as discrete and autonomous gender identities. These different categories are interconnected: it is impossible to succeed as a 'Christian' without also fulfilling the expectations imposed on 'men' and 'women,' but since the construction of each category entails differences of expectation and agency, it must also be conceded that in the interlocking of gender identities constructed in different gender regimes, there are areas of inconsistency in which persons can contest and change ideas about identity.

The official reading of the proverb of the head and the neck draws upon the ideal gender regime of the Christian family, only one possible pattern from among the range of Jamaican and African-Caribbean patterns of domestic organization. Here the construction of a male gender identity is premised on the legally sanctioned conjugal relationship between men and women in a 'Christian marriage,' with the result that men are narrowly defined as 'husband.' In fact, most men in the church have been brought into it by their wives, or were raised in it and found partners there. As husbands, men are vested with responsibility which is effected through an autonomous agency to lead, command and discipline others. However, these ideas are not necessarily reflected in the lived experiences of male members in Jamaica and Britain. First, by positing men's power and authority over women in the family, they deny or negate the experience of domestic marginality. Secondly, they say little about male sexuality and negate the lived experiences of men who can become fathers through a range of different conjugal unions by virtue of sexual maturity. Although some elderly men are referred to as 'father' out of respect and deference to their age, the role of father as genitor is not celebrated or institutionalized in the church. It is God who occupies the position of father. Thus within the gender regime of the church, men can enact gender roles as they 'should be' where the opportunity for agency is severely circumscribed or denied by secular social organization. However, there are also a few single men in the church, for whom a gender identity as husbands bears little relation to their circumstances. The construction of a pertinent gender identity for single men in the church remains unclear.

While the construction of a male gender identity can only be played along a single axis, the construction of a female gender identity is played along two axes. On one axis, women are narrowly constructed as wives in terms of their relationship with men in an ideal 'Christian marriage.' A wife can be a help or a hindrance to her husband; the ideal wife should be passive, submissive and demonstrably supportive of her husband. As a wife, a woman possesses little agency other than to yield to and thus support and ensure her husband's agency. A straightforward reading of the imagery of the head and the neck supports the neat patriarchal model of the 'Christian family.' However, as the excerpts from women's life histories and an examination of member's non-fictive kinship in chapter 1 have demonstrated, women's experiences and domestic circumstances do not always fulfill the 'model for' the family provided by the ideology of the church's gender regime. Elaine Foster (1992) is correct to point out the potential difficulty of a construction of women as wives in a denomination where many women may be single, divorced or separated, where they may be single mothers, unlikely to marry or remarry, or where they may be married to men who are not members of the church. Women can find that they are at the center of domestic organization whether or not their partners are present, they can find that they are mothers not necessarily by virtue of being married to a man or giving birth to a child, and for some women who are alone there is the painful reality that there is no family, 'Christian,' 'extended' or otherwise, of which to be or not to be the center.

It is in this context that the second axis, the construction of women as mothers, takes its force. This model does not invert or negate social reality but draws its strength from the lived experiences of women. The construction of a gender identity as mother acknowledges the Jamaican cultural concept that the role of mother is founded upon emotion, dispositions and the action of doing things for others. It does not tie motherhood to biological parturition or conflate it with the ideal conjugal role of wife in 'Christian marriage.' As mothers, women are vested with enabling agency to nurture, comfort, socialize, instruct, admonish and discipline others to develop into competent social actors.

Unlike the complementary roles of husband and wife which are described in an official reading of the proverb of the head and the neck, on this axis of gender there is no role of father to complement the role of mother. Despite this, an ambiguous reading of the proverb can still account for the role of the mother because it can accommodate her power and authority where it is read as enabling and supportive agency. Although women as wives and mothers possess different types of agency, the role of wife is invested with wisdom, which a wife can use in a crisis to prevent harm befalling her household. This aspect of a wife's agency intersects with the agency of mothers and can be accommodated in the ambiguous deployment of Biblical stories. While the power and authority of mothers can be read into the proverb, it is not done in a way which permits woman-centered Caribbean kinship and domestic organization to undermine the ideal of patriarchal gender relations, nor does it need to pathologize the role of mothers or contradict the experiences of many female members. The transformative power of conversion is crucial here. The NTCG does not condone the actions of men and women which result in single motherhood. As in middle-class Jamaican Pentecostalism, single motherhood is not the subject of disproportionate attention in lessons and sermons, but when women come into the church as single mothers, their circumstances are taken as given and their past sins forgiven. By emphasizing the enabling agency of mothers as the neck which allows the head to be held erect, the power and authority of women is acknowledged but knitted into the ideal model of gender relations. In the same way, the practical power of Mothers is acknowledged but remains 'officially unofficial.'

Although the ideology of gender in the church tempers the power and authority of women, it still permits women an avenue of power and a means for expressing their interests through the agency of saints. Although persons are differentially constructed as 'men' and 'women,' at the same time they are constructed as saints as a result of their 'Christian' identity. When a person is born again, he or she is born into a specific genderless regime which does not differentiate between the 'Christian man' and the 'Christian woman.' Both male and female saints must go through the same process of conversion and adhere to the same rules governing behavior. Unlike the differentiated agency of men and women, all saints possess the same agency, which originates from

God, though they may possess different amounts of agency based on differences in spiritual maturity. Saints may pray, sing, testify, study the Bible, evangelize and potentially prophesy, heal, discern danger and preach. Unlike the separate and complementary activities of men and women in the church these are joint activities. However, 'Christian' identity and agency as a saint cannot be completely divorced from the gendered roles of males and females, for in this androgynous gender regime there are also messages which convey information about the ways in which men and women are constructed in the church.

Male and female saints can be distinguished by reference to the terms 'Brother' and 'Sister.' Unlike the roles of husband, wife and mother, which convey both difference and inequality, in this case the fictive kinship terms 'Brother' and 'Sister' denote male and female difference. However, it is also important to note that, unlike Sicilian conceptions of brother and sister, all members stand in equal relations to each other as children of God who are potentially equally empowered. At the same time, the differential empowerment of male and female ministers and the differing roles of officers and Mothers of the Church highlight the articulation of gendered persons with persons as saints. One cannot be a saint without reference to the appropriate behavior of men and women respectively. Crucial to this is the reading of relations between men and women in the church in terms of the patriarchal gender regime of the 'Christian family.' Male saints are vested with the legitimate effectiveness to make decisions which affect the church and to represent the church to the wider society. Male saints are responsible for the financial running of the church, for calling members together for a meeting, and for organizing most of the transport, carpentry and structural maintenance of the church building. As ordained ministers, it is male saints who can exercise the authority to acknowledge the growth and unity of the church family, e.g., by acknowledging potential members through infant dedication, making public the 'Christian' identity of the person in baptism, and sanctioning unions between male and female saints by performing the sacrament of marriage.

By contrast, the agency of female saints is combined with the enabling agency of mothers in the role of Mother of the Church. Since authority and power as a mother results from the nurturing relationship one has with others, it can easily be extended to include others in the church for whom one does things. In the church women are always 'lifting up their hands': cooking, cleaning, sewing, etc. However, in order for a woman to exercise her enabling agency as a Mother of the Church, she must fulfill two other conditions. First, she must possess agency as a saint; she must possess spiritual maturity and be a good 'Christian' so that she can instruct others and set an example for others. Secondly, it is not enough to be simply a mother in terms of actions; to be a Mother of the Church a woman should also stand in relation to a man as his wife in a 'Christian marriage.'

While gendered identity as men and women can thus be seen to articulate with identity as a saint, the interlocking of a person's identity as a saint and as a woman can result in inconsistencies and contradictions, for example, the contradictions which arise when a woman must simultaneously fulfill her responsibilities as wife, mother, employee and saint, or the inconsistencies which arise with regard to the agency of female saints such that they cannot ordinarily perform infant dedication or baptize new converts. These discrepancies can be challenged and negotiated with an appeal to the agency of different identities. Some women mobilize an identity as mother to admonish men and demand that they are less controlling 'minimal men' and more nurturing and helpful in meeting domestic responsibilities. Or a male preacher can argue that since women are mothers, they should have the capacity to dedicate a baby. Alternatively, some women mobilize their identity as saints. As such, they can subvert the joint activities of saints to express their interests as gendered persons and express what it is like to be a woman through testimonies and the use of maternal imagery in sermons by women. Or they can argue that as saints they possess the spiritual agency necessary to fulfill ministerial roles such as dedicating babies and baptizing converts. Using an identity as saints, women can widen the scope of their agency piece by piece and thus effect a change from an agency of enablement to an agency of doing. After all, as was hinted at in the Saturday address of the 'District Ladies' Weekend,' if women were to restrict themselves in their capabilities and responsibilities, they 'would be calling God a liar.'

The gender regime of the NTCG is not fixed: gender identities are in the process of being made and remade by social actors themselves. 'Saints,' 'men,' 'women,' young and old are all equally valid social categories of the person in the NTCG. These categories are continuously differentiated, played off against each other and recombined. This manipulation of categories results in ambiguity which is used for the creation of meaning of ideas about gender and personhood. Nor are these meanings created in isolation: the creation of meaning draws upon the lived experiences of members, sometimes inverting or negating them and sometimes using them as a source of truth. Ideas about gender in the church mediate the contradictions inherent in a specific African-Caribbean tradition of marginal men and domineering matriarchs. They do this by appropriating the power and authority of mothers and fastening them to an ideal of patriarchal gender relations where women can be seen as both submissive wives and powerful mothers, necks supporting powerful men as heads. In mediating and resolving the contradictions between men and women's authority and power in this way, ideas regarding the construction of gender and personhood in the church displace the very basis on which the African-Caribbean gender regime of the family and the roles of Black men and women are pathologized in British society.

Racism and discrimination have both men and women as their object. The structuring of African-Caribbean women's engagement in the workforce conflicts with dominant conceptions of their sexuality and motherhood. The commonplace stereotypes of African-Caribbean women, in England which center on their engagement in the workforce, sexuality and motherhood are in turn reflected back onto African-Caribbean women, where their behavior is seen as deviant. Women's religious participation in the NTCG which first defines them as 'Christians' without a gender or ethnic identity, and secondly provides a construction of female gender where women are 'good,' caring mothers who are married to responsible men and yield to their authority and power, replaces the commonplace assumptions about African-Caribbean women and has implications for their prestige in the dominant gender order of the wider society.

Women's participation in the church cannot only be understood in terms of its implications for them in the dominant gender order: their participation must also be understood in terms of the implications for the prestige of Black men in the dominant gender order. Again it is necessary to raise the issue of conflict between a dominant gender and a minority gender order which not only constructs the gender of African-Caribbean women but of African-Caribbean men as well. Connell's insight into a core patriarchal structure based on a hierarchy of hegemonic masculinity, conservative masculinity and subordinated masculinity (1987: 109–10) applies to the position of African-Caribbean men. If the masculinity of African-Caribbean men has been emasculated or subordinated, then they are effectively prevented from participating in the politico-jural relations structured by the dominant gender order. Before they can represent themselves as the official voices of their community and articulate with the wider society, their legitimate masculinity must be reinstated. This is accomplished in the church where women as the neck, the wives and mothers in 'Christian marriage,' support and enable their men to possess a conservative masculinity of responsibility, sexual restraint, power and authority, thus negating a 'powerless' Black male gender identity of deviancy, irresponsibility and threatening sexual promiscuity.

The 'silent collusion' in which men and women are engaged in the church (Foster 1992) should be read exactly for what it is, collusion. It cannot be argued that in the construction of gender in the church women loose out. Women know what they are doing when, given the circumstances of racism and oppression, they support their men, but they also care whether or not their power is acknowledged. The fact that women in the church do not employ feminist rhetoric or tactics to attack a model in which they are constructed as women does not mean that they are not engaged in changing or cannot change and restructure the model. The pursuit for agency and respect in which women in the church are engaged should not be read as simply claims 'of the self' made 'for the self'; they are simultaneously claiming respect for African-Caribbean men and women within the dominant gender order.

Conclusion

On October 16th, 1995, a large yet debatable number of Black American men marched on Washington DC under the organizing aegis of the Nation of Islam's Minister Louis Farrakhan. The purpose of the march was to encourage Black men to take greater responsibility for their families and communities.[1] On the one hand the march was designed as a religious event, 'A Holy Day of Atonement, Reconciliation and Responsibility,' while on the other it was a display of Black identity. Minister Farrakhan's invocation of the religious postures of atonement, reconciliation and responsibility were purposeful, yet the event was secularly billed as an opportunity to reclaim a unified, strong, positive, Black male identity. Farrakhan utilized the African-American tradition where religious participation provides a forum for the construction of Black identity and a platform for political action. It is precisely because he used a religious discourse that he was able to attract such a large turnout. Many of the men in attendance were adherents of Islam, but significantly more men were not. He was also able to bridge potential rifts between Islam and Black Christian denominations by appealing to the patriarchal gender model inherent in both. However, because religion and identity are closely associated in the American imagination, what made this march appealing also made it controversial. Observers feared many of Farrakhan's controversial stances. If a million African-American men attended, did this mean they sympathized with Farrakhan? Would they convert from Black Christianity to Islam and slip further from the grasp of White American understanding?[2] Ambivalent feelings abounded. Black Methodist and Baptist leaders individually condemned and condoned the march and

1. J. F. Brown, 'Million Man March Fact Sheet,' *Washington Afro-American*, 9/30/95.
2. C. Power and A. Samuels, 'Battling for Souls,' *Newsweek*, 10/30/95.

265

White Americans looked on warily. Yet, Methodists, Baptists, other Christians and Whites attended. It quickly became clear that there was a disassociation of the message from the messenger.[3] The march moved from being a demonstration of support for Farrakhan and the Nation of Islam to a grass-roots movement incorporating men of different ages, classes and educational backgrounds as well as different sexual, religious and political persuasions. Some men attended not to atone, but to reaffirm their position in their families and communities. It was the wider message directed at every Black American male – that it was time to contest the destructive representations of the Black male current in the US – which drew these men. True, Farrakhan organized the event, but as a student at Lincoln University was quoted as saying, 'This goes way beyond Farrakhan.'[4]

Women were not officially excluded from the march, nor were they encouraged to attend. Instead, they were asked not to work or buy anything, but to remain at home, keep children home from school, teach and discuss the day's events with them, prepare food and pray.[5] While the majority of women did not attend, they supported the march by participating in organizing events prior to it and organizing events and meals and praying on the day. Some women attended:[6] Rosa Parks, Dorothy Height, President of the National Council of Negro Women, Dr. C. Delores Tucker, Chair of the National Political Congress of Black Women and Maya Angelou were invited to speak at the march. The ambivalent stance towards women's participation can be understood with reference to the multifaceted construction of women as mothers, wives and sisters, the segregated and complementary roles of men and women, and a religious grammar of patriarchy. Women did not

3. 'Million Man March not about Farrakhan,' *The Philadelphia Tribune*, 9/15/95; K. De Witt, 'Black Men say the March in Washington is about them, not Farrakhan,' *New York Times*, 10/15/95.

4. C. Shea, 'Good to be Black,' *The Chronicle of Higher Education*, 10/27/95.

5. S. Stone, 'Women Prepare to Play a Major Role in the March,' *The Philadelphia Tribune*, 10/13/95; G. Gilmore, 'Union Temple Women Sing Praises to March,' *Washington Afro-American*, 10/28/95; U. V. Battle, 'Standing behind their Men: African American Women displayed support for Million Man March,' *Baltimore Afro-American*, 10/21/95.

6. Patricia Elam Ruff, Letter to the Editor, *New York Times*, 12/13/95; V. K. Pryce, 'From a Woman in a Million Man March,' *The New York Beacon*, 10/25/95; K. Starling, 'I Got Your Back: A Renewed Faith for Sisters,' *About . . . Time Magazine*, 11/30/95.

need to be in Washington that day to support men; in fact the presence of many women would have attenuated the impact and aim of the event. The women who supported the event willingly subscribed to the model of gender where men are the public face of the family and community and are responsible, caring providers, while women in all their nonetheless important roles are invisible enabling supporters. These women literally justified their position by citing the maxim 'behind every good man is a good woman' or 'I got your back.'[7] A Baptist mother of two interpreted the position of women in the event with reference to her understanding of gender as constructed in the Black church, and she noted the tradition of services segregated by sex.[8] However, many notable Black women were offended by the exclusion of women, such as Angela Davis, Paula Giddings, Donna Franklin and Kristal Brent Zook.[9] Significantly, these women point out that the idea of the 'endangered Black male' is a racist stereotype, ignoring the range of Black male identities and the accomplishments of African-American men in history, well-known contemporary men as well as lesser known men. Further, they argue that in order to confront the image of the 'endangered Black male,' participants in the Million Man March have created a new Black patriarchy. African-American women are thus divided in their opinions between those for whom the Million Man March is a constructive response to a reality of the 'endangered Black male' and those for whom the 'endangered Black male' is a dangerous straw man who invokes a singular Black identity and Black authenticity.

Much of the meaning of the Million Man March will remain unfathomable if we fail to recognize and internalize the diversity of African-American identities, if we conflate religion, ethnicity and gender without investigating the nature of articulation among these manifestations of identity. The case of the Million Man March and the NTCG challenge Black authenticity. There are several Black identities across the African Diaspora (African, African-American, French African-Caribbean, Latin African-Caribbean, Dutch African-

7. 'Frederica Bey: Woman in Support of the Million Man March,' *The New York Beacon*, 10/11/95; Battle, ibid.; Starling, ibid.

8. M. Marriott, 'Black Women are Split over All-Male March on Washington,' *New York Times*, 10/14/95.

9. Marriott, ibid.; K. B. Zook, 'A Manifesto of Sorts for a Black Feminist Movement,' *New York Times, Magazine*, 11/12/95; D. Franklin, 'Black Herstory,' *New York Times*, 10/18/1995.

Caribbean, English African-Caribbean, etc.) and within each is a further diversification of identities, each possessing a different constellation of ethnicity, gender and religion. All are valid and present a challenge for research. Yet, there is also continuity in the themes and dynamics of identity across the African Diaspora such that the politics of identity and gender in the NTCG help reveal the meaning of the Million Man March.

The Million Man March and the NTCG highlight the role of religious belief and participation in structuring and giving meaning to gender. There is a religious revival of conservative gender constructs where new forms of masculinity are 'a feminist vision of manhood without machismo' ironically constructed through White Protestant patriarchy.[10] Hence, at first glance the Million Man March seems to fit in with the Promise Keepers Movement,[11] as well as Colombian, Bolivian and Sicilian Pentecostalism. It is doubtful whether the Million Man March can be understood simply as a revival without also considering the dynamics of African-American gender and how the gender of African-American women was redefined in that moment.

This study has examined some of the implications of participation in African-Caribbean Pentecostalism and the ways in which this religious framework provides its followers with a way of challenging the dominant representations of Black people and the terms of their interaction with others in contemporary British society. The members of King Street congregation share the same socio-economic characteristics as Birmingham's African-Caribbean population and participate in the same broad social and political context which has marginalized Black people in British society. Given members' similarity to other African-Caribbeans and their diversity of life histories and personal backgrounds, the variables of 'deprivation,' age, gender, kinship, economic status or 'life crisis' cannot, as Cucchiari (1988) argued for Sicilian Pentecostalists, be used to explain participation in this form of African-Caribbean

10. W. Kaminer, 'The Measure of a Man,' review of *Manhood in America: A Cultural History*, by M. Kimmel, *New York Times*, 12/31/95. Cf. the restructuring of gender in other forms of fundamentalism such as Islam.

11. The Promise Keepers is a predominantly White American movement where men pledge to honor Jesus Christ, remain spiritually, morally and sexually pure and faithful to their wives, and take on the mantle of leadership in their families and communities.

Pentecostalism. Participation must therefore be understood as one choice within a range of possibilities in which Black people may negotiate the terms of representation and interaction with others in British society.

The continued presence, popularity and growth of African-Caribbean Pentecostalism in Britain suggests that early interpretations of African-Caribbean Pentecostalism – that it is a retreat into familiar and comfortable cultural practice (Calley 1962, 1965; Eggington 1957; Patterson 1965), a solution to the relative status-deprivation experienced by Caribbean migrants in British society (Hill 1963, 1971a, 1971b, 1971c) or the passive resignation of the first generation (Cashmore 1979; Pryce 1979) – needs to be replaced with an alternative interpretation. A historical review of religious practice and the rise of Pentecostalism in Jamaica suggests that in the context of the late colonial period, Pentecostalism received a limited degree of popularity because it simultaneously addressed the issues of status and suffering and thus reconciled the characteristics of denominational Christianity on the one hand and African-Christian religious practices on the other. For the individual, Pentecostalism acted as a bridge which connected and integrated the polarized constellations of Jamaica's religious spectrum. In the British context, however, African-Caribbean Pentecostalism differs significantly. No longer capable of integrating the religious order, it (like its followers) is at once a part of society and apart from society. In England, the religious order was characterized by homogeneous congregations – open racial exclusivity – and a non-negotiable correspondence between religious behavior and status. Questions of suffering – especially racial disadvantage and oppression – could not be addressed, and there was little room for ambiguity that could be drawn upon to make claims about status. White churches did not 'share fellowship' and did not tolerate the expression of Caribbean forms of religious feeling. African-Caribbean Pentecostalism, by contrast, has been able simultaneously to address the issue of status, in its emphasis upon values which are compatible with the wider society, and the issue of suffering, where it draws upon Christian imagery to represent and transform the experiences of marginality and disadvantage in a racially divided society. The breadth of the Pentecostal message, therefore, makes the church appealing to old and young, to successful and impoverished. As the quote at the beginning of this work and the recurrence of race, nationality and ethnicity in actors' statements suggest, members are angered by the dominant terms of their representation in society and the resulting terms of their interaction with others. To participate in African-Caribbean Pentecostalism may not be a form of militant demonstration, but it is a means whereby people are actively engaged in the reworking of definitions and issues.

Crucial to the Pentecostal position are the ideas held about the nature of conversion. People become members following the spiritual rebirth of conversion, in which they believe they have been granted a new nature, deeply embedded in the physical substance of the body, the blood, stomach and heart. Thus a person is identified and identifies him- or herself as a 'Christian' on the basis of internal character. Identity as a 'Christian' cannot easily be assessed from the external appearance and actions of the individual, nor is it fixed; it requires constant discipline and religious work and is constructed and maintained through ritual participation. As a 'Christian,' one is tied through ties of sacred fictive kinship to a diffuse collective of other 'Christians' which transcends the boundaries of time and space. Because the members of this collective can only be identified on the basis of their internal nature, the group cannot easily be objectified. Thus belief not only remakes the nature of the individual, it challenges everyday ideas about the nature of the group to which he or she belongs. By replacing external appearance and action with internal nature as the basis of definition and identification and manipulating the categories of the individual and the group, the cosmology of the NTCG provides an incisive challenge to the logic upon which dominant representations of Black people are constructed.

The dominant representation of congregations such as King Street draws boundaries around the physical manifestation of the community as a 'Black Church'; it draws on the diacritics of race, national origin, status, material wealth, language, work, education and food to assign the group an identity on the basis of ethnicity. However, the cosmology of the NTCG posits membership in a diffuse community of 'Christians' whose members can only be defined on the basis of their internal nature. Thus, the placement of group boundaries and the symbolic markers used in the construction of community are contested. Members respond to dominant representations by mobilizing the same diacritics of nationality, status, material wealth, language, work, education and food in the symbolic construction of the community. However, no straightforward correlation between ethnic and religious identity could be claimed: religious identity is not an expression of ethnicity. These diacritics are given new symbolic meaning such that they can no longer be read as the border posts of exclusion but as the gateway to unity and inclusion and as a charter for behavior and interaction with others.

Where national citizenship is divisive and for some, at least, a way of challenging the position of Black people in Britain, in the church it is replaced with an inclusive spiritual 'citizenship with God.' Where status and material wealth can be used to divide and stratify people in society, the value of status and material wealth in the church is actively denigrated and replaced with an emphasis on equality among brethren. Equality among brethren provides a charter for behavior. The emphasis on equality can also be understood to be expressed in the predominant application of fictive kinship terms which precludes generational depth and hierarchical ranking. Similarly, the divisive and differentiating power of language is undermined in the church. Where 'Queen's English' is used in interaction with others who are different and in a public context, and Patois is used to convey trivial secular exchanges, the use of 'Authorized Worship Language' and potentially glossolalia serve as diacritics of identity and group membership because the capacity to use them are felt to be part of the new nature which a person receives in conversion. Although the serving and consumption of food constitutes a significant proportion of church activities, unlike the symbolic themes of nationality, status, material wealth, language, work and education, food was not manipulated as a verbal symbol of group identity and membership, and food as practice was found to be antithetical to religious worship.

These findings, supported by the various models of the relationship between ethnic identity and religious identity offered by members, suggest that although an ethnic identity is not inimical to a religious identity, there can be no straightforward reading of the ethnic in religious belief and practice. The themes of nationality and general status markers clearly exhibited the greatest distance between an 'essential Black identity' and religious identity, while the manipulation of Patois, education and food highlighted the difficulties which arise when ethnicity is conflated with religious behavior. The symbols which members of the NTCG utilize in the construction of the community not only invert the values of the dominant culture in society but also subvert the basis on which African-Caribbean people are deprived and excluded.

Since 'Christian identity' was understood as the remaking of the person and his or her relationships with others, following Strathern (1987a) and Connell (1987), gender is understood as culturally constructed difference which can be revealed through an examination of imagery, social practice and agency. Members do not distinguish between a 'Christian' man and a 'Christian' woman – in other words, identity as a 'Christian' is non-gendered. At a practical level, however, distinctions are made between men and women. Thus, there are three categories of the person in the church: 'men,' 'women' and 'saints.' The construction of gendered persons ('men' and 'women') and the construction of persons as undifferentiated saints employs two different models: one model rests upon both the 'model for' the family provided by patriarchal 'Christian marriage' and the 'model of' the practical range in African-Caribbean kinship and domestic organization, while the other model is based on the 'model for' 'Christian identity.'

The 'model for' the 'Christian family' defines husbands, wives and mothers as persons possessing different legitimate agency. The construction of male gender is narrowly based on ideas of the conjugal relationship in legally sanctioned 'Christian marriages.' Despite Caribbean cultural concepts, the role of men as genitors is not celebrated. Thus, in the church, the construction of male gender illustrates the distance between ethnic identity and religious identity which was found to exist for the symbolic construction of the community.

By contrast, the construction of female gender in the church operates along both the axes of 'Christian marriage' and the practical range of African-Caribbean kinship and domestic organization. In the idiom of 'Christian marriage,' women are constructed as wives who are subject to the authority of their husbands: they should be passive, submissive and supportive. The construction of women as wives, as of men as husbands, contradicts many of the experiences of women while denying them scope for legitimate power and agency. As 'wives,' women only possess agency to intervene in moments of crisis which jeopardize the family and the household. However, the practical range of African-Caribbean kinship and domestic organization also provides an idiom for the construction women as 'mothers' where women possess enabling agency within the sphere of domestic responsibilities to nurture, instruct and admonish juniors, cook, clean, sew, etc. Unlike the constructions of husband and wife, the construction of women as mothers can thus be seen to draw upon the experiences and strengths of women. The roles and agency of wives and mothers appear contradictory: however, the potential for contradiction and conflict is minimized by incorporating the role of women as mothers into the patriarchal relationship between husbands and wives. Once integrated into the 'model for' the family, the agency of mothers is emphasized as an enabling agency which must be subordinate to the autonomous agency of husbands. Thus, where the construction of male gender underscores the difference between ethnic identity and religious identity, the construction of female gender in the church draws upon the ambiguous unity of ethnic identity and religious identity which was also found to exist in the symbolic construction of the community.

The second model for the construction of personhood is that of undifferentiated saints. As 'Christian' persons, men and women have a relationship with God, and it is this relationship which gives them both equal access to power and agency. Both male and female saints possess the potential of power for service endowed by the baptism of the Holy Spirit. Once again there appears to be scope for contradiction in the different identities which the person possesses as an undifferentiated saint and as a gendered person. However, the model which constructs the gendered person is not entirely distinct from that which constructs him or her as a saint. The intersection of identity as a saint and as a gendered person, male or female, empowers the individual with particular kinds of agency which can be directed at other members of the congregation.

As husbands, men possess patriarchal authority as the head of the household. Thus male saints may become pastors, ordained ministers, licensed ministers, exhorters and church officers. They are vested with agency to lead, command, instruct and discipline members and are responsible for the physical and financial maintenance of the church. For women, by contrast, it is not the agency appropriate to wives which is combined with the agency of saint, but that of woman as mother. However, women can also serve as pastors, ministers and exhorters. In the past, the legitimate agency of female ministers was limited by their gendered identity as women: as female ministers and exhorters, women lacked the power to acknowledge the incorporation of members, denote potential members or unite members in marriage. Currently, however, some women are appealing to the contradictions between the model that constructs them as women and that which constructs them as saints in order to claim effective agency as saints to extend the scope of their ministerial authority.

Dominant representations of African-Caribbean men and women in British society contrast what is perceived to be the 'ethnic' construction of gender with the construction of men and women in the dominant gender order. The manipulation of ethnic identity and religious identity in the construction of gender in the church offers an effective, if subtle, rejoinder. It is significant that the social construction of gender for men and women does not incorporate the same articulation of ethnicity and religion. Men are no longer disempowered, sexually promiscuous, threatening members of society, but are empowered by a conservative masculinity defined through their relationship as husbands to women in patriarchal 'Christian marriage.' Women are no longer the sexually promiscuous, dominant matriarchs, and working mothers of 'common-sense' assumptions: instead, women possess conservative femininity in which they are subordinate wives and good mothers. Crucial to this re-definition of male and female gender, which effectively challenges dominant representations of Black men and women, is the laying aside of 'sexist and oppressive' conceptions in accounting for women in the church and an acceptance of the fact that, without the compliance of women, this gender regime would collapse.

Participation in African-Caribbean Pentecostalism provides members with an alternative basis for identity and difference, not as Blacks in a White society, but as 'Christians' in an imperfect society and world. Throughout this work, 'identity' has been understood as that which results from the dynamic interplay between externally imposed dominant representations and subjective perceptions (following Wallman 1978 and A. P. Cohen 1985a). Dominant representations assign identity to African-Caribbean people as generally undifferentiated members of a group which is then in turn differentiated and excised from British society on the basis of visible racial difference and its multiple synonymous attributes: nationality, language and culture. Identity as 'Christians' is a powerful rejoinder to dominant representations, because it strikes at the heart of the matter, contesting the nature of the object upon which representations are imposed by addressing both the individual and the group. It shifts the focus of objectification from the group to the individual and in so doing challenges the definition of the individual, gender and the group, and the meaning of diacritics like sex, race, nationality, language and culture. What 'Christian identity' asserts is an ideal view of society and social interaction where people are valued and respected as individuals who can be differentiated upon the basis of what they are inside – what they feel and believe themselves to be – and not in terms of the group to which they belong. Thus valued, the individual is free to interact with others in a society and world that is free from the hindrances of particularistic group membership and group differentiation. It is significant that in providing its followers with an alternative identity, African-Caribbean Pentecostalism engages and works through difference, thus demonstrating that one does not need to stop short at difference and adopt an active form of resistance, like Rastafarianism or the Nation of Islam, in order to claim the right to self-determination in the politics of representation.

Appendix I: Services

There are numerous forms of organized communal worship: Sunday morning and evening service; alternate prayer meeting or Bible study on Monday evenings; Family Training Hour on Wednesday evenings; and a range of smaller meetings, e.g., fasting meetings, bible-study groups held at members' homes, and the weekly or monthly meetings of church auxiliaries.

Most members attend the Sunday Divine services. These services follow a fairly regular pattern, beginning with choruses and the singing of hymns and followed by an opening prayer; music and prayer may be repeated. The moderator then leads the congregation in the reading of the lesson; this ends the 'devotional part of the service.' If children are to be dedicated, this usually follows the scripture reading. Visitors are called upon to stand and say a few words following the lesson or the dedication. If testimonies are offered in the morning services, they follow the lesson, the 'dedication of infants' and the noting of visitors. The noting of visitors may be followed by another period of music or prayer. The next section of the service is the collection of tithes and offerings. Three combined elements constitute this section: music from the youth choir, prayer for the offering and the collection proper. The prayer for the offering may be said either before or after the collection. This is followed by a hymn from the Sanctuary Choir, which marks the transition to the sermon. The sermon itself may be a simple oration or it may include prayers and song. It ends with an 'altar call' while the remainder of the congregation prays. Notices are read and the service is concluded with a 'closing benediction' which is recited in unison. If the service is a fasting service on the first Sunday of the month, it will continue throughout the day and there will be no benediction at the end of the morning worship. Though regular Sunday morning services are lively and energetic, it is only occasionally that the stereotyped ecstatic fervor of Pentecostalism is displayed.

Sunday evening services are usually smaller, less formal meetings characterized by more emotional behavior with extended periods of ecstatic behavior. The focus of Sunday Divine services is the raised pulpit, but in the evening the focus shifts to the floor of the congregation. The service is conducted from a podium behind the altar rail, from which the sermonette will be delivered. The members of the Sanctuary Choir who are present in the evening will move from the choir gallery to the pews normally occupied by the youth choir, and the smaller assembly will occupy the forward pews of the hall (see Figure 3.1). Evening services follow the same general pattern of morning services beginning with a devotional part, the transitional phase (when the collection is taken) and the final part, in which a sermon is delivered. However, there is greater scope for the manipulation of the elements of worship and for individual lay participation. Persons are invited to give their testimonies following the devotional part of the service and more members are called upon to speak and pray.

At one evening service, there were forty-nine adults, thirty-five women and fourteen men. We were told that most of the men were giving support to the men's program at Queenspiece. Mother Palmar moderated the service for the evening and called upon Sister Conneely to pray. The focus of Sister Conneely's prayer was for those who were on their way, and she asked God for a divine manifestation of the Holy Spirit that evening. This was followed by a chorus. Mother Palmar called upon Sister Bucks to give the devotion. Before the reading, a hymn was sung and Sister Cynthia Dwire prayed and took us to the 'throne of grace.' Sister Beaufort then read the scripture, which was Psalm 150. Following the devotion there were a total of sixteen testimonies, two of which were sung. Brother and Sister Montaigne both testified, as they were to return to Jamaica that week. The testimony of Brother Montaigne was short and simple. He thanked God and the members of the congregation for assisting his wife and himself during their bereavement. Sister Montaigne then testified. She approached the front of the hall; her testimony was very emotional and ecstatic. She used it as an opportunity to preach about separating the sheep from the goats (Romans 8). She was moved by the Holy Spirit and no one attempted to interrupt her or stop her. Brother Montaigne remained standing during his wife's testimony. There was also a testimony from a new woman, who spoke of her experience of salvation when her arthritic arms had been healed. She made it very clear that she wanted to become a member of the church. After the testimonies, two little girls came forward and sang the chorus 'I Love You Jesus.' Then the members of the Sanctuary Choir sang while the offering was collected. Sister Adler prayed that the offering may be used in the service of God's work. Sister Giddea Dwire came forward and prayed for Brother and Sister Montaigne. This was followed by an altar call to which eight women came forward. Sister Buchannan came forward to lay hands on the women while we prayed. Sister Giddea then gave her sermon on the theme of 'fighting like Goliath' and the protection of the Lord. The service ended with the hymn 'Got You any Rivers You Think Uncrossable?'

Although regular evening services, like morning services, are opportunities for collective worship, the service is characterized by the stress on the individual worshipper who has come to worship in the company of others. Evening services also tend to be used to highlight the achievements of individuals or groups within the church, as they are usually the time allotted for the celebration of baptisms, Lord's Suppers and 'send-offs.'

Sunday Divine and evening services are subject to manipulation and contextualization. Services are incorporated into special weekends, seminars or conventions which not only unite different congregations in the district, but also highlight and draw attention to different gender and age groups within the church. On these occasions, members who are involved in the auxiliary are responsible for organizing the service. The annual church calendar is filled with numerous programs which unite congregations at the district, regional and national levels. A district weekend in March focuses on the work of women in the church. Sisters from Queenspiece, Palace Walk and Eastleigh will convene at King Street for a two-day program of workshops and worship which ends at the close of the evening session on Sunday. Another event is the Easter weekend National Youth Convention, which celebrates the work of the Youth and Christian Education Board and the youth in the church. This youth convention is followed by a district-level youth convention. The Bible School holds its annual graduation on a Sunday afternoon in early July. In early Summer members from all congregations gather in the south for the National Convention. The lull of the Summer may be interrupted by a tent crusade in the park. September begins with the district-level church convention, which is followed in October by the 'Ladies' Ministry' Regional Seminar. The regional seminar celebrates the work of women in the church, uniting women from congregations throughout the northwest of England.

Appendix II: Declaration of Faith

We believe:

1. In the verbal inspiration of the Bible.
2. In one God eternally existing in three persons: namely, the Father, the Son, and the Holy Ghost.
3. That Jesus Christ is the only begotten Son of the Father, conceived of the Holy Ghost, and born of the Virgin Mary. That Jesus was crucified, buried and raised from the dead. That He ascended to heaven and is today at the right hand of the Father as the Intercessor.
4. That all have sinned and come short of the Glory and that repentance is commanded by God for all and necessary for forgiveness of sins.
5. That justification, regeneration, and the new birth are wrought by faith in the blood of Jesus Christ.
6. In sanctification subsequent to the new birth, through faith in the blood of Christ; through the Word and by the Holy Ghost.
7. Holiness to be God's standard of living for His people.
8. In baptism with the Holy Ghost subsequent to a clean heart.
9. In speaking with tongues as the Spirit gives utterance, and that it's the initial evidence of the baptism of the Holy Ghost.
10. In water baptism by immersion, and all who repent should be baptized in the name of the Father, and of the Son, and of the Holy Ghost.
11. Divine healing is provided for all in atonement.
12. In the Lord's Supper and washing of the saint's feet.
13. In the premillenial [sic] second coming of Jesus. First, to resurrect the righteous dead and to catch away the living saints to Him in the air. Second, to reign on the earth a thousand years.
14. In the bodily resurrection; eternal life for the righteous, and eternal punishment for the wicked.

Appendix III: Prayer and Testimonies

Intercessory prayer offered by the minister during a sermon on prayer:

> Father, in the name of Jesus, I thank you for your word. I thank you for your people. I thank you for this ministry of prayer which you put in our hearts, which you stamped in our hearts. I want to bring those who are standing right now to you in the name of your Son, Jesus. Men and Women whom you have called to yourself, we ask your forgiveness, because we have not been what you wanted us to be concerning our prayer, and tonight in the name Jesus I pray that you touch those who are on their feet. I pray even now that you will brave them with the spirit of intercession. Oh God touch them, I pray that from heaven you will send the Spirit in a new measure, Hallelujah! That you would anoint them to pray and teach them to make the necessary adjustments that their life in prayer will please you. In Jesus' name...say in Jesus' name with me (response: "In Jesus' name"). Say it again (response: "In Jesus' name"). Say it one more time (response: "In Jesus' name"). Hallelujah!

Testimonies given by women at a LM, YALM and YLM District Weekend:

> I Praise the Lord for saving my soul one day when I was lost: 'He came along and rescued my soul and onward as I go along.' I can say that I'll serve Him at all times 'as long as he lendeth me breath.' And as the songwriter say, 'Can a woman tender bear seed toward the child she bare, yes she may forget good deed, but still ideal women would be....' You know and as we look back, we know today is woman's day and we can know everybody thank God for the parents, thank God for the mothers, and we praise God and to know that Jesus is more than a mother to us; He's everything, He's our all in all. 'And onwards as I go along', I'm glad, really glad, giving God thanks and praise for saving my soul. I know I can depend upon God to see me through. When the 'tempest are raging and the billows are tossing

high,' I can surely depend upon Him. You pray for me while I pray for you (response: "Praise the Lord!").

Praise the Lord (response: "Praise the Lord!"). Let's praise him again (response: "Praise the Lord!"). I too am glad, very glad, deep down in my heart that I'm a part of the family of god. I love the Lord. I've been traveling with him for these many years and I don't find any fault with Him. I really love the Lord and I just need to continue with Him. You know, I saw a person last week, Monday, and the person took down very ill, and all through that time as she got her operation she couldn't talk any more. She was not in this world any more, she went on till she die last week, Monday night, so as I heard. Sister Lawrence was saying that it behooves us to give our testimony while we have the breath in us, while we are standing, while we are alive, for once our eyes close, and sometimes people go into a coma, we won't be able to testify what God has done for us, so while we have the breath we must give God thanks and we must tell the world what He has done for us and He has done great things for me, 'thereof I am glad.' I'm glad to be in Palace Walk working for the Lord and doing what I can for Him to be of his Kingdom and you know King Street, you know me well. I'm a part of King Street and I'm a part of every church, so let us praise the Lord (response: "Praise the Lord!"). And I mean to continue with Jesus until He calls me home, you pray for me (response: "Praise the Lord!").

Bibliography

Alexander, C. (1992), 'The Art of "Being Black": The Creation of Black British Youth Identity', D.Phil. thesis, Oxford University.

Allen, S. (1982), 'Confusing Categories and Neglecting Contradictions', in E. Cashmore and B. Troyna (eds), *Black Youth in Crisis*, London: George Allen and Unwin.

Amos, V. and P. Parmar (1984), 'Challenging Imperial Feminism', *Feminist Review*, vol. 17, pp. 3–19.

Anderson, B. (1983), *Imagined Communities*, London: Verso.

Anderson, R. M. (1979), *Vision of the Disinherited: The Making of American Pentecostalism*, Oxford: Oxford University Press.

Anthias, F. and N. Yuval-Davis (1992), *Racialized Boundaries*, London: Routledge.

Ardener, E. (1972), 'Belief and the Problem of Women', in J. S. Lafontaine (ed.), *The Interpretation of Ritual*, London: Tavistock.

Ardener, S. (1975), *Perceiving Women*, London: Dent and Sons.

Argyle, M. and B. Beit-Hallahmi (1975), *The Social Psychology of Religion*, London: Routledge & Kegan Paul.

Arnold, S. E. (1992), *From Skepticism to Hope*, Nottingham: Grove Books.

Austin-Broos, D. J. (1987), 'Pentecostals and Rastafarians: Cultural, Political and Gender Relations of two Religious Movements', *Social and Economic Studies*, vol. 36, no. 4, pp. 1–39.

—— (1991–1992), 'Religion and the Politics of Moral Order in Jamaica', *Anthropological Forum*, vol. 6, no. 3, pp. 293–319.

Baer, H. A. (1993), 'The Limited Empowerment of Women in Black Spiritual Churches: An Alternative Vehicle to Religious Leadership', *Sociology of Religion*, vol. 54, pp. 65–82.

—— and M. Singer (1981), 'Toward a Typology of Black Sectarianism as a Response to Racial Stratification', *Anthropological Quarterly*, vol. 54, pp. 1–14.

Bailey, B. L. (1966), *Jamaican Creole Syntax*, Cambridge: Cambridge University Press.

Baldwin, J. (1953), *Go Tell It on the Mountain*, New York: Dell Publishing.

Banton, M. (1955), *The Coloured Quarter*, London: Jonathan Cape.

—— (1959), *White and Coloured*, London: Jonathan Cape.

—— (1967), *Race Relations*, London: Tavistock.

Barrett, D. B. (ed.) (1982), *World Christian Encyclopedia*, London: Oxford University Press.

Barrett, L. E. (1977), *The Rastafarians*, Boston: Beacon Press.

Barrett, M. and A. Phillips (eds) (1992), *Destabilizing Theory*, Cambridge: Polity Press.

Barth, F. (1969), *Ethnic Groups and Boundaries*, Boston: Little Brown and Co.

Beckwith, M. (1923), 'Some Religious Cults in Jamaica', *American Journal of Psychology*, vol. 34, pp. 32–45.

—— (1929), *Black Roadways*, Chapel Hill: University of North Carolina Press.

Benson, S. (1981), *Ambiguous Ethnicity*, Cambridge: Cambridge University Press.

Berger, I. (1976), 'Rebels or Status Seekers? Women as Spirit Mediums in East Africa', in N. J. Hafkin and E. G. Bay (eds), *Women in Africa*, Stanford: Stanford University Press.

Berger, P. L. and T. Luckman (1985), *The Social Construction of Reality*, Harmondsworth: Penguin.

Blake, J. (1961), *Family Structure in Jamaica*, New York: Free Press of Glencoe.

Bloch, M. (1975), *Political Language and Oratory in Traditional Society*, London: Academic Press.

Bloch-Hoell, N. (1964), *The Pentecostal Movement*, London: George Allen and Unwin.

Bolles, A. L. and D. D'Amico Samuels (1989), 'Anthropological Scholarship on Gender in the English-speaking Caribbean', in S. Morgen (ed.), *Gender and Anthropology: Critical Reviews for Research and Teaching*, Washington: American Anthropological Association.

Booth, T. T. (1984), 'We true Christians', Ph.D. thesis, University of Birmingham.

Bott, E. (1957), *Family and Social Network*, London: Tavistock.

Bourne, J. (1980), 'Cheerleaders and Ombudsmen: The Sociology of Race Relations in Britain', (With A. Sivanandan), *Race and Class*, vol. 21, no. 4, pp. 331–52.

Bradley, H. (1989), *Men's Work, Women's Work*, Cambridge: Polity Press.

Braithwaite, L. (1960), 'Social Stratification and Cultural Pluralism', in V. Rubin (ed.), *Social and Cultural Pluralism in the Caribbean*, Annals of the New York Academy of Sciences, vol. 83.

Brathwaite, E. (1971), *The Development of Creole Society in Jamaica 1770–1820*, Oxford: Clarendon Press.

Brooks, I. V. (n.d.), *Another Gentleman to the Ministry*, Birmingham: Compere Press.

—— (1982), *Where do we go from here? A History of the New Testament Church of God in the UK, 1955–1980*, London: Charles Raper.

Broom, L. (1954), 'The Social Differentiation of Jamaica', *American Sociological Review*, vol. 19, no. 2, pp. 115–25.

Brown, A. L. (1994), 'Afro-Baptist Women's Church and Family Roles: Transmitting Afro-Centric Cultural Values', *Anthropological Quarterly*, vol. 64, no. 4, pp. 173–86.

Brown, C. (1984), *Black and White Britain: The Third PSI Survey*, London: Heinemann.

Brown, I. (*et al.*) (1990), *Here to Stay: A Collection of Stories by Women*, Oxford: Lion Paper Back.

Brierly, P. (ed.) (1992–93), *UK Christian Handbook*, London: MARC Europe.

Brusco, E. (1995), *The Reformation of Machismo: Evangelical Conversion in Columbia*, Austin: University of Texas Press.

Bryan, B., S. Dadzie and S. Scafe (eds) (1985), *The Heart of the Race: Black Women's Lives*, London: Virago.

Butler, J. and J. W. Scott (eds) (1992), *Feminists Theorize the Political*, London: Routledge.

Bynum, C., S. Harrel and P. Richman (eds) (1986), *Gender and Religion*, Boston: Beacon Press.

Calley, M. J. (1962), 'Pentecostal Sects Among West Indian Migrants', *Race*, vol. 3, no. 2, pp. 55–64.

—— (1965), *God's People: West Indian Pentecostal Sects in England*, London: Oxford University Press.

Carby, H. V. (1982a), 'White Woman Listen!' Black Feminism and the Boundaries of Sisterhood', in Centre for Contemporary Cultural Studies (ed.), *The Empire Strikes Back*, London: Hutchinson.

—— (1982b), 'Schooling in Babylon', in Centre for Contemporary Cultural Studies (ed.), *The Empire Strikes Back*, London: Hutchinson.

Cashmore, E. (1979), *Rastaman: The Rastafarian Movement in England* (reprinted 1983), London: Counterpoint, Unwin.

—— (1982), 'Black Youth for Whites', in E. Cashmore and B. Troyna (eds), *Black Youth in Crisis*, London: George Allen and Unwin.

—— and B. Troyna (1982), 'Black Youth in Crisis', in E. Cashmore and B. Troyna (eds), *Black Youth in Crisis*, London: George Allen and Unwin.

Cassidy, F. G. (1971), *Jamaica Talk*, London: Macmillan (2nd edn).

—— and R. B. LePage (eds) (1967), *Dictionary of Jamaican English*, Cambridge: Cambridge University Press.

Castles, S. and G. Kosack (1981 [1972]), 'The Function of Labour Immigration in Western Europe', in P. Braham, E. Rhodes and M. Pearn (eds), *Discrimination and Disadvantage in Employment*, London: Harper Row.

—— (1973), *Immigrant Workers and Class Structure in Western Europe*, London: Oxford University Press.

Clarke, E. (1966), *My Mother who Fathered Me*, London: George Allen and Unwin.

Coates, J. and D. Cameron (eds) (1988), *Women in their Speech Communities*, London: Longman.

Cohen, Abner (1974a), *Two-Dimensional Man*, London: Routledge & Kegan Paul.

—— (ed.) (1974b), 'The Lesson of Ethnicity', in A. Cohen (ed.), *Urban Ethnicity*, London: Tavistock (ASA Monographs, 12).

—— (1980), 'Drama and Politics in the Development of a London Carnival', *Man* (n.s.), vol. 14, pp. 65–87.

Cohen, Anthony Paul (1975), *The Management of Myths*, Manchester: Manchester University Press.

—— (1985a), *The Symbolic Construction of Community*, London: Tavistock.

—— (ed.) (1985b), *Belonging: Identity and Social Organisation in British Rural Cultures*, Manchester: Manchester University Press.

—— (1990), 'The British Anthropological Tradition, Otherness and Rural Studies', in P. Cowe and M. Bodiguel (eds), *Rural Studies in Britain and France*, London: Bellhaven Press.

Collins, P. H. (1990), *Black Feminist Thought*, Boston: Unwin.

Collins, S. (1957), *Coloured Minorities in Britain*, London: Lutterworth Press.

Comaroff, J. (1985), *Body of Power Spirit of Resistance*, Chicago: The University of Chicago Press.

Conn, C. W. (1955), *Like a Mighty Army Moves the Church of God*, Cleveland: Church of God Publishing House.

Connell, R. W. (1987), *Gender and Power*, Cambridge: Polity Press.

Constantinides, P. (1979), 'Women's Spirit Possession and Urban Adaptation in the Muslim Northern Sudan', in P. Caplan and J. Bujra (eds), *Women United, Women Divided*, London: Tavistock.

Cooper, C. (1988), 'That Cunny Jamma Oman: Female Sensibility in the Poetry of Louise Bennett', *Race and Class*, vol. 24, no. 4, pp. 45–60.

Cucchiari, S. (1988), ' "Adapted for heaven": Conversion and Culture in Western Sicily', *American Ethnologist*, vol. 15, no. 3, pp. 417–41.

—— (1990), 'Between Shame and Sanctification: Patriarchy and its Transformation in Sicilian Pentecostalism', *American Ethnologist*, vol. 17, no. 4, pp. 687–707.

Curtin, P. D. (1955), *The Two Jamaicas: The Role of Ideas in a Tropical Colony 1830–1865*, Cambridge, Mass.: Harvard University Press.

Danforth, L. (1995), *The Macedonian Conflict: Ethnic Nationalism in a Transnational World*, Princeton: Princeton University Press.

Daniel, V. E. (1942), 'Ritual and Stratification in Chicago Negro Churches', *American Sociological Review*, vol. 7, pp. 352–61.

Davie, G. (1994), *Religion in Britain since 1945: Believing without Belonging*, Oxford: Basil Blackwell.

Davis, J. (ed.) (1982), *Religious Organization and Religious Experience*, ASA Monograph 21, London: Academic Press.

Davis, J. M. (1942), *The Church in the New Jamaica*, New York: Academic Press/International Missionary Council.

Davison, R. B. (1962), *West Indian Migrants: Social and Economic Facts of Migration from the West Indies*, London: Oxford University Press.

Deakin, N. (1970), *Colour and Citizenship in British Society*, London: Panther Books.

Deakin, S. (1984–85), 'The Churches: Immigration and Race Relations', *New Community*, vol. 12, no. 1, pp. 101–15.

Devereaux, L. (1987), 'Gender Difference and the Relations of Inequality in Zinacantan', in M. Strathern (ed.), *Dealing with Inequality*, Cambridge: Cambridge University Press.

Dex, S. (1983), 'The Second Generation: West Indian Female School Leavers', in A. Phizacklea (ed.), *One Way Ticket*, London: Routledge & Kegan Paul.

—— (1985), *The Sexual Division of Work*, Brighton: Wheatsheaf.

di Leonardo, M. (ed.) (1991), *Gender at the Crossroads of Knowledge*, Berkeley: University of California Press.

Dodgson, E. (1984), *Motherland: West Indian Women to Britain in the 1950s*, London: Heinemann Educational Books.

Douglas, M. (1982), *Natural Symbols* (rev. edn), New York: Pantheon Books.

Drake, St. C. and H. Cayton (1962), *Black Metropolis* (rev. edn), New York: Harper and Row.

Durkheim, E. (1915), *The Elementary Forms of Religious Life* (Seventh Impression, 1971), London: George Allen and Unwin.

Edwards, J. (1991), 'The Growth of the Urban Black Church', *Racial Justice*, vol. 16, pp. 2–5.

Edwards, V. (1988), 'The Speech of British Black Women in Dudley, West Midlands', in J. Coates and D. Cameron (eds), *Women in their Speech Communities*, London: Longman.

Eggington, J. (1957), *They Seek a Living*, London: Hutchinson.

Eidheim, H. (1969), 'When Ethnic Identity is a Social Stigma', in F. Barth (ed.), *Ethnic Groups and Boundaries*, London: George, Allen and Unwin.

Fajans, J. (1985), 'The Person in Social Context: The Social Character of Baining "Psychology"', in G. M. White and J. Kirkpatrick (eds), *Person, Self and Experience: Exploring Pacific Ethnopsychologies*, Berkeley: University of California Press.

Falk, N. A. and R. M. Gross (1989), *Unspoken Worlds: Women's Religious Lives*, Belmont: Wandsworth.

Fauset, A. H. (1944), *Black Gods of the Metropolis*, London: Oxford University Press/Philadelphia Anthropological Society.

Fischer, M. J. (1974), 'Value Assertion and Marriage in Rural Jamaica', *Caribbean Studies*, vol. 14, no. 1, pp. 7–36; no. 2, pp. 7–37.

Fitzpatrick, J. (1987), *Puerto Rican Americans: The Meaning of Migration to the Mainland*, Englewood, N. J.: Prentice Hall.

Foner, N. (1976), 'Women, Work and Migration: Jamaicans in London', *New Community*, vol. 15, nos 1/2, pp. 85–98.

—— (1977), 'The Jamaicans: Cultural and Social Change among Migrants in Britain', in J. L. Watson (ed.), *Between Two Cultures*, Oxford: Basil Blackwell.

—— (1979), *Jamaica Farewell: Jamaican Families in London*, London: Routledge & Kegan Paul.

Forman, C. W. (1984), 'Sing to the Lord a New Song', in D. O'Brien and S. Tiffany (eds), *Rethinking Women's Roles*, Berkeley: University of California.

Foster, E. (1992), 'Women and the Inverted Pyramid of the Black Churches in Britain', in G. Sahgal and N. Yuval-Davis (eds), *Refusing Holy Orders*, London:Virago.

Frazier, E. F. (1964), *The Negro Church in America*, Liverpool: Liverpool University Press.

Freidl, E. (1967), 'The Position of Women: Appearance and Reality', *Anthropological Quarterly*, vol. 40, pp. 97–108.

Fryer, P. (1984), *Staying Power: The History of Black People in Britain*, London: Pluto Press.

Fuller, M. (1982), 'Young Female and Black', in E. Cashmore and B. Troyna (eds), *Black Youth in Crisis*, London: George Allen and Unwin.

Furley, O. W. (1965), 'Protestant Missionaries in the West Indies: Pioneers of a Non-racial Society', *Race*, vol. 6, no. 3, pp. 232–42.

Furnivall, J. S. (1948), *Colonial Policy and Practice*, Cambridge: Cambridge University Press.

Gans, H. J. (1994), 'Symbolic Ethnicity and Symbolic Religiosity: Towards a Comparison of Ethnic and Religious Acculturation', *Ethnic and Racial Studies*, vol. 17, no. 4, pp. 577–92.

Gardner, W. J. (1873), *A History of Jamaica* (Third Impression, 1971). London: Frank Cass.

Geertz, C. (1973a), 'Religion as Cultural System', in *The Interpretation of Cultures*, New York: Basic Books, Harper Torch Books.

—— (1973b), 'Ethos, World View and the Analysis of Sacred Symbols', in *The Interpretation of Cultures*, New York: Basic Books, Harper Torch Books.

—— (1973c), 'Internal Conversion in Contemporary Bali', in *The Interpretation of Cultures*, New York: Basic Books, Harper Torch Books.

Gellner, E. (1983), *Nations and Nationalism*, Oxford: Blackwell.

Gerth, H. H. and C. Wright-Mills (1991), *From Max Weber: Essays in Sociology*, London: Routledge.

Giddens, A. (1972), *Emile Durkheim, Selected Writings*, Cambridge: Cambridge University Press.

Gilkes, C. T. (1986), 'The Role of Women in the Sanctified Church', *The Journal of Religious Thought*, vol. 43, no. 1, pp. 24–41.

Gill, L. (1990), '"Like a Veil to Cover Them": Women and the Pentecostal Movement in La Paz', *American Ethnologist*, vol. 17, no. 4, pp. 708–21.

—— (1994), *Precarious Dependencies: Gender, Class and Domestic Service in Bolivia*, New York: Columbia University Press.

Gilroy, P. (1987), *'There Ain't no Black in the Union Jack'*, London: Hutchinson.

Glass, R. (1960), *'Newcomers'*, London: George Allen and Unwin/Centre for Urban Studies.

Goodman. F. D. (1972), *Speaking in Tongues: A Cross-Cultural Study of Glossalalia*, Chicago: The University of Chicago Press.

Goody, J. (1961), 'Religion and Ritual: The Definitional Problem', *British Journal of Sociology*, vol. 12, pp. 142–64.

Greeley, A. (1972), *The Denominational Society: A Sociological Approach to Religion in America*, Glenview: Scott Foreman.

Hacket, R. (1984), 'Women and New Religious Movements in Africa', in D. O'Brien and S. Tiffany (eds), *Rethinking Women's Roles*, Berkeley: University of California Press.

Hall, C. (1992a), 'Missionary Stories: Gender and Ethnicity in England in the 1830s and 1840s', in *White, Male and Middle Class*, Cambridge: Polity Press.

—— (1992b), 'Competing Masculinities: Thomas Carlyle, John Stuart Mill and the Case of Governor Eyre', in *White, Male and Middle Class*, Cambridge: Polity Press.

Hall, S. (1992), 'The New Ethnicities', in J. Donald and A. Rattansi (eds), *'Race', Culture and Difference*, London: Sage.

—— and T. Jefferson (1976), *Resistance Through Rituals*, London: Hutchinson.

——, C. Critcher, T. Jefferson, J. Clarke and B. Roberts (1978), *Policing the Crisis*, London: Macmillan.

Henriques, F. (1953), *Family and Colour in Jamaica*, London: Eyre and Spottiswoode.

Henry, B. I. (1982), 'The Growth of Corporate Black Identity Among Afro-Caribbean People in Birmingham, England', Ph.D. thesis, University of Warwick.

Hill, C. (1971b), 'From Church to Sect: West Indian Sect Development in Britain', *Journal for the Scientific Study of Religion*, vol. 10, pp. 114–23.

—— (1971c), 'Pentecostalist Growth-Result of Racialism?', *Race Today*, vol. 3, no. 3, pp. 187–90.

Hobsbawm, E. J. (1959), *Primitive Rebels*, New York: W. W. Norton.

Hogg, D. (1960), 'The Convince Cult in Jamaica', *Yale University Publications in Anthropology*, vol. 58, pp. 3–21.

Holden, P. (ed.) (1983), *Women's Religious Experience: Cross Cultural*

Perspectives, London: Croom Helm.

Hollenweger, W. J. (1972), *The Pentecostals,* London: SCM Press.

—— (1974), *Pentecost Between Black and White,* Belfast: Christian Journals.

Horton, R. (1967), 'African Traditional Thought and Western Science', in B. R. Wilson (ed.), *Rationality,* Oxford: Basil Blackwell.

Howard, A. (1985), 'Ethnopsychology and the Prospects for a Cultural Psychology', in G. M. White and J. Kirkpatrick (eds), *Person, Self and Experience; Exploring Pacific Ethnopsychologies,* Berkeley: University of California Press.

Husband, C. (1982), 'Introduction: "Race", the Continuity of a Concept', in C. Husband (ed.), *Race in Britain,* London: Hutchinson.

James, W. (1993), 'Migration, Racism and Identity Formation: The Caribbean Experience in Britain', in W. James and C. Harris (eds), *Inside Babylon,* London: Verso.

—— (1989), 'The Making of Black Identities', in R. Samuels (ed.) *Patriotism: The Making and Unmaking of British National Identity,* vol. II, London: Routledge.

Johnson, M. R. D. (1988), 'Resurrecting the Inner City: A New Role for the Christian Churches', *New Community,* vol. 15, no. 1, pp. 91–101.

Jones, C. E. (1983), *A Guide to the Study of the Pentecostal Movement* (Vol. I, Parts I and II), London: American Theological Library Association and Scarecrow.

—— (1987), *Black Holiness,* London: American Theological Library Association and Scarecrow.

Jones, P. N. (1970), 'Some Aspects of the Changing Distribution of Coloured Immigrants in Birmingham, 1961–1966', *Transactions of the Institute of British Geography,* vol. 50, pp. 199–219.

—— (1976), 'Coloured Minorities in Birmingham, England', *Annals of the Association of American Geographers,* vol. 66, no. 1, pp. 89–103.

Katzin, M. F. (1959a), 'The Jamaican Country Higgler', *Social and Economic Studies,* vol. 8, no. 4, pp. 421–35.

—— (1959b), 'Partners: an Informal Savings Institution in Jamaica', *Social and Economic Studies,* vol. 8, no. 4, pp 436–40.

Kerns, V. (1983), *Women and the Ancestors: Black Carib Kinship and Ritual,* Urbana: University of Illinois.

Kerr, M. (1952), *Personality and Conflict in Jamaica,* Liverpool: Liverpool University Press.

King, U. (ed.) (1987), *Women in the World's Religions: Past and Present,* New York: Paragon House.

—— (ed.) (1995), *Religion and Gender,* Cambridge: Blackwell.

Kitzinger, S. (1969), 'Protest and Mysticism: The Rastafari Cult of Jamaica', *Journal for the Scientific Study of Religion,* vol. 8, no. 2, pp. 240–62.

Kuper, A. (1976), *Changing Jamaica,* London: Routledge & Kegan Paul.

Lamphere, L. (1974), 'Strategies, Cooperation and Conflict among Women in Domestic Groups', in M.Z. Rosaldo and L. Lamphere (eds),*Woman, Culture and Society*, Stanford: Stanford University Press.

Lawless, E. J. (1983), 'Shouting for the Lord: The Power of Women's Speech in the Pentecostal Religious Service', *Journal of American Folklore*, vol. 96, no. 382, pp. 434–59.

—— (1987), 'Piety and Motherhood: Reproductive Images and Maternal Strategies of the Woman Preacher', *Journal of American Folklore*, vol. 100, no. 398, pp. 471–8.

—— (1988), *Handmaidens of the Lord: Pentecostal Women Preachers and Traditional Religion*, Philadelphia: University of Pennsylvania Press.

—— (1991), 'Rescripting their Lives and Narratives: Spiritual Life Stories of Pentecostal Women Preachers', *Journal of Feminist Studies in Religion*, vol. 7, no. 1, pp. 53–71.

Lawrence, E. (1982a), 'Just Plain Common Sense: The Roots of Racism', in Centre for Contemporary Cultural Studies (ed.), *The Empire Strikes Back*, London: Hutchinson.

—— (1982b), 'In the Abundance of Water the Fool is Thirsty; Sociology and Black "Pathology"', in Centre for Contemporary Cultural Studies (ed.), *The Empire Strikes Back*, London: Hutchinson.

Leach, E. (1976), *Culture and Communication*, Cambridge: Cambridge University Press.

Leacock, E. (1978), 'Women's Status in Egalitarian Society: Implications for Social Evolution', *Current Anthropology*, vol. 19, no. 2, pp. 247–75.

Leech, K. (1985), 'Correspondence; The Churches: Immigration and Race Relations', *New Community*, vol. 12, no. 2, pp. 352–3.

Lewis, G. (1993), 'Black Women's Employment and the British Economy', in W. James and C. Harris (eds), *Inside Babylon*, London: Verso.

Liebow, E. (1967), *Tally's Corner*, Boston: Little Brown and Co.

Lincoln, E. and L. Mamiya (1990), *The Black Church in the African American Experience*, Durham: Duke University Press.

Linton, R. L. (1979 [1943]), 'Nativistic Movements', in W. A. Lessa and E. Z. Vogt (eds), *Reader in Comparative Religion*, New York: Harper and Row.

Little, K. L. (1947), *Negroes in Britain*, London: Kegan Paul.

Llobera, J. R. (1994), 'Anthropological Approaches to the Study of Nationalism in Europe: The Work of Van Gennep and Mauss', in V. Goddard, J. R. Llobera and C. Shore (eds), *The Anthropology of Europe*, Oxford: Berg.

Lowenthal, D. (1972), *West Indian Societies*, London: Oxford University Press.

Lutz, C. (1985), 'Ethnopsychology Compared to What? Explaining Behavior and Consciousness', in G. M. White and J. Kirkpatrick (eds), *Person, Self and Experience: Exploring Pacific Ethnopsychologies*, Berkeley:

University of California Press.

MacCormack, C. and A. Draper (1987), 'Social and Cognitive Aspects of Female Sexuality in Jamaica', in P. Caplan (ed.), *The Cultural Construction of Sexuality*, London: Routledge.

Madsen, C. (1994), 'A God of One's Own: Recent Work by and about Women in Religion', *Signs*, vol. 19, no. 2, pp. 480–98.

Martin, D. (1990), *Tongues of Fire: The Explosion of Protestantism in Latin America*, Oxford: Basil Blackwell.

Moore, H. (1988), *Feminism and Anthropology*, Cambridge: Polity Press.

Morris, B. (1987), *Anthropological Studies of Religion*, Cambridge: Cambridge University Press.

Morris, M. (ed.), (1982), *Louise Bennett: Selected Poems*, Kingston: Sangster's Book Stores.

Morrish, I. (1982), *Obeah, Christ and Rastaman*, Cambridge: James Clarke.

Naipaul, V. S. (1967), *The Mimic Men*, Harmondsworth: Penguin.

Nelsen, H. M. and A. K. Nelsen (1975), *Black Church in the 60s*, Lexington: University Press of Kentucky.

Nettleford, R. M. (1965), "National Identity and Attitudes to Race in Jamaica", in *Race*, vol. 7, no.1, pp. 59–72.

Nettleford, R. M. (1972), *Identity, Race and Protest in Jamaica*, New York: William and Morrow.

Newnham, A. (1986), *Employment, Unemployment and Black People*, London: Runnymede Trust.

O'Brien, D. and S. Tiffany (eds) (1984), *Rethinking Women's Roles*, Berkeley: University of California Press.

Ortner, S. B. and H. Whitehead (eds) (1981), *Sexual Meanings: The Cultural Construction of Gender and Sexuality*, Cambridge: Cambridge University Press.

Orum, A. M. (1966), 'A Reappraisal of the Social and Political Participation of Negroes', *American Journal of Sociology*, vol. 72, pp. 32–46.

Parmar, P. (1982), 'Gender, Race and Class: Asian Women in Resistance', in Centre for Contemporary Cultural Studies (ed.), *The Empire Strikes Back*, London: Hutchinson.

Patterson, S. (1965), *Dark Strangers*, Harmondsworth: Penguin (2nd edn).

Peach, C. (1968), *West Indian Migration to Britain*, London: Oxford University Press.

——, V. Robinson and S. Smith (eds) (1981), *Ethnic Segregation in Cities*, London: Croom Helm.

Pearson, D. G. (1976), 'West Indian Communal Associations in Britain: Some Observations', *New Community*, vol. 5, no. 4, pp. 371–81.

Philpott, S. B. (1973), *West Indian Migration: The Montserrat Case*, New York: Athlone Press.

Phizacklea, A. (1983), 'In the Front Line', in A. Phizacklea (ed.), *One Way Ticket*, London: Routledge & Kegan Paul.

—— (1988), 'Entrepreneurship, Ethnicity, and Gender', in S. Westwood and P. Bhachu (eds), *Enterprising Women*, London: Routledge.

Phoenix, A. (1988), 'Narrow Definitions of Culture: The Case of Early Motherhood', in S. Westwood and P. Bhachu (eds), *Enterprising Women*, London: Routledge.

Poblete, S. J. R. and T. F. O'Dea (1960), 'Anomie and the "Quest for Community": The Formation of Sects among the Puerto Ricans of New York', *The American Catholic Sociological Review*, vol. 21, no, 1, pp. 18–33.

Post, K. (1978), *Arise Ye Starvlings*, The Hague: Martinus Nijhoff.

Prescod-Roberts, M. and N. Steele (1980), *Black Women: Bringing it all Back Home*, Bristol: Falling Wall Press.

Pryce, K. (1979), *Endless Pressure: A Study of West Indian Life Styles in Bristol*, Harmondsworth: Penguin Books.

Ramdin, R. (1987), *The Making of the Black Working Class in Britain*, Aldershot: Wildwood House.

Reese, L. and R. Brown (1995), 'The Effects of Religious Messages on Racial Identity and System Blame among African Americans', *The Journal of Politics*, vol. 57, pp. 24–44.

Reiter, R. R. (ed.) (1975), *Toward an Anthropology of Women*, London: Monthly Review Press.

Rex, J. (1973), *Race, Colonialism and the City*, London: Routledge & Kegan Paul.

Rex, J. and R. Moore (1967), *Race Community and Conflict: A Study of Sparkbrook*, London: Oxford University Press.

—— and S. Tomlinson (1979), *Colonial Immigrants in a British City: A Class Analysis*, London: Routledge & Kegan Paul.

Rhys, J. (1995), 'Let Them Call it Jazz', in *Let Them Call it Jazz*, London: Penguin.

Richmond, A. H. (1973), *Migration and Race Relations in an English City: A Study in Bristol*, London: Oxford University Press.

Riley, J. (1987), *Waiting in the Twilight*, London: The Women's Press.

Roberts, G. W. and S. A. Sinclair (1978), *Women in Jamaica*, New York: KTO Press.

Roberts, P. A. (1988), *West Indians and their Language*, Cambridge: Cambridge University Press.

Rogers, S. C. (1975), 'Female Forms of Power and the Myth of Male Dominance: A Model of Female/Male Interaction in Peasant Society', *American Ethnologist*, vol. 2, pp. 727–56.

Rosaldo M. Z. and L. Lamphere (eds) (1974), *Woman, Culture and Society*, Stanford: Stanford University Press.

Rowe, M. (1980), 'The Women in Rastafari', *Caribbean Quarterly*, vol. 26, no. 4. pp. 13–21.

Rubin, V. (ed) (1960), *Social and Cultural Pluralism in the Caribbean*, Annals of the New York Academy of Science, vol. 83.

Ruel, M. J. (1982), 'Christians as Believers', in J. Davis (ed.), *Religious Organization and Religious Experience*, London: Academic Press.

Runnymede Trust (1980), *Britain's Black Population*, London: Heinemann/ Runnymede Trust and the Radical Statistics Race Group.

Saghal, G. and N. Yuval-Davis (1990), 'Refusing Holy Orders', in *Marxism Today*, March.

—— (eds) (1992), 'Introduction: Fundamentalism, Multiculturalism and Women in Britain,' in G. Saghal and N. Yuval-Davis (eds), *Refusing Holy Orders*, London: Virago Press.

Saunders, G. R. (1995), 'The Crisis of Presence in Italian Pentecostal Conversion', *American Ethnologist*, vol. 22, no. 2, pp. 324–40.

Selvon, S. (1993 [1956]), *The Lonely Londoners*, London: Allan Wingate.

Sered, S. S. (1994a), 'Ideology, Anatomy and Sisterhood: An Analysis of the Secular Consequences of Women's Religions', in *Gender and Society*, vol. 8, no. 4, pp. 486–506.

—— (1994b), *Priestess, Mother, Sacred, Sister: Religions Dominated by Women*, Oxford: Oxford University Press.

Silberman, C. E. (1964), *Crisis in Black and White*, New York: Random House.

Simey, T. S. (1946), *Welfare and Planning in the West Indies*, Oxford: Oxford University Press.

Simpson, G. E. (1955), 'The Ras Tafari Movement in Jamaica: A study of Race and Class Conflict, *Social Forces*, vol. 34, no. 2, pp. 167–71.

—— (1956), 'Jamaican Revivalist Cults', *Social and Economic Studies*, vol. 5, no. 4, pp. 321–442.

—— (1972), 'Afro-American Religions and Religious Behaviour', *Caribbean Studies*, vol. 12, no. 2, pp. 5–30.

SISTREN (eds) (1986), *Lionheart Gal: Life Stories of Jamaican Women*, London: The Women's Press.

Smith, I. and W. Green (1989), *An Ebony Cross: Being a Black Christian in Britain Today*, London: Marshall Pickering.

Smith, M. G. (1965a), *The Plural Society in the West Indies*, Berkeley: The University of California Press.

—— (1965b), 'Some Aspects of Social Structure in the British Caribbean About 1820', in *The Plural Society in the British West Indies*, Berkeley: The University of California Press.

—— (1965c), 'A Framework for Caribbean Studies', in *The Plural Society in the British West Indies*, Berkeley: The University of California Press.

—— (1965d), 'The Plural Framework of Jamaican Society', in *The Plural Society in the British West Indies*, Berkeley: The University of California Press.

Smith, R. T. (1973), 'The Matrifocal Family', in J. Goody (ed.), *The Character of Kinship*, Cambridge: Cambridge University Press.

—— (1975), 'Religion in the Formation of West Indian Society: Guyana and Jamaica', in M. L. Kilson and R. I. Rotberg (eds), *The African Diaspora: Interpretive Essays*, London: Harvard University Press.

—— (1987), 'Hierarchy and the Dual Marriage System in West Indian Society', in J. F. Collier and S. J. Yanagisako (eds), *Gender and Kinship*, Stanford: Stanford University Press.

—— (1988), *Kinship and Class in the West Indies*, Cambridge: Cambridge University Press.

Smith, S. (1989), *The Politics of Race and Residence*, Cambridge: Polity Press.

Solomos, J. (1989), *Race and Racism in Contemporary Britain*, Basingstoke: Macmillan.

Spanos, N. (1986), 'Glossolalia, a Learned Behavior: An Experimental Demonstration', *Journal of Abnormal Psychology*, vol. 95, no. 1, pp. 21–3.

Stack, C. (1974), 'Sex Roles and Survival Strategies in an Urban Black Community', in M. Z. Rosaldo and L. Lamphere (eds), *Woman, Culture and Society*, Stanford: Stanford University Press.

Steady, F. C. (1976), 'Protestant Women's Associations', in N. J. Hafkin and E. G. Bay (eds), *Women in Africa*, Stanford: Stanford University Press.

Stone, K. (1983), 'Motherhood and Waged Work: West Indian, Asian and White Mothers Compared', in A. Phizacklea (ed.), *One Way Ticket*, London: Routledge & Kegan Paul.

Strathern, M. (1980), 'No Nature, No Culture: The Hagen Case', in C. MacCormack and M. Strathern (eds), *Nature, Culture and Gender*, Cambridge: Cambridge University Press.

—— (1981), 'Self-interest and the Social Good: Some Implications of Hagen Gender Imagery', in S. Ortner and H. Whitehead (eds), *Sexual Meanings*, Cambridge: Cambridge University Press.

—— (ed.) (1987a), *Dealing with Inequality*, Cambridge: Cambridge University Press.

—— (1987b), 'Producing Difference', in J. F. Collier and S. J. Yanagisako (eds), *Gender and Kinship*, Stanford: Stanford University Press.

—— (1988), *The Gender of the Gift*, Berkeley: The University of California Press.

Sutton, C. R. and S. R. Makiesky-Barrow (1980), 'Social Inequality and Sexual Status in Barbados', in F. C. Steady (ed.), *The Black Woman Cross Culturally*, Schenkman: Cambridge.

—— (1994), 'Migration and West Indian Racial and Ethnic Consciousness', in C. R. Sutton and E. M. Chaney (eds), *Caribbean Life in New York City: Sociocultural Dimensions*, New York: Centre for Migration Studies.

Toulis, N. (1985), 'She Looks One Hundred Percent! Dress and Adornment as a Salient Diacritical marker of Afro-American Ethnicity among

Women at Bryn Mawr, Bethel African Methodist Episcopal Church',
B.A. thesis, Bryn Mawr College.

Turner, B. S. (1971), 'Belief, Ritual and Experience: The Case of Method-
ism', *Social Compass*, vol. 18, no. 2, pp. 187–201.

Turner, V. (1967), *The Forest of Symbols*, Ithaca: Cornell.

Wallace, A. F. C. (1979 [1956]), 'Revitalization Movements', in W. A. Lessa
and E. Z. Vogt (eds), *Reader in Comparative Religion*, New York: Harper
and Row.

—— 1970, *Culture and Personality*, New York: Random House.

Wallman, S. (1978), 'The Boundaries of Race: Processes of Race and
Ethnicity in England', *Man* (n.s.), vol. 13, no. 2, pp. 200–17.

—— (ed.) (1979), *Ethnicity at Work*, New York: Macmillan.

—— (1984), *Eight London Households*, London: Tavistock.

Ware, V. (1992), *Beyond the Pale: White Women, Racism and History*, London:
Verso.

Washington Jr., J. R. (1972), *Black Sects and Cults*, New York: Doubleday.

Watson, J. L. (ed.) (1977), *Between Two Cultures*, Oxford: Basil Blackwell.

Weber, M. (1965), *The Sociology of Religion*, London: Methuen.

—— (1978), *Economy and Society*, vol. I, Berkeley: The University of
California Press.

—— (1985), *The Protestant Ethic and the Spirit of Capitalism*, London:
Counterpoint, Unwin.

Wedenoja, W. (1980), 'Modernization and the Pentecostal Movement in
Jamaica', in S. D. Glazier (ed.), *Perspectives on Pentecostalism*, Washington DC: University Press of America.

Westwood, S. (1984), *All Day Every Day: Factory and Family in the Making
of Women's Lives*, London: Pluto Press.

—— and P. Bhachu (eds) (1988), *Enterprising Women: Ethnicity, Economy
and Gender Relations*, London: Routledge.

White, G. M. and J. Kirkpatrick (eds) (1985), *Person, Self and Experience:
Exploring Pacific Ethnopsychologies*, Berkeley: University of California
Press.

Williams, J. J. (1933), *Voodoos and Obeahs*, New York: Dial Press.

Williams, M. D. (1974), *Community in a Black Pentecostal Church: An
Anthropological Study*, Pittsburgh: University of Pittsburgh Press.

Wilson, A. (1978), *Finding a Voice: Asian Women in Britain*, London: Virago.

Wilson, B. R. (1961), *Sects and Society*, Westport: Greenwood Press.

—— (1970), *Religious Sects*, London: World University Library.

Won Moo Hurh and Kwang Chung Kim (1990), 'Religious Participation
of Korean Immigrants to the US', *Journal for the Scientific Study of
Religion*, vol. 29, no. 1, pp. 19–34.

Young, M. and P. Willmott (1962), *Family and Kinship in East London*,
Harmondsworth: Penguin Books.

Yuval-Davis, N. (1992), 'Fundamentalism, Multiculturalism and Women in Britain', in J. Donald and A. Rattansi (eds), *'Race', Culture and Difference*, London: Sage.

Official Publications

African Methodist Episcopal Church (AME) (1980), *The Book of Discipline* (1980–1984 edn), Nashville: H. A. Berliner Jr Publications/Compilation Committee.
Birmingham City Council, Area Study Group (BCC) (1987), *Area Studies Information Package*.
Birmingham City Council, Development Department (BCC) (1988), *Birmingham Population by Birthplace of Head of Household*.
Birmingham City Council, Development Department (BCC), Urban Policy Team (1989), *Poverty in Birmingham: A Profile*.
Commission for Racial Equality (CRE) (1985), *Ethnic Minorities in Britain*.
Central Statistical Office (CSO) (1991), *Regional Trends* 26, London: HMSO.
Central Statistical Office (CSO) (1993), *Social Trends* 23, London: HMSO.
Church of God (COG) (1988), *Minutes of the 62nd General Assembly*, Cleveland: Church of God Publishing House.
Hill, C. (1963), *West Indian Migrants to the London Churches*, London: Oxford University Press/Institute of Race Relations.
—— (1971a), *Black Churches: West Indian and African Sects in Britain*, Community Race Relations Unit of the British Council of Churches.
Lancaster, E. M. (1990), *The Real Me and Other Poems*, Birmingham City Council, Social Services.
Labour Market Trends, February 1996.
Office of Population and Census Statistics (OPCS) (1981a), *Census: Small Area Statistics for Birmingham Wards*, London: HMSO.
—— (1981b), *Labour Force Survey*, London: HMSO.
—— (1984), *Labour Force Survey*, London: HMSO.
—— (1991a), *Census: National Report, Great Britain, Part I*, London: HMSO.
—— (1991b), *Census: National Report, County Report West Midlands, Parts I and II*, London: HMSO.
West Midlands City Council (WMCC), Low Pay Unit (1988), 'Last among equals'.

Other Sources

Employment Gazette, March 1988.
Law Report, 'Rastafarians not ethnic group', *The Independent*, 5/3/91.
New Testament Church of God, *Welcome: Quarterly Magazine*, (n.d.).

Unpublished Sources

Cross M. and J. Johnson (1981), 'Household Survey', Warwick University/Centre for Ethnic Relations.

Hall, S. (1992), 'Identity and African Caribbean Political Action', Address delivered at the 'Culture, Identity and Politics: Ethnic Minorities in Britain' Conference, St Antony's College, Oxford.

Howard, V. (1987), 'A Report on Afro-Caribbean Christianity in Britain', University of Leeds: Community Religions Project Research Papers (n.s.).

Index

African American church, 165, 167, 247
African Methodist Episcopal church, 245–6
Afro-Baptist church, 54, 57, 247
  agency, 97, 219, 235–350
  female, 241, 250, 256–62 *passim*, 272–3
  male, 241, 258, 261, 273
  negotiated, 262
  of Holy Spirit, 241
  Rastafarian men, 216
  saints 258, 260–1
alcohol, 198
Alexander, C., 15
Allen, S., 16
'altar call', 132n4, 159
Amos, V. and P. Parmar, 23
Anderson. B., 180n12
Anglican church, 95–96
appearance, 134
  see also social practice
Argyle, M. and B. Beit-Hallahmi, 115–6
Arminian doctrine, 103n25
assimilation, 6, 10, 25, 28–9, 82, 112–5, 167
  see also religious participation, assimilation
associations, 9–10, 10n2,48
attitudes towards racial difference, 4–5, 9, 11
Austin-Broos, D., 109–10, 169, 216–217
'authorized worship language', 186–90, 208, 271
auxiliaries, 250–7
AWL,
  see 'authorized worship language'

'backslide', 63n25

Baker, Moses, 96
Baldwin, J., *Go Tell It on the Mountain*, 128–9
'balmyards', 98n20
Banton, M., 6
baptism, 145, 146–50, 157, 233, 234, 244
  Church of God, 125n2
  previous, 150
Baptists, 94, 96
  American Baptist, 96
  Native Baptists, 96–7
Barr, Edmund, 104, 105
'barrel', 183n13
Barrett, L., 232
Barth, F., 170
behavioral commitments, *see* ritual
belief, 123, 125–6, 132–3, 135–7
  see also declaration of faith
Bible, 139–142
  concordance 140n7
  Institute, 195
  interpretation of 30–1, 141
  School, 52
  scriptural explication, 248
Birmingham, 37–40
  see also King Street congregation
Bloch, M. 236–7
blood, 132–3
Black,
  academics, 14–7 *passim*
  see also feminism; identity, Black
  'Black Church', 32–3, 32n12, 167
  label contested, 178–9, 205, 210–11, 270
  'brother', 55–7 *passim*, 261
Brown, A. L., 54, 57
Brusco, E. 222, 223
'building program', 65n26

Calley, M., 28–29, 61, 108, 112, 121,

143–4, 149
Carby, H., 24
Cashmore, E., 30–1
Christ, 123, 135, 162, 222–3, 226
'Christian dedication', 156–7
Christianity,
    Caribbean vs. English, 26
    Jamaica, 94–95
    non-conformist, 94–6
'Church and Pastor's Council', 245
Church of God,
    Black congregations, 104–5
    development, 102–6
        in Jamaica, 105–6
        in United States, 102–5
    see also New Testament Church of
        God
Church of the Cherubim and
    Seraphim, 247
citizenship,
    see nationality
cleanliness, 177–8
clothing,
    see social practice
Cohen, Abner, 172
Cohen, Anthony, 172, 209
collective vs. individual,
    123–5, 138, 146, 163
color, 85–6
Comaroff, J., 206
conjugal unions,
    see color; family; marriage; women,
        relationships with men
Connell, R. W., 219–21, 263–4
conversion, 53, 125, 126, 132, 168,
    210, 225, 270
    crisis of presence, 126–8, 162
    testimonies (narratives), 128–32
conviction, 128–32
cosmetics,
    see social practice
Creole,
    see Patois
Cucchiari, S., 223, 224
culture, 5, 88n10
    see also religion and culture; race
        and culture
cultures of disaffection, 12
Curtin, P., 92

Davie, G., 115
declaration of faith, 125, 280
DeMartino, E., 126–7
devotion, 141, 240
'discernment'
    see Holy Spirit, gift of discernment
discourse,
    see also multiculturalism;
        representations
Douglas, M., 60–1, 163
'duppies', 93n14
Durkheim, E., 121, 123–4, 138–9

education, 192–6, 208–9
    and employment, 46
Edwards, J., 205
Edwards, V., 237n19
Eggington, J., 18–9, 27
elderly, 41, 42
Elim Foursquare Gospel Church, 117
employment, 42–7
    restructuring of, 39–40
    see also King Street Congregation,
        congregational employment
English churches,
    migrant's rejection of 26–8, 66, 111,
        114–5
    racism, 26, 28, 111
    see also Elim Foursquare Gospel
        Church
ethnic,
    absolutism, 14–5
    church,
        see 'Black Church';
            Pentecostalism, Puerto Rican
            sects; Protestantism, Korean
            sects
    identity
        see identity
ethnicity, 172–4, 270–1
    'new ethnicity', 15–8
ethos, 135–6

family, 23–4, 224, 227
    Christian, 57, 101, 226, 259, 261,
        272
    see also kinship; women, domestic
        circumstances
'family altar', 100

Farrakhan, Louis, 265, 266
fasting, 199
feminism,
  Black, 23, 24, 215
  Western 214
  White, 23, 24
fiction,
  identity, 7–8
  women, 20–2
Fitzpatrick, J., 116
Foner, N., 19–20
food, 196–200, 208–9, 271
Foster, E., 214–5, 259
funerals, 157

Gardner, W. J., 98
Geertz, C., 135, 136, 137
gender, 13, 212, 218–21
  African Caribbean religious
    practice, 216–8
  and ethnicity, 272, 273, 274
  females, 257, 259–60, 272–4
  imagery, 225–30, 240–1
  males, 257, 258–9, 272
  order, 219–20
  and Pentecostalism, 221–5
  regime, 219–20
  and religion, 95, 97–8, 212–6, 268
  roles in church 242–50
generational continuity and
  differences, 6, 12–7 *passim*, 30–1,
  172
Gibb, George, 96
Gill, L., 222
Gilroy, P., 14, 170
glossolalia, 158–9, 159n19, 188, 236,
  271
God, 123, 135, 217, 222–3, 226, 258
'Godparents', 156, 156n16

hair,
  see social practice
Hall, S. 4, 7, 11, 16
healing, 142
heaven and hell, 136, 137
Henriques, F., 86–7
Henry, B., 12–3, 31
Hill, C., 29–30, 82, 111–2, 113–4
Holy Ghost, *see* Holy Spirit

Holy Spirit, 69
  baptism of, 63, 103, 104, 157–61,
    236
  gift of discernment, 161
  gift of interpretation, 160
  gift of prophecy, 160
  tarrying for, 159
housing, 47–9
  see also King Street congregation,
    residential distribution and
    housing
Husband, C., 83n4
husbands,
  see agency, male; gender, males

identity, 3–4, 82–3, 108, 127, 170–2,
  274
  African Caribbean, 162
  alternatives, 7–16 *passim*, 24, 78,
    218, 268–9
  as Black, 10–5, 16, 83, 174, 208,
    215–6, 265, 271
  as Christian, 134–135, 161–4, 168,
    206, 210, 225–6, 270, 274
  maintenance of, 133–5, 163–4,
    200, 210, 233, 270
  ethnic, 171
  members' models of religion and
    ethnic identity, 200–6
  members' self-image, 171, 177–9
  post-war Jamaica, 83–92
  religious, 110–1, 117, 119–20, 169,
    271
  as West Indian, 4–10, 198
  see also education; fiction; food;
    language; self
imagined community, 180
immigrant labor, 39, 39n3
immigration 1, 4, 9, 10
  see also women, immigration
individual, the, 126–7
infant dedication, *see* 'Christian
  dedication'
interaction, social, 5–9, 171–2, 210,
  275
  see also language, social interaction

Johnson, M. R. D., 32
Jesus,

see Christ
jewelry,
    see social practice

King Street congregation, 49–51
    congregational employment, 67–9
    membership, 52–3
        equality of, 55, 271, 181
    residential distribution and
        housing, 75–6
    summary of, 77–8
kinship, 53, 54–61, 138, 179, 226, 261,
    270
Kuper, A., 90

'Ladies' Ministry', 251–7
Lancaster, E., 215
language, 184–90, 208, 271
    choices, 185–6
    social interaction, 187, 188
    women, 235–42
    see also 'authorized worship
        language'; Patois; 'Queen's
        English'
Lawless, E., 144, 224
Lawrence, E., 14, 16
Lincoln, C. E. and L. Mamiya, 165,
    167, 247
Lisle, George, 96
Little, K., 26
Llewelyn, 106
'Lord's Supper', 145, 146, 151–4
    see also 'Mother of the Church'
Lyseight, O. A., 114, 117, 118

machismo, 222, 223
marriage, 243, 258
men,
    see agency, male; 'brother'; gender,
        males; saints
'Men's Fellowship', 251
Methodists, 95–6
'Million Man March', 265–8
ministerial roles, 242–4
Moravians, 94, 98
Morrish, I., 30
mother, 19, 22, 228–30, 254, 256–9,
    272–3
    see also agency, female; single

mothers
'Mother Church', 49
motherhood, 19, 22
'Mother of the Church', 56–7, 246–50,
    261
    role in baptism, 149
    role in 'Lord's Supper', 152, 249
    role at 'washing of the saints' feet',
        154, 249
    see also agency, female
multiculturalism, 13–5
    see also Black church
Mundle, 106
Myalism, 92, 93, 93n15, 95, 97, 98n20

Naipual, V. S. *The Mimic Men*, 7, 8, 15
nationality, 173, 179–81, 179n10, 207,
    271
New Testament Church of God, 25,
    49, 102, 118
    recruitment to, 57
'nine-night', 177, 177n8

Obeah, 92–3, 95, 97, 98n20
'officers of the church', 244–6, 261
    role in baptism, 149
    role in 'Lord's Supper', 153
outline of study, 34–6

parenthood, 229
Parsonian theory of society, *see*
    Henriques, F.
'partners', 69, 69n20
Patois, 184–5, 208, 237n19, 271
Patterson, S., 18–9, 26, 27
Pentecostalism 2, 104, 136
    African American, 235
    African-Caribbean,
        alternate interpretation, 119–20,
            206–7, 209–11, 274
        appeal interpreted, 10, 17, 25, 28,
            29, 33–4, 80, 82
        development, 9, 25, 28, 29, 80
    Caribbean, 169
    English, *see* Elim Foursquare
        Gospel Church
    Jamaican, 80, 102, 106–11, 217, 269
    Latin American, 222, 223
    Sicilian, 222, 223, 224, 268

United States, 224
Puerto Rican sects, 116–7
see also Church of God; gender;
New Testament Church of God
personhood, 95, 127, 210, 218–9, 257, 272
plural society theory,
see Smith, M. G.
Poblete, S. J. R. and T. F. O'Dea, 116–7
population,
African-Caribbean in Britain, 2, 11
Birmingham, 40–2
practical commitments, *see* ritual
prayer, 142–4, 159, 240, 252, 281
Prescod-Roberts, M., 21
prophecy,
see Holy Spirit, gift of prophecy
Protestantism,
Korean sects, 112–3
Pryce, K., 30, 31

'Queen's English', 185–6, 208, 271

race, 4, 83n4, 274, 275
and consciousness, 6, 7
and culture, 14, 83
racism, 1, 21, 82, 164, 201
see also attitudes towards racial
difference; English churches,
racism
Rastafarianism, 30–1, 169–70
women, 216–8
see also social practice
'reception of members', 145, 150–1
religion, 121
Britain, 115–6
and culture, 25, 26, 210
political expression, 29
and slaves, 92–5 *passim*, 94n16
religious differentiation,
colonial Jamaica, 92–9
postwar Jamaica, 99–102
religious participation,
and assimilation, 10, 25,
28–9, 82, 95, 112, 167
dual, 101, 109
Jamaica, 100
previous, 53, 64
status assertion/deprivation, 29,

95, 99–101 *passim*, 113–4, 181
representations, 4, 7, 9, 11, 267, 274
challenged 6, 15, 17, 206–11, 263–4,
266, 275
see also women; youth, Black male
research area,
religious institutions, 48
ward description, 37–9
ward housing, 47–8
ward population, 42
residential distribution, 9, 41
see also King Street congregation,
residential distribution and
housing
revivalism, 98
Rex, J., 9
and S. Tomlinson, 32
Rhys, J., *Let Them Call it Jazz*, 22
'right hand of fellowship',
see 'reception of members'
Riley, J., *Waiting in the Twilight*, 21
ritual, 123, 124, 137–9, 137n6, 145

saints, 273
see also agency
sanctification, 103, 104, 137–8, 157,
236
Saunders, G., 126
seating arrangements, 233–4
segregation
see interaction; residential
distribution; seating
arrangements
self, the, 127
Selvon, S., *The Lonely Londoners*, 7–8,
15, 20
'send-off' 154–5
sermons, 187, 189–90, 236–9
services, 276–9
sexism, 215
sharing, 177, 182
of food, 200
Simmons, E. E., 106
sin, 125–6, 161–2, 164
single mothers, 217, 260
sister, 55, 56, 57, 261
Smith, I., 215
Smith, M. G. 87–9
social practice, 220–1, 230–4, 241

speaking in tongues
   see glossolalia
Spurling, R. G., 102, 103, 104
Standard British English
   see 'Queen's English'
status, 102, 111, 119, 181–3, 207, 269,
      271
   Jamaica, 83–92
   see also religious participation;
      education
suffering, 102, 111, 119, 169, 209, 269
symbolic transformation, 207–9
syncretism, 97–8
   seeing through the Spirit see Holy
      Spirit gift of discernment

testimonies, 128–131, 144–5, 281–2
   at baptism, 147, 149
   at 'Lord's Supper', 153
   at 'washing of the saints' feet', 154
time, 61
Tomlinson, A. J. 104

vision, a, 128, 129
visitors, 51–2

Wallman, S., 172
'washing of the saints' feet', 145,
      151–4
wealth,
   see status
Wedenoja, W., 106–8

Wesleyan doctrine,
   see Arminian doctrine
'White bias', 85, 87
Williams, M. D., 235, 247
Wilson, B., 80, 117
Won Moo Hurh and Kwang Chung
      Kim, 112–3, 117
women, 16–25, 227, 256, 259, 272,
      273
   domestic circumstances, 62, 64, 66
   immigration, 62, 64, 66, 72
   relationships with men, 226–227,
      258
   religious participation, 62–7
      see also individual denominations
   representations, 18–9, 263
   wives,
      see agency, female; gender,
         female
   women in Bible, 227–8
   see also agency; language; mother;
      motherhood; Rastafarianism;
      single mothers
work, 190–2, 207
   and childbirth, 74
   and motherhood, 256
   and racism, 70, 72, 73
   and religion, 70, 71, 73,
world view, 135–6, 175–6

youth, 11, 29–30
   Black male, 11, 12, 15